ANDREW

GOODWIN

DANCING

IN

Music Television and Popular Culture

THE

DISTRACTION

FACTORY

University of Minnesota Press

MINNEAPOLIS

Published by the University of Minnesota Press
2037 University Avenue Southeast, Minneapolis, MN 55414
Printed in the United States of America on acid-free paper

Library of Congress Cataloging-in-Publication Data

Goodwin, Andrew, 1956–
    Dancing in the distraction factory : music television and popular
culture / Andrew Goodwin.
        p.   cm.
    Includes bibliographical references and index.
    ISBN 0-8166-2062-8. — ISBN 0-8166-2063-6 (pbk.)
    1. Music videos.   2. MTV Networks.   3. Television and music.
4. Television—Semiotics.   I. Title.
PN1992.8.M87G66   1992
791.45'657—dc20   92-13861
                                                               CIP
                                                               MN

For my mum and dad, Sally and Jim,
with love and gratitude

Contents

Acknowledgments

This book has its origin in a research project undertaken in the United Kingdom in 1983, with Justin Lewis and Pete Sketchley, as part of a local government policy-making initiative on cable TV sponsored by the Greater London Council and Sheffield City Council, titled *Cable and Community Programming*. I am grateful to Justin and Pete for an especially pleasurable period of collective work, and to Nick Garnham, whose work at the GLC took care of our economic base.

Since then, this research has taken on a life of its own, as these things do. In the mid-1980s I came to the United States, and spent some time marking out a distance between my own writing and the conventions of the academy. This shift from the prose and pose of academia to the riffs and rhythms of listening to (and then writing about) an awful lot of music was transformative mainly because of the people I met.

I am especially grateful to Joe Gore (now an editor at *Guitar Player*), who was first a friend, then a music teacher, and then later an occasional musical collaborator. He has been extremely generous in sharing the contents of his musical heart and soul with me. J. H. Tompkins (a senior editor at the *San Francisco Bay Guardian*) gave me my first chance to write serious pop music criticism, which was a liberating process that I recommend to anyone who feels intellectually "stuck." Bill Wyman (now a staff writer at the *Chicago Reader*) was also very generous about sharing his knowledge with me. Brenda and Glenn Johnson-Grau's work as editors of *ONETWOTHREEFOUR: A Rock and Roll Quarterly* helped me to complete my first effort at serious, accessible music television criticism ("From Anarchy to Chromakey: Music, Video, Media"). Parts of chapters 1 and 7 of this book are taken from that essay. I must also thank engineer/producer Paul "PK" Kendall of Mute Records for a view from behind the mixing desk that spawned many insights into matters aesthetic and technological.

I owe a special debt to Simon Frith, who in 1983 was kind enough to send a page of thoughtful, supportive comments in response to an unsolicited manuscript and who was thereafter always generous with his time and expertise.

The following people have also helped me, in a variety of different ways, including information, critique, invitations to give talks, and the loan of books, articles, and videos: Judianne Atencio (MTV Networks, Los Angeles), Mark Booth (MTV Europe), Alex Coronfly (California Music Channel), John Fiske, Christine Gledhill, Todd Gitlin, Lawrence Grossberg, Philip Hayward, Val Hill, Sut Jhally, John Hess, Laura Hynes (Tommy Boy Records), Simon Jones, Holly Kindel, Dave Laing, Richard Leppert, James Lull, Maureen McNeil, Graham Murdock, Tony Platt, Joel Rudinow, Cathy Schwichtenberg, Sarah Thornton, Toni Urbano, and Michelle Wolf.

Many of the ideas discussed here were tried and tested in lectures and papers presented at the International Television Studies Conference, the International Conference on Critical Thinking and Educational Reform, the annual meetings of the International Communication Association, the meetings of Global Options (San Francisco), the University of Minnesota's Humanities Seminar in Comparative Studies in Discourse and Society, the University of Rochester's Comparative Arts Colloquim, and the Eastman School of Music.

My sister, Susan Goodwin, helped me by collecting dozens of videotapes in the United Kingdom, which were consumed with varying degrees of relish and repulsion during visits home. And Sally Goodwin kept her son entertained with a regular supply of research materials, in the form of British music newspapers, which have been invaluable.

I am grateful to two colleagues who have been of special importance in the development and completion of this book. Richard Johnson's patient and careful supervision greatly enriched my thinking during the time I worked on the doctoral thesis version of this project in the Department of Cultural Studies at the University of Birmingham. And Janaki Bakhle, my editor at the University of Minnesota Press, has been both a supportive presence and a careful critic.

Finally, my personal and professional debt to Janet Wolff is enormous, and pleasantly indistinguishable. Her comments on a draft of this book were extremely important, although not as significant as her encouragement in making it all seem possible in the first place.

The bum notes remain, of course, all mine.

—Andrew Goodwin, San Francisco

Author's Note

There is a stylistic problem in knowing how to identify music video clips that is as yet unresolved. In the absence of any general conventions, titles of video clips appear here in small uppercase letters (for example, NOTHING COMPARES 2 U), in order to distinguish them from the songs, the titles of which appear in quotation marks (for example, "Nothing Compares 2 U"). Following the conventions of scholarship and cultural criticism, album titles and the titles of films and television programs are italicized (for example, *Fear of a Black Planet*, *A Hard Day's Night*, *Top of the Pops*). Video anthologies are also identified this way (for example, *Michael Jackson: The Legend Continues*).

This should help the reader to distinguish between analysis of songs and analysis of video clips. It does, however, often involve an illegitimate implication of authorship; when I write about Sinead O'Connor's NOTHING COMPARES 2 U (i.e., the video clip), I do not of course mean to imply that the singer/musician has authorial control over the clip—nor, indeed, that she or he is the author of the song (in this instance, of course, Prince has that honor).

Usually it is the clip's director (and the record company whose product is being promoted in the clip) who is chiefly responsible for the clip itself. To switch to talking of John Mayberry's NOTHING COMPARES 2 U, in order to acknowledge the director, would, however, be confusing for the reader and in any case merely implies another auteurism, which I wish to refuse. For the sake of clarity, then, the video clips are generally identified with reference to the musicians they promote—in much the same way we might write about "the new Levi's commercial." It should be clear soon enough that the analogy is carefully chosen.

Introduction

Watching *MTV 10* on a November evening in 1991, I sat and pondered the problem of how to introduce this book—or, rather, the issue of to *whom* it is addressed. *MTV 10* was an hour-long celebration of MTV's tenth anniversary, screened in prime time on the ABC TV network. In this show MTV invaded the network space that it had implicitly critiqued for a decade, in an orgy of self-celebration that could leave no one in any doubt as to which of the two institutions (ABC or MTV) thought it owned our past, our present, and our future. The show kicked off with a performance of "Freedom 90" by George Michael, featuring the following lyric: "We won the race / Got out of the place / Went back home / Got a brand new face / For the boys on MTV." Delivered with a smirk, these lines embodied both MTV's self-consciousness and its cultural centrality. Also performing for *MTV 10* were R.E.M., Aerosmith, Michael Jackson, and Madonna. The show's hosts included Cher, Tom Cruise, Spike Lee, and Mel Gibson. Original VJ Martha Quinn was seen boasting that the term *video jock* had now entered *Webster's Dictionary*. On the cover of the current issue of *TV Guide*, Madonna was hyping an interview with MTV presenter Kurt Loder, in which she discussed her own fascination with television.

As MTV, the most visible and frequently discussed embodiment of music television and music videos, trumpeted its victory, I recalled my first encounter with the new service, in the summer of 1982. Back then, watching an obscure and embryonic televisual form that did not yet have its own voice, I think it took me about half an hour to realize that one day I would find myself watching its tenth anniversary celebration.

At the time, this was a hunch—not the kind of thing that one can own up to in a scholarly essay or defend as a scientific practice, even in the social sciences. But my informed speculation did emerge out of two reasonably educated guesses, and these remain the dual riffs (a kind of double bass line) that run throughout this book. First, there is the issue of pleasure. No matter how corny it was, no matter how transparently manipulative, no matter how crass its images (many music video directors are clearly in need of some serious metaphor therapy), MTV was fun to watch. I think that MTV was, and is, fun to watch because it brings a rock sensibility to television—as I suggest later in this book, it makes television *musical*.

Second, and every bit as important, was the obvious fact that MTV had invented one solution to the perennial problem of cable television— how to generate enough revenue for new programming. MTV sidestepped this difficulty to some extent by having someone else pay for the "programs," as its video clips were financed by record companies.

Frankly, I was awestruck by the cynical brilliance behind these two features of MTV, and I have been thinking about the relation between them ever since that first encounter. On the one hand, there is the question of how music television mediates between a sometimes countercultural aesthetic and the institution of television. On the other hand, there is the question of the political economy of the media, and how new forms such as MTV operate politically.

Despite these opening thoughts triggered by *MTV 10*, this book is not in fact primarily concerned with MTV. It takes music television as its object of study, by which I mean both the individual music video clips that became increasingly pervasive in the promotion of popular music during the 1980s and the televisual context in which these clips are seen. That framing context includes cable and satellite services exclusively dedicated to music television (such as MTV: Music Television, VH-1, and the Jukebox Network in the United States, and MTV Europe and Sky TV's The Power Station in Europe) and other areas of television programming, including blocks of music video programming used to construct a show (in the United States, NBC's *Friday Night Videos*, or in the United Kingdom, ITV's *The Chart Show*) and those more conventional pop music broadcasts, such as the BBC's *Top of the Pops* or America's syndicated program *Soul Train*, that both screen video clips and act as a model structure for some programming on the dedicated networks.

MTV: Music Television has received the most critical attention in the scholarly and more popular literature so far, and this is not just because it is the first 24-hour all-music television network (available, since August 1981, on cable television in the United States). MTV's visibility stems less from its quantitative reach (its audiences are far smaller than those for broadcast television's music programming) than from its intrinsic qualities as a different kind of television—television that attempts to incorporate aspects of a rock music aesthetic. Therefore, my analysis will not be confined to the music video portions of such programming but will extend beyond them, to consider their televisual framing.

The most interesting and important point about MTV lies in what it stands for—on the one hand, it signifies new relations between popular music and the mass media (R.E.M. on ABC, in prime time, during *MTV 10*); on the other, it represents a trend in American television toward making new appeals to young audiences, and to the "baby boomer" generation (MTV as the "logic" of a generation; see Pittman, 1990). Thus, while many of the clips analyzed here are screened on MTV, this book seeks a wider purchase. In particular, it aims to describe and explain the emergence of music video in its British context, and most of its analysis is pertinent to British and European broadcast institutions, since it concerns texts that are screened in that context (for instance, on *Top of the Pops*, MTV Europe) and discourses that are now a part of a global pop music culture.

In that respect my own history in relation to this topic is relevant. I grew up in a British pop culture environment heavily influenced by music from America (and its iconography), and I have been involved in producing and consuming pop music now for about twenty years. My first encounter with MTV occurred less than one year after its inception, in the summer of 1982 during a trip to the United States. I was already familiar with music videos in their British context, but it was following that trip that I became interested in understanding this new phenomenon. I continued to follow the development of music videos in Britain (while making occasional visits to the United States) until the autumn of 1986, when I moved to California. Now my earlier experience is reversed: I watch music television in its American context routinely and catch up on British developments on visits home. This transcontinental experience facilitates, I believe, an analysis of music television that takes account of both the British and American contexts.

In this project I also attempt an interdisciplinary synthesis of historical/economic institutional analysis, text analysis drawing on research in film and television studies, and musicology (a term I am using in its broad sense to refer to the analysis of contemporary musics). Of the three tasks undertaken here, the first is largely based on institutional analysis, while the other two are both textual and critical in nature. In a historical and economic analysis of recent developments in the music and media industries, I will explain the emergence of music television and, in doing so, explicate the relation between text and institution. While I do *not* argue that textual meanings can be "read off" from institutional context, I suggest that the organization of the music and media industries sets clear pressures and limits, partly due to the essentially promotional rhetoric of the music video clip.

Second, I will offer a textual analysis of music video clips that is rooted in the sociology of popular music, and in musicology itself. I will deploy concepts from television and film studies, but subject to a critical evaluation in light of what we know about the music industry and the audience for popular music. It is here in particular that I draw on my own experience as a fan of popular music, and as a musician. I view music television very much from *within* the field of pop consumption, and have tried to construct credible readings that are founded on both research on the music industry and my own observations of the pop music audience.

In particular, I have been struck by the numerous ways in which music television seems to correspond to aspects of the rock and pop aesthetic that I recognize as both a fan and a musician. Some of these features are formal (I have always been interested in the question of how pop songs defy the terms of the "realism" debate in film and television studies); some are sociological (ideologically, rock and pop speak to an idea of "youth" that marks itself out from the paternal and parental addresses of broadcast/network television); some are musicological (in that respect I am especially interested in rhythm and song structure, and how these elements structure video clips); and some concern the content of a rock aesthetic, the ways in which it embodies a Romantic aesthetic (see Frith, 1983, 1986; Pattison, 1987; Stratton, 1983) of intensity, vulgarity, and immediacy that once again implies a break with the traditions of television. This book investigates these connections, and then explores the interrelations between that project and our understanding of the narrative codes and conventions of television and cinema.

Third, I want then to connect up the specific questions about music with the wider issue of what rock culture *means* and how this relates to music television. I believe that these parts of the book are necessarily more speculative, but remain essential to the overall project of understanding music television. It is not enough to be able to detail the ways in which music television inhabits the realm of a new mass-mediated music culture; we must also investigate the social (and perhaps political) implications of that culture. Here I try to move beyond the individual music video clips to consider the overall context of music television, including some of its nonmusic programming, through a case study that centers on MTV. I then use this textual study as the basis for thinking through questions about the politics of music television in general and the current situation in terms of the interplay of some of the political discourses within pop music at large.

It is here in particular that the limitations of text analysis in a cross-cultural context occur, whatever the bicontinental practices of its author. For, while one might plausibly argue that the audience for music television inhabits a culture that has in common various discourses, attitudes, and structures of feeling, it is also true that different national-popular cultures, and subcultures within such formations, will inflect the meanings of music television texts differently. I have tried to explore the music television text in light of the possible reading formations that exist currently in Britain and the United States, choosing to emphasize the necessarily polysemic nature of music television texts, while insisting that the published literature on this topic is far too narrow in its interpretation of these formations.

The three levels of analysis attempted here are not discrete. The institutional/historical analysis is not confined to "setting up" the project, but offers a basis for a reading of music television that applies throughout the book, including the research into the televisual context of MTV itself. The effort to understand the social and political discourses in play in the music television text similarly tries to take account of the institutional context in which these messages are produced. Correspondingly, the musicological analysis is deployed not only in relation to the individual clips, but as a way of explaining the televisual context — in this instance, via a case study of MTV.

Mass-mediated rock and pop texts contain both visual and aural codes that are often inseparable. My project here is to suggest, first, that analysts of popular music have tended to neglect the importance of what we see (and how it relates to what we hear), while, on the other hand, analysts of music television have tended to overlook what we hear (and how it relates to what we see). In that regard the book should offer some insight of a more general nature into the relationship between sound and vision in popular music, which technological developments (for instance, sampling music computers) have helped to disrupt and which I have written about elsewhere (see Goodwin, 1988, 1991c).

In particular, it should be noted that the project of constructing a musicology of the music video image is presented as the basis for understanding how to undertake a credible textual study. Issues regarding the sound-vision relation, the formal organization of music videos, questions of pleasure, and so on need to be related to the musical portion of text. This work may in its turn generate research into the audience, but it does not claim to be a substitute for that inquiry.

During the course of this research one cluster of concepts in particular has become dominant in the analysis of this topic—postmodernism. While it remains unclear, in my view, whether advocates of postmodern theory understand this idea to be a new social theory, a new social formation, a new aesthetic, or perhaps a revision of an older one, there can be no doubt that the paradigm has been of enormous importance in the study of music television. My investigation of this area will thus inevitably involve an engagement with these ideas, as they relate to music television. I do not in this book offer any kind of assessment of postmodern concepts *tout court* or theories of postmodernity in general. I seek, rather, to undertake the more modest task of coming to terms with the postmodern analysis of music television. This is important, because my critical thoughts about the usefulness of this paradigm should not be taken as a statement about postmodernism in other contexts.

The book's title reveals its wider ambition—an engagement with the *politics* of music television.[1] Rather than encounter this issue on the grand terrain of abstract theory, I want to explain some things about music television and then use that empirical analysis to make an argument about popular culture. I will construct an argument about how music television is produced and consumed and then use that analysis to illuminate what I believe are some of the forgotten questions in contemporary cultural studies. Many of these questions reveal my continuing concern with how one might use historical materialism and a Marxist theory of ideology in an era when the base-superstructure model is rightly discredited. This is not, however, a defense of Marxist philosophy through a reading of Billy Idol. That would be absurd. What I do attempt is an exposition of how we can recover the usefulness of historical, sociological, and materialist studies in what is supposedly the age of either postmodernism or MTV, or both. To the limited extent that I find merit in postmodernism, I am concerned not with the theory behind it (and its poststructuralist roots), but with postmodernism as a cultural discourse. I am happy to follow Fred Pfeil (1986, 1988), Lawrence Grossberg (1988), and Todd Gitlin (1989), who have each suggested ways of seeing postmodern culture that defy postmodern theorizing.

A continuing theme will be the conceptual development of an ever-expanding field of something called cultural studies. The trend in recent cultural studies work has been toward making a conflation between political economy and cultural pessimism on the one hand, and text/audience analysis and cultural optimism on the other.[2] This setting up of the terms of debate is often the hidden assumption that structures academic work on popular culture. Yet it elides two important possibilities. First, textual interpretations that buttress existing power relations become increasingly invisible. Second, the actual, material relations of cultural production are unexamined, and explorations of institutional contexts that could help to explain counterhegemonic readings are never delivered. Thus, text analysis and/or audience readings that seem resistant to the dominant inequalities of class, race, and gender relations are repeatedly thought to defy any concrete relations of text and production—a connection that need not be envisaged through the metaphor of base-superstructure, but that does, surely, need to be theorized in some way.

I take up the issue of postmodernism in chapter 1, exploring it partly in relation to a major absence in the literature on music television, namely, the silence about music. In this opening discussion I aim to set the scene for the subsequent analysis, and to clear some ground through a critique of postmodernism and visually oriented studies of music television deriving from film and television studies.

Chapter 2 explores the institutional development of music television in order to lay the ground for the subsequent analysis. At this point I will discuss the emergence of music videos and show how an understanding of their economic function helps explain their textual construction, partly through a reformulation of the role of performance within the pop music economy. I will argue that music videos are an unusual kind of commodity that demands some rethinking of traditional ideas about the relations among institutions, texts, and audiences, in particular with regard to the conventional application of the terms *use-value* and *exchange-value* in cultural analysis.

The question of textual analysis of video clips is taken up in the following three chapters. My premise here is that in terms of their use-value to the audience, music videos need to be studied primarily in relation to popular music, rather than in relation to television or cinema. Chapter 3 initiates this project by applying concepts developed in the analysis of music to video clips. This work will include a brief consideration of the concept of synaesthesia (the process of visualizing music), which (I will argue) enters into the production of meaning in popular music prior to the emergence of music television.

In chapter 4 I will explore the possibilities for the narrative analysis of individual video clips. Here my task will be to critique those accounts that derive from film studies and to show correspondences between the construction of video clips and the organization of popular songs. I will argue that the production of meaning in popular music does not necessarily occur at the level of individual songs and that more attention needs to be paid to the role of characterization and *persona* that takes place at the level of the star-text. In chapter 5, I will develop this idea through an analysis of how stardom operates in music television.

The text analysis can be complete, however, only if we also consider the televisual context in which the clips are exhibited. In chapter 6, therefore, I offer a case study of one such site — MTV. This undertaking is not restricted to the specific framing of the clips themselves, but broadens out to consider other areas of MTV programming and the roots of these elements in that institution.

Chapter 7 concludes my analysis with a more detailed investigation of the politics of music television that returns to the subject of postmodernism. My particular focus here will be the thorny issue of ideology and the relationship between the formulation and application of that concept in postmodernism and in Marxist cultural studies. I am especially interested here in the uses to which irony and parody are put in music television, and how postmodern and Marxist approaches might theorize this. It needs to be reiterated that the method here is text analysis, albeit one that attempts to situate the text of music television in its actual social context, and there is no claim to provide a definitive account of textual reception. What is possible, however, is a more firmly grounded account of how pleasure and ideology work in music television, through an acknowledgment of the form's multidiscursivity, and via an engagement with the music that underpins it and the representations of stardom that surround it.

There are two sets of choices implied within the dominant understandings of how intellectual life and popular culture interact that I find to be banal and intend to refuse in this book. The more public division is the notion that some people (artists, musicians, young people) actually "live" the culture of pop and therefore know more about it than the poor unfortunates who can only analyze it. Simon Frith has described this, in another context, as the "arrogance" of the fan.

A second dilemma has increasingly presented itself as the only way to "think" the field, within academic cultural studies. On the one hand there is the crusty, elitist professor who writes about "communications" with a secret (or not so secret) hatred of popular culture. This person will usually be categorized as a "cultural pessimist." On the other hand, there are the bright young things of cultural studies who understand its pleasures and its possibilities for empowerment, and who take up popular culture as a political cause, to be brandished against the conservatism of "bourgeois" high Art. (One version of this debate is playing itself out in the United States around the current arguments concerning multiculturalism and Eurocentric curricula.) What is limiting about this paradigm is its assumption that one cannot enjoy popular culture and understand its appeal while also seeing at work its mechanisms of manipulation and its relationship to political power, as well as its more liberatory aspects. Like the more public choice (experiential pleasure versus cerebral criticism), this setting of the intellectual agenda presents a false choice—in fact, it merely *repeats* the terms of the more common attitude, by implying that the people who have really understood pop culture are those who *don't* "see through" it.

Whatever the merits or otherwise of the arguments that follow, I do hope that I have successfully refused these two possibilities for being set up, either by pop fans or by academic populists. Characterized either as the Critic Who Reads Too Much or as Dr. Crusty, one is denied the right to enjoy *MTV 10* and criticize it at one and the same time. But if millions of viewers were doing precisely this during that evening telecast in November 1991, that would come as no surprise to me.

ONE

Silence!
Academics at Work

Writing about music is like dancing about architecture. It's a really stupid thing to want to do.

—Elvis Costello[1]

Notwithstanding Elvis Costello's warning, in this book I will indulge in the stupidity of attempting to write about music—and its relation to the iconography of popular music. I am concerned as much with the *aural* content and logic of music television as with its visual aspects. As I shall argue in this chapter and the next, we need to locate music television within its contexts of production and consumption in order to construct plausible critical analyses; both sites demand an engagement with sound and its organization—respectively, with the music itself and with the music industry. This introductory chapter locates the purposes and aims of my study of music television by investigating not only the neglect of sound, but also the wider problem of the role of the visual in popular music.

In this review of some approaches to music television I do not attempt to survey the entire range of scholarship on this topic. In particular, I will not engage with the empiricist tradition of content and audience studies on music television that are often to be found in the pages of U.S. journals of "mass communication." [2] I choose instead to concentrate on the three (related) themes in the literature that seem to me to be conceptually dominant and in need of revision. First, there is the film studies/television studies approach to the topic, which tends to emphasize the *visual*. Second, there is the paradigm of postmodernism. And third, there is

1

the problem of textual analysis that has lost its necessary connections with the spheres of production and/or consumption. I will also attempt to demonstrate where ideas in the academy connect with assumptions in the industry itself.

In the study of music television, a number of major lacunae are evident, but underlying many of them is the neglect of the music itself. This deafening silence in the corridors of the academy combines with an overestimation of the power of the visual to disfigure the study of music television. The situation is not unlike that confronted by Roland Barthes (1961/1982) in his analysis of press photography. The familiar territory of words, argued Barthes, had tended to be more hospitable for critics than the more problematically polysemic construct of the photograph. Hence, analysis of newspapers and magazines often *overlooked* their most important visual component. Ironically enough, the analysis of the visual has been developed (partly as a result of Barthes's influence) to the point where it is these codes that now yield up their meanings with relative ease (or apparently so) — at least when compared with the *aural* codes of music found in music video clips, which remain oblique, enigmatic, and somewhat impervious to many established forms of cultural analysis. Unlike the photograph, however, music often appears to be less a "message without a code" (Barthes, 1961/1982: 196) than the reverse: the problem of music is that it appears to be *all code and no message*. Barthes pointed to the extraordinary polysemy of the photographic image, and to the framing nature of words, in the context of newspapers and magazines. In the case of music television, it is worth remembering Barthes's point about the open-ended nature of the photographic image, since so many analysts seem to think that it is *this* part of the message that somehow *determines* meaning! But the analogy with newspaper photography soon breaks down, partly because meaning in pop music is dispersed over so many media sites. It may be that music sometimes functions like the newspaper photograph: as a code that is framed by its context (in this case, visual imagery). But it can equally well be the case that the visual images are framed by the networks of interpretation suggested by words and music on the sound track that would function as aural "captions," in this instance, in just the manner identified (and explored more thoroughly) in another essay by Barthes (1977b).

In the literature on music television, misunderstandings about visuality in pop generate two related myopias: first, music scholars (and musicians and critics) have tended to neglect the importance of visual discourses in pop, and consequently exaggerate the significance of music video clips, which are too often studied (and dismissed) in isolation from the necessary analysis of pop's visual representation. On the other hand, students of the visual (whose work usually derives from film studies and related cultural studies paradigms, such as postmodern theory) have tried to analyze music television in iconographic, semiotic, and narrative terms, while paying insufficient attention to the sound track. Here the problem is that music video clips, and music television services such as MTV, are studied in isolation from the music itself, and with too little regard for their important foundations in the music industry.

The Sounds of Silence

For a cultural form that has been around for only a decade or so, the promotional music video has generated an extraordinary amount of textual analysis; it also has attracted readings that refract it through a remarkably diverse set of metaphors, concepts, and fields of theory. Music videos have been read as though they might be best understood as cinematic genre (Holdstein, 1984; Mercer, 1986), advertising (Aufderheide, 1986; Fry & Fry, 1986), new forms of television (Fiske, 1984), visual art (J. Walker, 1987), "electronic wallpaper" (Gehr, 1983), dreams (Kinder, 1984), postmodern texts (Fiske, 1986; Kaplan, 1987; Tetzlaff, 1986; Wollen, 1986), nihilistic neo-Fascist propaganda (Bloom, 1987), metaphysical poetry (Lorch, 1988), shopping mall culture (Lewis, 1987a, 1987b, 1990), LSD (Powers, 1991), and "semiotic pornography" (Marcus, 1987).

Strangely enough, very few analysts have thought to consider that music television might resemble music.[3] It is remarkable that so many of the analogies cited above are forms that *cannot* be listened to.

Whatever the merits of these arguments, music has barely been discussed. Marsha Kinder (1984) typifies the research to date when she writes of the discontinuous visual structure of music video that "this structure insures that the visuals will be the primary source of pleasure, for it is the lush visual track that will be withdrawn, withheld or suspended, when the spectator is no longer watching television but *only listening* to the song on the radio or stereo" (p. 3). I will take issue with that non sequitur throughout this book, but especially in my attention to the televisual sound track, in chapter 6.

The effects of this odd silence in music television research are far-reaching. When music videos are read as silent minimovies whose narratives might be understood in isolation from the music and its wider significance in pop culture, the result is enormous confusion about how audiences might actually make meaning from the video clips. In a famous early passage from *Film Comment,* Richard Corliss (1983) characterizes MTV thus: "It is all about the death of context; it is the shotgun annulment of character from narrative" (p. 34). As I will try to demonstrate in this book, characters can in fact be found in the video clips, but only if one pays attention to the sound track and to the culture of pop stardom. Critics whose eyes are glued to the screen, in the manner of cinema criticism, often miss the point. (The question of characterization developed through the personas of pop stars is explored in chapter 5.)

Pop music iconography has sometimes been misread. The implications of pop music genres are often downplayed or neglected altogether, so that the videos are read as if their only generic significance lay in their referencing of cinematic conventions. (Backlighting effects, to provide just one such example, are often interpreted as a reference to film noir, although the more reasonable association is clearly with the lighting conventions of live performance.) The meaning of pop stars as icons and characters is analyzed as though the tools developed in understanding Hollywood movies can simply be transferred into the quite different aesthetic environment of pop. The analysis of form is applied to musical texts as if categories such as "realism" transfer unproblematically. The music—if discussed at all—is usually relegated to the status of sound track, as though it illustrates the images (as in cinema), although the reverse is arguably far closer to the actual reading formations brought to these texts (as, Laing, 1985a, has argued).

During the period of music television's ascendancy, the academic literature on this new topic has swollen from a few untheorized tinklings to an enormous (one might say operatic) cacophony that rivals Queen's six-minute clip BOHEMIAN RHAPSODY (so often cited as the "first" music video) in bluster, complexity, and overblown pretension. "Pop video," writes Simon Frith (1988a), "is now more heavily theorised than pop music" (p. 205). The problem, of course, is that it is extremely difficult to theorize video clips without an adequate conceptualization of the music and its relation to pop iconography.

The neglect of music in music video analysis has been so pervasive that few writers seem to have noticed that a cultural form centered on its aural component has been analyzed by critics without ears. When two authors happily stated in a *Journal of Communication* content analysis of music video that "only the visual dimension was coded; the audio portion was not taken into consideration" (Sherman & Dominick, 1986), they were merely being explicit about a methodological deafness that normally goes unnoticed.

This silence can be traced back to the very earliest attempts to classify video clips. First, a division was constructed between performance clips and those that told a story—"concept videos" (Wolfe, 1983). Then, building on this, distinctions were commonly made among three kinds of structure—the performance clip, narratives, and antinarratives (Lynch, 1984). These were necessarily simple beginnings, but the limitation of such a tripartite categorization is immediately clear to anyone involved in listening to pop: the narrative/antinarrative distinction takes no account of music or lyrics, since the three categories derive entirely from a film studies foundation that privileges the analysis of visual signs. (Indeed, it is interesting to note the extent to which formalism in film theory is similarly visually specific, with its emphasis on a system of "looks"—for instance, see Mulvey, 1975, 1989. The "content" that is often overlooked or downplayed is of course frequently located on the sound track—in the dialogue, and in the music.)[4] Lynch (1984) finds most aesthetically valuable and intellectually interesting those clips that most closely resemble "experimental film."

A more sophisticated three-way distinction is made by Deborah Holdstein (1984: 12), who distinguishes among videos that politicize the song, those that "revive the traditional American film musical," and "fantasy videos," which are based "entirely or in part on the spirit and lyrics of the song" and place the performers in exotic/mythical situations and locales. Holdstein's analysis is superior to most of the research published at the time, in that she attempts to locate her analysis of three video clips within the framing context of star image. Yet it is also noticeable that her broad classification and text analyses alike say nothing about music.

The reasons for this neglect are not difficult to discern. Music, more than any of the arts, is commonly thought to be somehow above and beyond rational analysis.[5] A paradigmatic breakdown of the terms that make up the label "music television" yields some insight into the assumptions that underpin the debate:

Music	*Television*
natural	mediated
subjective	social
expression	communication
timeless	linear

My effort to provide a diagram that indicates the underlying *ideological* assumptions behind the neglect of music was suggested by John Fiske's (1986: 75) description of the differences between broadcast television and MTV, for this analysis precisely and uncritically *reproduces* the ideology I wish to explore in this volume:

MTV		*TV*
Signifier	:	Signified
The Senses	:	Sense
Body	:	Mind
Pleasure	:	Ideology
Freedom	:	Control
Resistance	:	Conformity

Fiske is positively restrained, however, in comparison with some postmodern analysts. For instance, one account of MTV draws on the work of Baudrillard and Foucault in order to conclude: "We have to STOP MAKING SENSE" (Chen, 1986: 68). The abandonment of reason in the face of music has rarely been so explicitly stated.

Clearly the central problem for cultural commentators is the notorious difficulty of finding the appropriate conceptual tools for analyzing music. Yet this difficulty, shared by all of us who seek to write about music (and articulated very cleverly in Elvis Costello's comparison with "dancing about architecture"), is no excuse for evacuating the territory. As McClary and Walser (1990) have noted, the analysis of popular music poses multiple problems for researchers. And yet while a more sophisticated musicology of pop remains to be worked out (probably in tandem with semiological methods; see Nattiez, 1990), there *are* standard terms of music criticism that might be applied in this field. However, even such extremely basic musicological terms as *rhythm* and *timbre* are usually missing from the lexicon of music video analysis, despite the fact that the most elementary understanding of the form requires us to recognize that there is a correlation between sound and image—most obviously in camera movement and editing techniques, but also in lighting, mise-en-scène, and gesture. (I explore those questions in chapter 3.)

Disregarding even these simple points, students of communications studies, sociology, and cultural studies often look at music television as if it were a purely visual form. Music video emerged into a media environment that seemed to have succumbed to the "imperialism of the image" (Baudrillard, 1988b: 167–71). Postmodern theorists and mainstream critics alike agreed on the apparent triumph of the visual: this McLuhanesque theme provides the foundation for Neil Postman's best-selling book *Amusing Ourselves to Death* (1985) and is a recurring motif in postmodern theory.[6] Indeed, there is an interesting connection between E. Ann Kaplan's (1987) application of postmodern theory to MTV and Postman's use of Marshall McLuhan: both writers see television as potentially schizophrenic.[7]

Assumptions about the ascendancy of visuality will be challenged in this book, but they do at least help to explain the marginalization of the sound track in music television research. Indeed, this work often reads as a more sophisticated parallel line of argument to dominant assumptions in the music industry, and among popular music critics and scholars.

Picture This

The debate about music video in the rock music community has been characterized by a sense that music has been taken over by visual imagery, packaging, and media marketing. This notion underwrites the hostility toward music video that continues to inform most rock criticism on the topic. It also has led some rock musicians, such as Joe Jackson and the Smiths, to repudiate the use of promotional videos.[8] The chief objection here concerns the supposed "fixing" in the mind's eye of a set of visual images, which—it is sometimes assumed—closes off the options for listeners to construct their own imaginative interpretations of songs.

Musicians and critics alike often seem to share two common assumptions: first, that visual images inevitably dominate and act to frame the aural codes of popular culture; and second, that visual signs are somehow less polysemic, more fixed, than aural signs. It is to those questions that I now turn.

Many myths surround music video, not the least of which is the notion that it single-handedly transformed the pop soundscape, because of its ability to overwhelm the aural codes of pop music. This perspective combines a misunderstanding of the meanings of pop and the sites of its discourses with an approach to visual media that is sadly reminiscent of the literary critics of an earlier era, who bemoaned the intrusion of radio and TV into the culture of the written word, and who similarly overstressed the power of the image.

Indeed, this initial period of music television recalls earlier moments in the history of broadcasting. Then, as now, critics and professionals were apprehensive about the introduction of the visual. Television professionals, such as Grace Wyndham Goldie (1977), have recounted their anxiety about the introduction of *picture value* into the selection of television news stories. Likewise, early critics of music television wondered whether the gatekeepers of the music industry would soon sign up only "videogenic" acts (for discussion of this issue, see Denisoff, 1988; Shore, 1985). It was implied that the "true" values of pop musicianship were being diluted by the importance of video, and many musicians publicly expressed their lack of enthusiasm for the form—a fact that must in part derive from the relative lack of control enjoyed by most musicians in this area, and from an ideology of rock that leads its musicians (publicly, at least) to denigrate promotional practices such as the use of "packaging" and the construction of "image." [9] Indeed, this strategy is actually staged as a fiction in Deep Purple's CALL OF THE WILD, where members of the band are called by an "agent" and asked to take part in a video for their song "Call of the Wild." In this narrative, the musicians refuse to participate, and so the video is lip-synced by extras.

The major problem with this approach is that it uncritically accepts a mythical, Romantic vision of the music industry, and is based on the related assumption that the emphasis on imagery is a new development in pop. This is a difficult view to sustain in light of what we know of pop history. Pop has always stressed the visual as a necessary part of its apparatus—in performance, on record covers, in magazine and press photographs, and in advertising. [10] In its very earliest days rock and roll was promoted via film; indeed, many teens first discovered rock at the movies, when Bill Haley and the Comets appeared in *The Blackboard Jungle* in 1955. The career of rock's first superstar, Elvis Presley, is a case study in pop's interaction with the media, as Presley's national identity was formed on American television (which generated the controversy about shooting him from below the waist)[11] and then, internationally, in his films (on rock movies, see Marcus, 1980). If Presley was the 1950s media pop star, then the 1960s and 1970s brought us the Beatles and Abba, respectively. The commodity form of pop has always needed other discourses of visual pleasure that are unavailable on disc. The implications of this for an understanding of pop videos are discussed in chapter 2.

The central importance of performance imagery in pop history has been evident in the numerous instances (long before the emergence of music television) when visual image, and its promotion of pop's commodities, has taken precedence over verisimilitude in the sound-vision relation. A typical and notorious example occurred in January 1968, following Pink Floyd's dismissal of its songwriter and vocalist Syd Barrett (one of his crimes, significantly, was failing to lip-sync "See Emily Play" on an *American Bandstand* television appearance the previous year). When the band came to make a promotional film for their single "Apples and Oranges," bassist Roger Waters mimed to Barrett's vocals, while new guitarist Dave Gilmour faked his guitar part (Schaffner, 1991). Since then, this question of visualizing musical parts not created by the performer has become more complex, in part because of sampling technologies that confuse the relationship between the origination of a sound and the moment of "creativity." [12] But the fundamental importance of performance imagery in establishing meaning in pop culture, and in promoting its commodities, is not new.

A related complaint is often made, that promotional video clips somehow kill off the imaginative aspect of music. Pop musicians themselves make this point on occasion—Joe Jackson used the argument to explain his own refusal to make promotional clips. Musicologist Richard Middleton (1985) makes a similar argument when he states:

> The video "boom" is being used to try to "fix" musical
> meanings, close off listeners' interpretative autonomy, and at the
> same time focus attention on a new technology under the control
> of the music leisure industries and the advertisers. (p. 41)

There is a great deal of truth in the second half of that statement, but the initial premise about "fixing" meaning implies two processes: a dominance of vision over sound, and the presence of very strong preferred meanings within the visual discourse. Neither statement has been shown to be true of music video.

There is some evidence to suggest that music video colors our memory and visualization of pop songs. Apart from independent and MTV-funded market surveys, academic research has shown that exposure to music video is widespread and is prevalent among pop music consumers: a study in San Jose, California, reported that 80 percent of 600 high school students surveyed watched MTV, averaging an astonishing two hours a day viewing music video. Not surprisingly, a number of the students looked to the videos to provide either the dominant or an additional element of meaning to their favorite songs (Sun & Lull, 1986).

But to what extent can music video be said to determine interpretations of pop? Consider this comment, from a Culture Club fan: "I picture George singing. And I think about the videos—the videos are in my mind as I listen to the songs" (quoted in Vermorel & Vermorel, 1985: 61). This probably captures very well one way in which video is used by pop fans. This fan imagines Boy George singing the song and has the video image in her or his mind. Neither observation requires that this visual discourse should dominate the music and lyrics. Even a fan who owns the videos of a particular act is still likely to spend more time listening to the music on record or cassette and on the radio than watching the videos. This analysis is crudely quantitative, but it cannot be irrelevant to note that music and radio remain pervasive as a part of our soundscape, where videos do not.

It might still be possible that visual discourses dominate, however. I want to turn to a comment by Graeme Turner (1983: 109), who suggests that the video for Culture Club's song "Do You Really Want to Hurt Me?" may shift the song's meaning. This clip is often cited as one that politicizes its audio track. The song appears to be a simple tale of romantic loss, but the video introduces a new element, as gender-bending Boy George sings the refrain to a courtroom judge. Thus, it can be read as an attempt to address homophobic attitudes and the persecution of gays—or, more correctly perhaps, of anyone who defies dominant gender roles—in a manner that is absent from the song itself.

Turner is not advancing a simple "fixing" thesis (and I happen to agree with his reading of the video and song), but his concluding remarks reveal an assumption that illustrates a pervasive difficulty in the literature on music television. He concludes that the video contains meanings "totally unrecoverable from the song's lyrics." This is undeniably the case. However, very few people would have consumed "Do You Really Want to Hurt Me?" through its lyrics alone. Millions of people in the United Kingdom would have seen Culture Club's performances on *Top of the Pops*, featuring George in drag, and millions more would have seen and read about the band in the popular press, the music papers, and teen magazines. The "new" meanings teased out in the video are already a potential reading of the song, because we know from George's performance imagery that he signifies sexual "deviance." [13] As Turner correctly notes, the video makes this reading explicit. My point is that this is not a case of video imagery transforming pop meanings so much as an example of a video clip building on the visual codes already in play. It is an important point for the argument about "fixing" meaning, because such a phenomenon would be significant only if it could be shown that video routinely offers a closing off of the range of potential readings of songs. In order to study that hypothesis, critics would have to consider discourses that already intervene between the lyrics and the video, including discourses of performance, promotion, and image.

This is not to deny that there might be instances of a music video clip freezing the meaning of a song. Perhaps the most likely example of this concerns the visual shifts encountered by the Cars' song "Drive." Heard on the radio, the song seems to be a narrative of lost love. Only in the original video clip (directed by Tim Hutton, and available on *Heartbeat City*, Warner Home Videos, 1984) do we discover that the girl being addressed by the singer appears to have been institutionalized in a mental home. The refrain "Who's gonna drive you home?" thus takes on a new pathos. The song's meaning shifted again in 1985, when "Drive" was used by the Canadian Broadcasting System as part of its contribution to the Live Aid event. The refrain "Who's gonna drive you home?" now sounds spectacularly incongruous; nonetheless, it is the images of Ethiopian famine that were then "fixed" for many listeners. Since then, the original DRIVE clip has been aired from time to time (for instance, on MTV); there is no research as yet on the duration of impact for video meanings, so there is no way of knowing whether the images in the Live Aid clip or the original video images have persisted. Most interestingly, no research has addressed the question of whether an "innocent," video-free, experience is recuperated once the clips are no longer in widespread circulation, or whether it may indeed disappear altogether.

Something similar may have occurred in the consumption of the clips that promote Robert Palmer's songs "I Didn't Mean to Turn You On" and "Addicted to Love." [14] These clips used mannequinlike female models who transparently and unconvincingly mimed the guitars-drums-keyboards parts of the musical backing. Soon the images of these women had become so popular that a pastiche of these representations was deployed in other videos (Robbie Neville's C'EST LA VIE, Tone Lōc's WILD THING, Paula Abdul's FOREVER YOUR GIRL, and Bell Biv Devoe's DO ME) and in the 1989 Pepsi commercials that used Palmer's hit "Simply Irresistible." Eventually, the female mannequin shots were parodied through gender inversion, in Michelle Shocked's clip ON THE GREENER SIDE, which mounts a scopophilic look at male models (who pose and mime guitar playing in some shots) to illustrate the music of a female narrator/musician.

It is also possible to think of instances of *fusion* of song/video text, as opposed to these examples of *transformation*: the most obvious examples would be the Band Aid/USA for Africa clips DO THEY KNOW IT'S CHRIST-MAS and WE ARE THE WORLD, which, by virtue of simultaneous song/video media saturation (coupled perhaps with a relative lack of investment in the songs themselves, as opposed to the cause they promoted, and the fact that investment in star indentities is dispersed, paradoxically enough, by their abundance), achieved a more symbiotic relationship than is usual.[15]

In order to understand the relation between sound and image, song and video, we need first to consider whether some visual signifiers are stronger than others (clearly this is so) in "fixing" meaning. One impor-tant factor here would be the different emotional investments that listeners/viewers bring to a song or video, depending on whether they are "fans" of that artist (or perhaps, just as important, harbor a strong dislike for the act in question). Second, we would need to remember that visual images are polysemic, too, and that meanings will never be frozen in time, or fixed for everyone. In order to demonstrate that video is es-tablishing a narrower range of meanings, one would have to show both that visual signification in the video itself routinely dominates the song and that it is not open to the same degree of interpretative frameworks as the music. This has yet to be shown by any of music television's critics. Furthermore, it would be necessary to show how video meanings oper-ate independent of other forms of visual promotion. (I will argue in the next chapter that this is an impossible task.)

It would also be important to consider the relative impact of song and video in the years following the heavy airplay only briefly enjoyed by some clips. Indeed, for videos that utilize rapid-fire cutting of apparently unrelated images (which often turn out to be extremely condensed or enigmatic metaphors), it needs to be asked whether in fact the more readily accessible and more frequently repeated audio portion is likely to dominate our memory of the clip from the outset. As Kinder (1984) suggests (contradicting the argument for visual dominance) in her analysis of Whitesnake's clip SLOW 'N EASY: "Although this video clip is dominated by performance, the fast pace of the montage makes it anything but easy to recall the chain of visual images that accompany the music" (p. 8).

A useful approach in thinking through these questions is suggested by the concept of "inner speech" developed by V. N. Volosinov (1929/1986) in *Marxism and the Philosophy of Language*. Volosinov's critique of socially dislocated linguistic analysis (in both semiotics and individualistic psychologism) is a model for one of the tasks attempted here. In Volosinov's account of the problem of analyzing "reported speech," he notes:

> Everything vital in the evaluative reception of another's utterance, everything of any ideological value, is expressed in the material of "inner speech." After all, it is not a mute, wordless creature that receives such an utterance, but a human being full of inner words. All his experiences — his so-called apperceptive background — exist encoded in his inner speech, and only to that extent do they come into contact with speech received from the outside. Word comes into contact with word. The context of this inner speech is the locale in which another's utterance is received, comprehended and evaluated; it is where the speaker's *active orientation* takes place. (p. 118; emphasis added).

In the context of music television, this comment is highly relevant, although it also needs amending. The music television viewer is full of sounds and images, as well as words, and I will follow Elvis Costello (rather than Volosinov) in arguing that these experiences cannot always be reduced to words (although they may be *understood* through them). However, if we widen Volosinov's terms of reference this way, it is clear that the "inner speech" of the music television audience is significant for the intertextual moment of interpretation, for it is a moment that must take account of the words, sounds, and images that have already "filled up" the viewer.

My point is that the dominance or otherwise of vision over sound can be understood only if we approach the matter sociologically (as Volosinov suggests), by investigating the signs that interact in an internal "dialogue" when a music video clip is watched. The extent to which a clip's imagery may be primary will therefore be dependent on the prior availability for that inner dialogue of (a) the song itself, (b) performance imagery already established by that artist, and (c) other video clips to which it might be related. It is slightly misleading, therefore, to present the analysis of music video in the terms set out by one researcher who sought to collect empirical evidence on how music television is watched, coming up with some revealing conclusions that were nonetheless posed in terms of the "problem" of "situational variables":

> I went to high schools and showed pre-selected videos to teen audiences and demanded they give me feedback. Their responses varied from hostility to amity, triggered less by content and more by situational variables such as was the artist hot, had the artist recently appeared in concert locally, or whether there was an avid fan in the classroom. (Lehnerer, 1987: 75)

The author goes on to note the inadequacy of this approach, and to undertake an interesting and more ethnographically oriented project, yet what is troublesome here is the whole concept of "situational variables." In popular music culture, these "variables" *are* the content, more often than not. The meaning of a given clip may lie precisely in prejudice, fandom, competence, expertise, familiarity, and fashion generated beyond the limits of the music video "text." Therefore, scholars need to invent techniques of critical speculation that take account of this; I will be especially concerned with that issue in chapter 5.

These points lay the basis for two of my concerns in this book: to elaborate, at a variety of levels, the relations between music and image in the pop industry, and to consider how music television intersects the production of meaning that is inextricably built into the sound-vision relation in contemporary pop. In approaching this work, I will falter if I make the error of assuming that video images are imposed on songs in a culture that is otherwise visually "innocent." This work must also involve a critical engagement with what are largely just *assumptions* about the primacy of the image.

But it is important to note that this position does not involve the slippage that sometimes occurs when the moment of meaning production is located in the act of reception—namely, the tendency for audiences to be given *too much* autonomy, as though individual subjects (in a return to the psychologism that Volosinov rejected) could construct meanings from media texts at will. This recent populism in cultural studies is no more helpful than the inflexible search for textual monosemy that it sought to replace, for it is clear that in Volosinov's model, individual subjects have been structured socially in such a way as to make only certain kinds of inner dialogue possible. While in this book I do not tackle the question of investigating reading formations in a wider social context, I will attempt to establish some ground rules for understanding how music and media discourses interact when music television is consumed. The weakness of the structuralist and post-mass communications model of media reception is that, in its emphasis on the relative autonomy of the *audience* vis-à-vis the culture industries, it too infrequently explores the ways in which media discourses help construct the subject's reaction to media discourses. (I explore this point in more detail in chapter 7.) Clearly this is an important nuance for any analysis that tackles a form such as popular music, whose media sites are multiple, and where the interpretation of a music video clip is going to depend in part on exposure to other media texts (for instance, songs, performances, other video clips). The range of possible reactions to a clip will depend in part on readings that are, inevitably, partially structured through those other media texts.

I will now detail some of the absences that arise from a neglect of the musical context of video clips.

The Seduction of the Visual

In a review of Jean Baudrillard's *America* (1988a), Meaghan Morris (1988a) has noted that Baudrillard's postmodern critique of America from behind a windshield is totally visual—he *talks* to no one. The silence in the world of postmodernism is rarely clearer than when we consider its analysis of music television. In cultural studies circles, the study of music television has been characterized by a dominant association with this one paradigm (Aufderheide, 1986; Fiske, 1986; Kaplan, 1987; Tetzlaff, 1986; Wollen, 1986). Postmodern critics see in MTV a mirror image of the ideal postmodern text: "Fragmentation, segmentation, superficiality, stylistic jumbling, the blurring of mediation and reality, the collapse of past and future into the moment of the present, the elevation of hedonism, the dominance of the visual over the verbal" (Tetzlaff, 1986: 80). The emergence in August 1988 of a program titled *Post Modern MTV* would seem to be the final confirmation of the intimate ties between the text and the theory. By the time of the 1990 MTV Video Music Awards, a new category of "post modern video" had been established, and the music industry itself had appropriated the term in the generic category of "postmodern rock."

Postmodern theory is notorious for an eclecticism that addresses not only its objects of study but the theory itself (see Goodwin, 1991b). For my purposes here it is possible to identify a number of key themes in the effort to relate postmodernism and music television:

1. Music television is thought to defy the categories of cultural capital. It is seen to constitute a typically postmodern development, in its fusion of high art and popular cultural discourses (or, perhaps more accurately, its refusal to acknowledge such cultural boundaries).

2. The abandonment of grand narrative structures present in postmodern culture is identified both in the nonrealist construction of the video clips and in the televisual text of, for example, MTV, which supposedly eschews discrete programs organized around traditional narrative regimes. MTV in particular is described as a service that favors continuous, seamless transmission—both factors imply an unstable text, and perhaps the production of an unstable self.

3. The borrowing from other texts prevalent in music videos and in MTV programming is viewed as a form of "intertextuality" typical of postmodern culture, which often finds an outlet in "pastiche"—in Fredric Jameson's (1984b) words, "blank parody."

4. Intertextuality and pastiche are assumed to blur historical/chronological distinctions, so that conventional notions of past, present, and future are lost in the potpourri of images, all of which are made to seem contemporary.

5. Music television is considered to be a "schizophrenic" abandonment of rational, liberal-humanist discourse that creates a nihilistic, amoral universe of representation on a par with other postmodern texts, such as the Bret Easton Ellis novel *Less than Zero*, or in the work of David Lynch (*Blue Velvet, Twin Peaks*). It therefore abandons the realms of political and social engagement as they are generally recognized, leading either to a pessimistic diagnosis (Tetzlaff) or to the suggestion that postmodern culture constitutes new forms of political resistance (Fiske, Kaplan).

While I concur with Dick Hebdige's (1988: 182) assertion that the postmodern debate has become so pervasive that it must be describing something real, and with Todd Gitlin's (1989) guarded endorsement that "something must be at stake in the edgy debates circulating around and about something called postmodernism" (p. 100), I take issue with postmodern analysis of music television. While there is a good case to be made for seeing some cultural forms in terms of postmodernity (e.g., twentieth-century architecture, postwar literature, 1980s political discourse), the current fashion for conflating the specificities of different media and genre into a ragbag category of "postmodernism" does injustice in equal measure to both the conceptual field and the object of study. Television programs such as *Miami Vice* (Gitlin, 1986), *Moonlighting* (Grossberg, 1987), and *USA Today: The Television Show* (Glassner, 1991) can be analyzed in these terms, and there is a good argument for discussing contemporary pop music in terms of new, possibly postmodern, relations between past and present. But music video in general and MTV in particular both represent poor choices of case studies for advocates of postmodern theory. I will pursue this line of argument further in chapters 6 and 7; at this stage I merely wish to note some of the broad limitations and problems of the burgeoning postmodernist literature on the topic, as they relate to the neglect of music and the music industry.

The postmodern analysis of the convergence of avant-garde/ modernist and popular/realist texts, for instance, is insufficiently grounded in an understanding of pop music debates. Because their categories of analysis usually derive from film studies, postmodern critics do not take account of the different ways in which modes of address operate in cinema and pop music. For instance, pop songs are often performed through a direct and/or first-person mode of address, thus breaking with the illusionism of the "fourth wall" of naturalistic cinema and television. There has as yet been very little analysis of pop music narratives — an absence that I will attempt to redress, specifically in chapter 4. Reading the dozens of postmodern accounts that celebrate the fragmentary visual discourses of MTV, one might never notice that MTV's sound track is organized around regimes of repetition and tonality that are highly ordered and predictable. Again, detailed discussion of the music itself, and its relation to image, remains largely unexplored. I will attempt such discussion later, in chapter 3. Both these points should lead us to question analyses that focus on the textual disruption and disorder sometimes evident at the visual level only.

In addition, postmodern classifications of pop often work by defying generic categories in ways that are hard to understand either musicologically or sociologically. Like many writers on the topic, Marsha Kinder (1984) analyzes music videos exclusively in terms of their visual components, which are assumed to dominate the aural level of the text, thus opening the way for her to draw out some intriguing connections between music television and dreams. Yet the founding assumption of the analysis is certainly open to question. As I have shown, in pop music culture visuals are clearly central—but it has never been demonstrated that they routinely dominate the music itself.

Like the postmodernists, this psychoanalytic reading offers, to paraphrase Leo Lowenthal, mass cultural history in reverse: "Most concert promotions currently being aired on MTV stress the extravagance of the visual spectacle as much as the music—spectacle designed to match what is being seen on television" (Kinder, 1987: 232). Using the same observation, Simon Frith (1988b) makes the link with postmodernism, in identifying the "simulation" at the heart of this process:

> For an increasing number of rock fans the meaning of "live"
> performance, the look of music "in reality" therefore comes
> from its ubiquitous simulation. This is an example of what we
> might call the Baudrillard effect: a concert feels real only to the
> extent that it matches its TV reproduction: even Bruce
> Springsteen's shows are now experienced in terms of their video
> imagery. (pp. 124–25)

The danger here is of exaggerating the impact of music video; the more important pheonomenon here is surely the presence of live video relays at major concerts, including those of Bruce Springsteen, since this technology certainly *does* influence the practice of attending a live performance. The argument is constructed around a chronological sleight of hand. The problem with both Kinder's and Frith's arguments is that they conflate those artists who present live music based on representations from music videos (Madonna, for instance) with a more common phenomenon: artists whose live performances look like their videos because the video clips are closely based on their stage acts. My point is that visual spectacles (dancing, gesture, the display of virtuosity, lighting, smoke bombs, dry ice, back projection, etc.) have always worked in tandem with the music itself. Performance videos on music television mirror many of these codes and conventions (established in more than thirty years of rock and pop concerts), yet academic theorists frequently relate this iconography to filmic, postmodernist, and (in Kinder's case) psychoanalytic categories without taking account of its more prosaic intention— that of evoking the excitement of live pop performance. Those discourses will surely merit further study, including perhaps psychoanalytic interpretation, but we cannot understand them if we reverse the actual chronological relation that sometimes exists between rock music and television. In other words, we should not assume that the signs and conventions of live performance are an imitation of television (except in those cases where this *is* so); instead, it is necessary to investigate the relations among music, live performance, and video imagery. That concern will be an important underpinning of this book, where I will attempt to show the close relations between music and image, particularly in chapter 3.

In another instance E. Ann Kaplan (1987) develops a different connection between postmodernism and the observations cited above when she writes:

> Most often the rock video world looks like noplace, or like a
> post-nuclear holocaust place — without boundaries, definition or
> recognizable location. Figures are often placed in a smoky, hazy
> environment . . . the sudden, unexplained explosion is a
> common feature." (p. 145)

Concertgoers will, however, recognize each of the "postnuclear" features of the rock video as elements in the staging of live rock shows. The "unexplained" explosions remain unexplained only if our ears are closed — otherwise we will notice that they tend to coincide with the pulse of the music and occur at moments of dramatic crescendo. What video effects and live staging have in common is, as I will show in chapter 3, an illustrative relation to aspects of the music, especially rhythm.

Likewise, Margaret Morse (1986) writes:

> The videos condense a considerable amount of narrative material
> into approximately four minutes, either through editing or also
> by spacing different elements related to a mood or story within
> one large room. It seems often to be a warehouse, a parking
> garage or an abandoned factory or hospital. (p. 17)

But it is, of course, a *rehearsal room* that is usually represented here: an element of the mise-en-scène that has important implications for the meaning of video clips, especially in relation to stardom, the construction of community, and the portrayal of musical professionalism.

These problems do not lie solely in the absence of musical and music industry-related analysis. Indeed, they arise from a more fundamental problem concerning assumptions about the role of theory. It is to that issue that I now turn.

From Texts to Contexts

One explanation for the poverty of music video analysis lies in the absence of a field of concepts adequate to this new form. And that problem has its roots in the *visual bias* of the theories that have been employed to date. The approaches that derive from film studies have their basis in paradigms drawn from the study of photography, iconography, and psychoanalysis, and necessarily neglect the analysis of sound.[16] Even in the field of television studies, whose conceptual development has largely been overlooked by music video theorists, there remains a marginalization of the audio element that has been identified and very fruitfully explored by Rick Altman (1987).

These difficulties have opened the way for a plethora of "readings" that generate some of the problems criticized above. Yet to cite the fact of visual bias is not in itself a complete explanation, for the limitations of some music video analysis lie also in a mutation of textual analysis that is now prevalent in cultural studies. This is the practice of constructing textual readings not on the basis of a theorized relation between text and production, or between text and consumption, but rather between text and *theory*. This represents an abandonment of the original intentions of textual analysis, which were to illuminate the conditions of production (Brunsdon & Morley, 1978), to engage in ideological critique (Gitlin, 1987; Hall, 1977), and to explore possible reading formations in the audience (Hobson, 1980; Morley, 1980a).

Text analysis was thus firmly rooted not in the "disinterested" project of literary or aesthetic criticism, but in the sociological (and, sometimes, psychoanalytic) project of understanding the social production and consumption of culture. Since that task is my concern in this book, it is important to address the purposes and methods used in my textual analysis of pop music and music television. I assume in the research that follows that the purpose of providing textual readings is not merely to establish fascinating, diverting, and perhaps even intelligent connections between cultural theories and texts. My purpose is to show how the conditions of production of music television are written into the text, and then to establish some possible reading formations that elaborate (in what I hope is a nonreductive fashion) the aesthetic and political implications of music television.

This should be an unremarkable statement of intent. It is based upon a critique of formalistic semiotic analysis that has been stated on many occasions and in a variety of scholarly contexts (for instance, Eagleton, 1983; Garnham, 1979b; Rodowick, 1988; Scholes, 1981; Volosinov, 1929/ 1986; Williams, 1977a). Yet consider how it differs from the literature published to date on this topic, which typifies a problem characterized thus by Meaghan Morris (1988b) in a critical account of recent developments in cultural studies:

> The kind of explanation from "production" so cheerfully rejected in cultural studies usually boils down to one based on a model of good old-fashioned, family-company industrialism. You can't derive your analysis of what people make of a record from finding out that capitalists own the factory. You can't deduce our uses of TV knowing who makes the programme and who owns the channels and how they link to other companies and agencies of state. Indeed, you can't. But in an era of de-industrialisation and increasing integration of markets and circuits alike, the problem of theorising relations between production and consumption (or thinking "production" at all) is considerably more complex than is allowed by a reduction of the effort to do so to anachronistic terms. (p. 24)

This is precisely the strategy of "post-Marxist" postmodern analysis of music television. And so, paradoxically, the textual analysts of music television are surprisingly crude when the conditions of production are considered. Kaplan (1987) reverts to simple forms of auteur theory at key moments in her text, for instance, in her account of MTV as the "creation" of one person (Robert Pittman). Other postmodern writers tend to opt for an economism, in which MTV in particular is condemned as a "twenty-four-hour advertisement" and in which music videos are seen as an incorporation of the true spirit of rock and roll music. I take up this issue in more detail in chapters 2 and 6.

In the research that follows, the attempt to read music television for traces of the "pressures and limits" (Williams, 1973) of the production context implies an effort to *open up* our understanding of the politics of music television, not a project of economic reductionism. As I will show in the next chapter, this production context is complex and defies many taken-for-granted assumptions about the relations between texts and institutions.

In addition to assuming that the production context of music television involves a very full engagement with the *music industry*, I assume that because most consumers of music video are music fans, the best route to outlining contemporary reading formations lies in an engagement with the shifting aesthetics of rock and pop music. The point is an important one: analysis informed by an understanding of music and the music industry is offered here as a more explanatory account of music television not because it produces richer readings of texts, or because its conclusions are closer to the orthodoxies of rock criticism. I argue for the superiority of this hermeneutic on the grounds that it more accurately corresponds to the actual reading formations of the audience for music television.

A great many of the textual readings published so far have been based on unfounded assumptions about "pastiche," usually involving reference to cinema, that may have little empirical basis in actual reading formations. The problem here is not just that music television analysts have neglected the referencing of rock's codes and conventions in favor of spotting cinematic (and televisual) references, but that the audience itself comprises many consumers who simply do not know what film noir is. Much the same can be said of references to high art, avant-garde aesthetics, and so forth. Postmodern critics who have been saturated in decades of cultural analysis have sometimes forgotten to consider how texts will actually be consumed by the audience, even where they invoke the polysemy of cultural consumption.

Kaplan (1987), for instance, expends a great deal of energy analyzing the pastiche involved in the Mary Lambert-directed video clip MATERIAL GIRL, noting the various ways in which it references *Gentlemen Prefer Blondes*. This reading is appropriate only if it can be shown that the Madonna audience read the clip through knowledge of the Howard Hawks movie. And yet MATERIAL GIRL is intertextual in a wide variety of ways: not only through the general use of its Marilyn Monroe/"dumb blonde" stereotyping, but also through Madonna's media reworking of that image, through the film *Desperately Seeking Susan*, which was released around the same time, and—more recently—when it is read retrospectively in the light of arguments about Madonna's "feminism" (see Lewis, 1990).[17] Just how relevant are the references to a film made in 1953 for an audience comprising many Madonna fans who are unaware of its existence, and would therefore be blind to the elements of pastiche? Of course, it would be foolish to deny that pastiche is involved here, to the extent that the Hawks movie and the Monroe image remain current in popular culture. My point is simply that this is not the only referent, and that it will, for *some* viewers, be an irrelevant one.

I use this example as one of dozens that might be chosen from the literature on music television. (The question of pastiche is taken up in more detail in chapter 7.) My aim is to establish the *materiality* of my earlier critique of the neglect of the music industry, and to buttress the applicability of Volosinov's ideas. Here, in his terms, music video analysts have paid insufficient attention to the "inner speech" of the music television audience. The problem is not just that one possibly interesting way of studying music television has been missed, it is that this is often the *dominant* framework for reading video clips and music television networks. For this reason, in the following chapters I will attempt to build on a discussion of the context of music production with detailed readings that explore possible relations among music, image, and popular music narratives.

TWO

From Anarchy to Chromakey
Developments in Music Television

> I feel like I've been an adman for the past year. I don't feel like a
> singer.
>
> —Roland Gift, Fine Young Cannibals[1]

Accounts of music television that begin by telling us that music video
was "invented" in a given year (or that imply such a position by using a
chronology that starts with the moment of birth of MTV) miss out of an
important step in thinking about this topic, namely, what *is* "music television"? It is essential that we engage this question because it encompasses many other issues regarding the nature of music video texts, and in
particular the relation between their economic status and ideological significance.

I begin this chapter, therefore, by asking two different kinds of questions. First, how and why did promotional music videos emerge? And
second, what definitions and understandings of popular music are implied by that first question? In other words, what are the defining properties of "music television"? I will answer these questions with a central
premise that runs counter to many recent attempts to understand this
new area of cultural studies: I assume that we cannot make sense of music
video without locating its development within a nexus of far-reaching
changes inside the mass media, including the pop music industry. The
analysis of music television presented here is predicated on the assumption that since the cultural industries are currently in a state of increasing
convergence, it will repay media analysts to make greater efforts toward

the integration of critical concepts drawn from the various disciplines that inform media and cultural analysis.

The media industries are currently involved in processes of convergence, both at the level of institutions (e.g., mergers, cross-media marketing deals, new forms of advertising and sponsorship) and at the level of the text (generic fusions and crossovers within media and between them). Music television is a classic case of such fusion, representing both the blurring of two hitherto separate (indeed, sometimes hostile) media and a new hybrid of programming and promotion that mixes media and genres at the level of the text.

In order to understand music television, therefore, it is necessary to probe ways of combining analyses normally left to their own devices — in pop music, television, and advertising studies. The first step in understanding music television must be to move beyond the analysis of television deriving from film studies and begin to grapple with the questions raised by popular music scholars such as Franco Fabbri (1982) and Antoine Hennion (1990), who have investigated the problem of locating the correct objects and levels of study. The key points that arise out of this kind of investigation are that the production of meaning in the sphere of pop music occurs across a variety of textual sites and in an unusual relation to its commodity form. This in turn leads us into an investigation of the commodity and promotional status of music television — without which, I will argue, the correct questions to pose in textual analysis cannot be known.

Performance as Promotion

It is important to establish from the outset that pop music is, and always has been, a multidiscursive cultural form, in which no one media site is privileged. The implication of this for music video analysis is that it becomes impossible to understand the meaning of any individual clip without considering its relation to the wider world of pop culture. The pop industry has always differed from other media in one crucial aspect that places its ancillary industries (TV, radio, cinema, publishing, advertising) at the center of any analysis: most other media forms have traditionally been sustained economically by direct commodity production, by advertising, or by a mixture of the two, but this is not quite true of the music business. The commodity forms of the music industry are records, cassettes, and compact discs. These are the products that have to be shifted in order to make profits. And yet these products do not sustain pop meaning, which has always had to draw on other forms — including posters, teen magazines, live performances, film, radio, and TV. As Alan Durant (1984) notes:

> Within what is commonly referred to as rock or "popular music," there is no obvious, single format or mode of presentation. When thinking about this area of music . . . what is in question is not simply a well-established corpus of either records, performances, groups or images. Unlike television, film or arguably theatre, the forms of this music irreducibly involve an intersecting range of practices, without an obvious primacy of any one discourse or text. To isolate gramophone discs as the "text" of rock music, for example, is to marginalise or dismiss a very considerable range of activities . . . which never accede to reproduction by way of the recording process. . . . It would also be to neglect the important way in which rock's musical forms have spread over a variety of technical means other than gramophone recording — "live" performance itself, of course; cassettes; television and film soundtrack; currently "promotional" videos. (p. 168)

Durant's argument is supported by recent trends in the music industry, where a proliferation of formats and configurations and the growth of mass media-related pop products lend further emphasis to his point. This comment, from music industry lawyer Alexis Grower, indicates the breadth of media involved in promoting today's popular music:

> When I've seen non-music lawyers look at music contracts they don't know what they're doing. . . . There are now an increasing number of ways of exploiting an artist's work. Twenty years ago they didn't have videos, cable TV, satellite, pop songs used in adverts, jingle-writing, compact discs, cassettes, the 12-inch market, merchandising, and they didn't have TV advertising to sell records. The contracts have become more complicated because the whole industry has become more complicated, and you want to make sure that your client gets the benefit of it all. (quoted in Garfield, 1986: 255-56)

The point is made also by Island Records founder Chris Blackwell:

> I don't think there are any record companies now in the real

sense of the word. We're all in the fashion business. You used to be able to sell records purely on music and musicianship. Now it's packaging, media, television and video. (quoted in Garfield, 1986: 244)

These trends in the music industry are not unique. It is also the case that other media are increasingly multitextual (in Durant's terms) — a process that was exemplified, for instance, in the selling of the 1989 Warner Bros. film *Batman*, which involved tie-ins with the music industry (Prince's *Batman the Movie* LP, and the sound track from the film itself), publishing (including the Batman comic books, published by Warner Communications subsidiary D.C. Comics), television (through home video sales and rentals, and — eventually — cable and broadcast television rights), and merchandising (Batman bubble gum, breakfast cereal, and so on).

It is useful here to consider an important distinction emphasized by Nicholas Garnham (1983: 2), following Theodor Adorno, between those media industries that distribute products that are essentially mass-produced, recorded forms (film, TV) and those media — including music — that are based on the mass circulation of preindustrial cultural forms (including also books). Why is this important? Because it points to a contradiction inside the music industry, between inherently mass-produced commodity forms such as records and cassettes (which produce profit but insufficient meaning) and preindustrial forms of promotion such as live performance (which help to "complete" the package of meaning, but which until the 1980s generally failed to generate profit even when organized on a mass scale). These observations also demonstrate why isolated analysis of individual texts is inadequate for our understanding of the increasingly intertextual processes of the mass media — textual processes that of course result in part from increasing concentration and integration at the level of ownership in the cultural industries. (The selling of *Batman*, like the selling of Michael Jackson, has employed vertically integrated economies of scale to improve profitability.)

Music video clips must be contextualized within a framework that explains the role of pop performances in terms of their essentially *promotional* role within a multidiscursive industry. Jacques Attali (1985) has noticed this phenomenon, but without explaining it:

For those trapped by the record, public performance becomes a simulacrum of the record: an audience generally familiar with the artist's recordings attends to hear their live replication. What

> irony: people originally intended the record to preserve the
> performance, and today the performance is only successful as a
> simulacrum of the record. (p. 85)

Ironic or not (and rock does, after all, continue to pay homage to the primacy of the "live," raw-sounding recording),[2] this process very obviously derives from the commodification of popular music. Live performances must resemble recordings because it is from the sale of those
commodities that profit is generated. However, as I will show, Attali's
analogy of the "simulacrum" is inadequate, because pop performances
do not merely imitate previously consumed, recorded, commodified ar-
tifacts; they must also promote as-yet unsold commodities (other
records, or perhaps old music in new configurations, as in the case of
consumers buying music they already possess, perhaps on CD).

Pop performance is therefore not only a commodity in itself but also
an essential adjunct to the business of selling T-shirts, records, tapes, and
compact discs. The emergence of promotional music videos must be understood in light of this fact: that pop performance has always had a
largely promotional role.[3] The development of the promotional music
video can thus be seen in part as a means of more effectively commodi-
fying the business of promotion—a trend that is also exemplified in the
increasing use in the 1980s and 1990s of corporate sponsorship and the
expanding economic role of merchandising (the sale of T-shirts, programs, and other tour paraphernalia) in tour budgets (see McRobbie,
1986b; Mower, 1986; Sandall, 1988; Savan, 1987; *Variety*, 1989: 58;
Young, 1986; Zimmer, 1988).

From this perspective music video can be seen as an attempt on behalf
of the music industry to find a more efficient and cost-effective method
of promoting pop music internationally. It must also be seen in the context of related developments, such as the corporate sponsorship of pop
concerts (and radio and TV slots) and the growth of pop merchandising.
That last development has reached such a stage of importance that sales
of T-shirts at major concerts sometimes outstrip the revenue gained from
ticket sales. A further area of profitability has emerged in the shape of
spin-offs from video recordings of live performances, distributed via
videocassettes, cable television, pay-per-view television, and—on occasion—broadcast television.

The history of pop is thus the history of a form that has become increasingly commodified via the recording and media industries, while it

is still wedded to the discourses of performance that are essential to pop meaning. Aspects of visual performance have always been provided via television and movies: what is new about music video is not just its pervasiveness and potential for cost-effective international circulation, but the fact that the record companies themselves control the funding of these new performance texts. Music video therefore lacks the degree of cultural autonomy enjoyed by most previous forms of pop performance, as Dave Laing (1985a) has pointed out. For instance, when a record company helps underwrite the cost of a national tour, it enjoys none of the influence over the performance that it does when it hires a director to shoot a music video clip. While this certainly does not mean that we can automatically "read off" music video meanings from what we know of their conditions of production, I will try to show later in this book (especially in the discussion of stardom in chapter 5) that the promotional demands of music video explain many of its textual features.

Having located music video clips within this context of performance, and having placed performance itself in its essentially promotional relation to pop commodities, I can now turn to the question of the emergence of music television, which has its roots in five developments in the music and media industries: (a) changes in the pop music performing and recording processes; (b) shifting ideologies of pop, organized around the development in Britain of the "New Pop"; (c) expansion of television services, especially in cable television in the United States; (d) recession in the music industry and related concern about the rise of competing audiovisual leisure services; and (e) changing demographic patterns in rock and pop music consumption.

From Anarchy to Chromakey

The question of the origins of music video is a matter that has received considerable academic and journalistic attention. Following Shore (1985), a BBC-TV program tracing the history of promotional videos once cited a short film made in 1934 as an antecedent of the form.[4] Journalists writing about the subject routinely mention the promotional jazz film clips made in the 1940s, sometimes referred to by their brand name of Soundies, and the Scopitone jukebox developed in France in the 1960s.[5] Other sources cited are the various 1950s movies about youth culture and rock and roll that contain sequences not unlike today's promos.[6] On television, in the 1960s, there was *The Monkees* TV series, and other televisual pop, such as *The Archies* and *The Partridge Family*, is often mentioned. The Beatles are often introduced into the debate, as critics cite the early Beatles films (*A Hard Day's Night, Help!*), later promotional film clips ("Penny Lane," "Strawberry Fields Forever"), and the *Magical Mystery Tour* TV special. But the most popular candidate for the title of "first" music video is the Jon Roseman/Bruce Gowers six-minute clip for Queen's number-one hit record "Bohemian Rhapsody," made in 1975.

Yet the hunt for origins is a fruitless exercise, like the pointless debate about labels (is it *pop video, music video, music television,* or *promotional video/clip?*). Certainly many of these earlier fusions of sound and vision are very interesting and tell us a great deal about pop—most important, that music television and pop cinema are as old as pop itself. But if we want to identify the beginnings of music video in its contemporary form, we need to know what is significant about it. If pop sounds and visions on celluloid and videotape date back to Bill Haley and Elvis Presley, to the Monkees and the Beatles, to Abba and the Sex Pistols, then why is it only in the 1980s that critics and industry insiders begin to discuss something called "music video"?

Is it the device of lip-syncing (miming to a song) that is new? No. This technique is as old as Hollywood and commonplace when pop stars appear on TV. (However, I will suggest later that technological changes in music making have subsequently altered its meaning.) Is it the break with "realism" in image making? Once again, no. The aural codes of pop have often made such a break, and attempts by some critics to apply the debate about the cinematic "classic realist text" to pop performance are, as I will show in chapter 4, largely unconvincing.

What is really important about music video is its emergence in the 1980s as a routine method for promoting pop singles. (As long as this is so, music television will always be able to survive the demise of MTV, which many critics seem to view, consciously or not, as coterminus with the form—a slippage that MTV itself is keen to encourage.) This is why the development of music television is inextricably tied into the moment known as the "New Pop"—those acts, including the "New Romantics," who represented a shift in pop's attitude to music-making technologies and promotional strategies.[7] Before going on to discuss the complicated interaction of developments in the music and media industries, I want to sketch out the initial moment of the emergence of music video in the United Kingdom and its connection with the New Pop.

Neither *The Monkees* nor PENNY LANE nor BOHEMIAN RHAPSODY had any consistent or long-lasting effect on the way pop was sold. The promotional clips that accompanied the music of acts such as Duran Duran, the Thompson Twins, ABC, Wham!, and Culture Club did. As Simon Reynolds (1985) and Dave Rimmer (1985) have shown in their analyses of the New Pop, this was a movement organized around new understandings of the relations among music, image, and business that developed partly in reaction to the perceived "failure" of punk rock.

The question of the music itself is central to my argument, since it was changes in the process of production that helped to lay the foundations for video promotion. The ideology of punk was one of "do it yourself," in which "amateurs" were encouraged to learn the very basics of pop song production and then form a band. In the d-i-y language of punk fanzine *Sniffin' Glue*: "Here's a chord. Now go and form a band" (quoted in Laing, 1985b: 22; see Laing's book generally for more on punk). To this end, some groups (for instance, Cabaret Voltaire, the Human League) used synthesizers, sequencers, and drum machines to produce rudimentary avant-punk music. In performance, however, despite the occasional use of machines, the emphasis in punk was always on *real* performance. Punk's ideology of workers' control placed the musicians themselves at the center of things, and while amateurism was celebrated, this was usually in the context of actual, human, performance. Indeed, an overreliance on advanced technology was taken as a sign of "progressive rock"—the very music that punk was supposed to displace.

But when the moment of punk passed, in the late 1970s, musicians began to take a new interest in the mainstream, and in particular in dance music. New acts who formed after punk, or who simply failed to gain commercial success during punk, turned to the movement of the New Pop, just as some members of successful punk bands shifted their musical locus toward dance music, partly via a new interest in drum machines and sequencers. The shift from punk do-it-yourself sounds to a sleeker, machine-based music is typified in the careers of Joy Division/New Order, the Thompson Twins, the Human League/Heaven 17, and Scritti Politti. Newer acts who exemplified this machine age were Depeche Mode, Thomas Dolby, and Frankie Goes to Hollywood.[8]

By 1980 drum machines had become so sophisticated that their use in music production was routine. Sequencers had become more advanced and it became possible to store songs and whole sets in the memory of a bank of synthesizers and then take them on tour, to perform "live."

Computer sampling devices such as the Fairlight CMI and the Synclavier began to usurp the musician's role in the studio, and were increasingly used on stage. It was becoming commonplace for producers to store all the appropriate sounds in a computer, which could then be programmed to an astonishing degree of sophistication—thus obviating the need for the musicians to play at all. Often they did not even need to be present.[9]

This *displacement of the musician* eventually culminated in the controversy about lip-syncing and miming in live performance. From the New Pop moment onward, distinctions between automated and human performance were increasingly blurred. Bands that used sequencers in their recordings began to play back these automated sounds in the live context, thus integrating the "recorded" and "live" moments. Rap music totally undermined the distinction between the creation of music and its appropriation. As samplers were used in performance, it became more and more difficult for the concertgoer to perceive the *source* of the sounds heard over the PA. (This is a facet of attending live performances that exactly corresponds to the "sound hermeneutic" function developed in Rick Altman's 1987 analysis of television's aural addresses, in which a sound asks us to look at the screen—in this case, the stage—to find its source.) Throughout the 1980s, pop, rock, and rap audiences became habituated to the idea that some of the music being heard "live" might be on tape, or might emanate from a machine, and/or might consist of a sample of music recorded elsewhere.

Eventually, in late 1990, it was revealed that some singers were actually miming to prerecorded vocals in concert, and legislators in New Jersey and other U.S. states threatened legal action to make it mandatory for promoters to inform the audience of this practice (see Giles, 1991; Handelman, 1990). Soon thereafter, Milli Vanilli were stripped of their 1990 Grammy award for Best New Artist when it was found that the duo (Rob Pilatus and Fab Morvan) sang neither on their own album nor in "live" performance. Other, associated, disruptions of the contract of faith implied when we *see* a vocalist singing or a musician playing (the truth-performance nexus, which very much parallels traditional notions in broadcasting ideology, such as the BBC's injunction of professionalism to "keep faith with the viewer") occurred. For instance, in 1989 vocalist Loleatta Holloway was obliged to take out a lawsuit against the Italian Euro-disco act Black Box when her voice was extensively sampled on the single "Ride on Time," and lip-synced to in a video clip and in television performances by a model (Katrin Quinol).[10] Indeed, on the

Black Box video compilation *Video Dreams 1991* (BMG Video) Quinol is listed as one of the four members of Black Box, even though the credits make it clear that the vocals are performed by Holloway, by Martha Wash, and by Heather Small—none of whom are in the "band"!

Why are these developments relevant to the emergence of music video as a routine sales mechanism? Because the new music-making technologies demonstrated to musicians, critics, and audiences more forcefully than ever before that pop performance is a *visual* experience. If performing pop music could mean singing across recorded sounds that are almost identical to the music on record and tape, then it was only a small step to accept as a legitimate pop practice the miming of a performance for a music video clip. The changing uses made of technology thus sanctioned and legitimated the practice of lip-syncing as a valid part of pop culture. Importantly, this argument suggests that the later development of acts such as Milli Vanilli was *not* a "result" of MTV and music television. Rather, both Milli Vanilli and MTV were effects of the uses to which the new pop technologies were put. (I will analyze the economic roots of this shift in the final section of this chapter.)

Until the moment of the New Pop, musicians on television had either attempted to hide the fact that they were miming (bands on the BBC's *Old Grey Whistle Test* often did this) or poked fun at the whole charade, by miming badly or by introducing extraneous performers not present on the record (tactics used by Marc Bolan of T. Rex and Roy Wood's Wizzard, respectively, on *Top of the Pops* in the 1970s). The New Pop openly acknowledged pop performance as a visual medium with a sound track. My point is that this has always been true, but it was made increasingly apparent by changes in music-making technology. Music video did not create this change; it was validated by it.

The second important postpunk development was a shift in artists' attitudes toward marketing and the media. Again, Dave Rimmer's (1985) account is very revealing here: he shows how many of the New Pop acts were inspired by punk, even as they created sounds and images that seemed to be its antithesis. Music video must also be placed in these contexts of changing pop ideologies. The moment of music video coincides with the rise of the New Pop—those acts (such as Duran Duran, Culture Club, Wham!, Howard Jones) who refused the downbeat style and oppositional politics of punk. Some bands even spanned the shift themselves. The Thompson Twins, for instance, began as a radical independent Afro-punk group and went on—via the dance floor success of "In the Name of Love" in the United States—to become a mainstream teeny-pop act. Scritti Politti started out as a neostructuralist punk band and, after splitting up, were resurrected as a sleek, studio-based pop group. Joy Division began as a guitar-based, dirgelike punk group and remade themselves (following the death in 1980 of lead singer Ian Curtis) as New Order, with danceable, machine-based pop music. What is significant about this trend is not, however, the process of incorporation or "selling out" that is often the focus of (misplaced) criticism. What is important is the shift in pop/rock ideologies that accompanied these postpunk trends.

The New Pop existed in cultural territory where notions of "selling out" no longer made sense, and sounded increasingly like a countercultural accusation from another age. The New Pop bands did not just introduce new images and music into pop, they also shifted its attitudes toward business and commerce. The key here lies in new attitudes toward media marketing. A central development lies in the formation in 1983 of ZTT Records, a company founded by producer Trevor Horn and rock writer Paul Morley, whose main success was with Liverpool band Frankie Goes to Hollywood (see Jackson, 1985). But the ZTT strategy of the self-conscious, ironic hype that served so well in marketing Frankie Goes to Hollywood had a precursor in another band produced by Horn—ABC.

ABC were a Sheffield band who used dance music and machine-based rhythms as a starting point for self-conscious, tongue-in-cheek romanticism and a celebration of abundance that marked one beginning of the new way of making and selling pop. The band's approach was based on a knowing use of glamour, with songs that seemed to be jokes *about* "falling in love;" their most widely known hit was a song appropriately titled "The Look of Love." This strategy dovetailed perfectly with video promotion, and it is significant that it was ABC who made one of the very first long-form, conceptually linked video productions, *Mantrap* (RCA/Columbia, 1983), directed by Julien Temple. The New Pop aesthetic embodied in ABC fractured the relation between sound and image in a fashion that was to typify postpunk pop—and that in some ways paralleled the strategies of rap music.[11]

Punk and rock shared an ideology of performance codes that assumed a correspondence between creativity and performance. That is partly why it is so important for rock artists to write their own material. Performance was seen as an "authentic" event in which musicians communicated their music to an audience.[12] Writers and producers who did not perform could not really be accommodated into an act's public image, despite efforts to acknowledge some record producers as an additional member of the band (George Martin and the Beatles, Eddie Offord and Yes, Chris Thomas and the Pretenders). Where this correlation was severed, rock ideology denied the act in question any true musical credibility and withheld the possibility of an image of authenticity (the Monkees and the Archies are two famous examples).

The New Pop constituted a timely acknowledgment that this ideology did not make sense. By the time Frankie Goes to Hollywood emerged in the United Kingdom in 1983, nobody any longer cared whether or not the musicians played on their own records. In the United States, rock and roll notions of "authenticity" were more entrenched, but by the end of the 1980s Madonna had crossed over into the mass marketplace with strategies that closely resembled those of the New Pop. On her 1990 Blond Ambition tour, she made a point of announcing her intention to do something "naughty," and then lip-synced through the song "Hanky Panky" (which, fittingly, both derived from and promoted the movie *Dick Tracy*). In artists such as Madonna and the Pet Shop Boys, the idea of authenticity still operated to a high degree, but it was located in an act's perceived ability to manipulate and construct media imagery, and could be understood separately from the music-making apparatus. In the British context, as Frith and Horne (1987) have shown, the art schools of Britain had a significant impact in framing this response, as a part of their continuing contribution to rock culture.

By the mid-1980s British pop music had produced many successful acts who did not perform live, and often could not play live, since the music was reproducible only through the use of the multitrack studio and its machinery: Heaven 17, Scritti Politti (in their second, New Pop, phase), the Human League, and Wham! each did little or no live performing in their early days, thus breaking with the accepted rock tradition of "paying your dues" through hard work on the club/college circuit. These acts made studio recordings and personal appearances by means of the mass media—including video clips. The New Pop eventually marketed a band with no identifiable members at all—ZTT's the Art of Noise—and a group in which one member apparently made almost no contribution to the music—Wham! The culmination of these trends was the most critically acclaimed development of this music, the Pet Shop Boys (see Heath, 1990). Their emergence, in a second wave of dance-oriented pop associated with house music and hip-hop, bridged the gap between the

New Pop and rap (their first hit, "West End Girls," was a self-described "English rap" song) and raised the stakes of the challenge to rock authenticity when lead singer Neil Tennant bluntly stated: "It's kinda macho nowadays to prove you *can* cut it live. I quite like proving we *can't* cut it live. We're a pop group, not a rock and roll group" (quoted in *Rolling Stone*, 1988). The context of Tennant's remarks is revealing. At the American Music Awards, the Pet Shop Boys had not only mimed to musical backing, but even lip-synced the vocal parts, rather than singing live over a taped accompaniment, as is increasingly the practice on television and in many live rock performances (for example, the concerts given by New Order, which rely heavily on sequenced/taped backing tracks).

It was thus through video clips that the New Pop acts established themselves as "performers," often miming to music they did not actually play. The New Pop was therefore the precursor to the later trend, noted by Théberge (1989), in which artists such as Prince, whose music was often the result of a one-person multitracking process, used performers to mime parts they did not play in order to create the impression of a group performance. This development is by no means reserved for self-consciously "artistic" musicians like Prince: it has been utilized, for instance, by the heavy metal band Whitesnake, when leader Dave Coverdale hired musicians after the completion of the recording process in order to manufacture the image of a new group line-up. A similar situation occurred with the Replacements' video WHEN IT BEGAN. The album from which the song comes (*All Shook Down*, Sire, 1990) was originally intended as a solo release by songwriter Paul Westerberg; his record company insisted, however, that it be promoted as a Replacements product, even though the band plays on only one track (not "When It Began"). In WHEN IT BEGAN (which was airing as the band were touring to promote "their" album), the whole group appear, miming to parts they did not play. (Occasionally, however, a video clip does reveal the multitracking process; for instance, when Phil Collins is seen performing each of the parts in the clip MISSED AGAIN, this works to promote his virtuosity.)

Changing music-making practices and new attitudes toward marketing and the manufacture of image thus constitute two foundations for the development of music television. The new music-making technologies enabled lip-syncing to be read as a legitimate part of pop performance, and the new attitude to marketing matched the up-front, and often self-conscious, strategies used in promotional clips. These two shifts made the development of video and television as an integral part of pop culture a real possibility. Music video did not, therefore, create the conditions of its own success; that success was made possible by these changes in the music industry. But this in itself does not account for the rise of music television. Promotional video clips were made because there was an audience, but for an explanation of the link between music and television, it is necessary to address other trends inside the media industries.

The Happy Marriage of Music and Television

The changes within the music-making community in the United Kingdom help to explain how the conditions for the development of music video as a routine promotional tool were laid: they do not of course establish a full account of the ascendancy of music television, and they constitute a necessary rather than a sufficient set of explanations. In order to understand why music videos developed so rapidly in the 1980s, it is important to explore the political economy of the media industries, because it was here (rather than in audience demand) that the impulse to produce music video clips on a mass scale was generated.

A major factor in the development of music television lies in the global increase in the quantity of television programming. The most obvious example of this is the expansion of cable television in the United States, but even in the more carefully regulated and restricted markets of Europe, broadcast, cable, and satellite television services experienced a significant increase in the number of programming hours needed to fill the schedule. Since advertising (and license fee) revenue did not and could not increase proportionate to the proposed increases in the number of hours broadcast, it follows that television entrepreneurs were concerned with finding cheaper forms of programming, either through a reduction in the average cost of production or through the economies of scale enjoyed via vertical integration that are available to global media organizations. While the second strategy has been pursued by, among others, Rupert Murdoch's News International group, the first alternative is simpler and less risky. It is that demand, for relatively inexpensive programming, that music television initially met.

That the development of music television was broadcasting led (rather than generated by the music industry) is made clear in Denisoff's (1988) research into the origins of MTV in the United States. MTV probably would never have reached the airwaves without the embryonic promotional video industry developed in the United Kingdom and elsewhere, and in its first eighteen months the new service had some difficulty persuading record companies of the viability and profitability of promotional clips. The music business was nervous about the investment needed in the clips—which ranged upward from about £20,000 per clip at that point[13]—and anxious that music television would turn out to be a fad, like video games.[14]

MTV's incentive to develop music television was of course advertiser led. Its budgets were underwritten by an expectation that an all-music service would deliver to advertisers those younger consumers (12-34-year-olds) who were traditionally difficult to reach through television. MTV was to be the "environment" that would narrowcast the right kind of music and thus target an elusive socioeconomic group. Denisoff's (1988) work shows that in its early months MTV's main problems were access to viewers (through local operators) and access to programming. Its task was to convince each constituency that there was a market for music television: in doing so, MTV had to *construct* an audience for music television. The key point here is that it was the television industry, rather than the record business, that led this development.

The situation in Britain was rather different, but not entirely so. Although broadcasting policy did not allow for the same degree of expansion of hours as in the United States, television in the United Kingdom did substantially increase in quantity during the 1980s. Some of those hours were filled with pop music programming, within existing studio-based formats (e.g., *The Tube*), in exclusively video clip-based shows (e.g., *The Chart Show*), and within other areas of programming (breakfast television, sports programs, and in new late-night programming).

Subsequent to these beginnings in the early 1980s, which drove the enormous expansion of video clips, music television developed in the United States on broadcast television (for instance, NBC's *Friday Night Videos*, which first aired in June 1983) and cable (WTBS's *Night Tracks*, the Nashville Network, Black Entertainment Television's *Video Soul*, the Video Jukebox Network) and on European cable services (for instance, Music Box, the Power Station, and MTV Europe). There is also an important connection with the movie industry, which in the 1980s began increasingly to use pop sound tracks in order to recruit young audiences, with films such as *Flashdance, Pretty in Pink*, and *Dirty Dancing*. Such sound tracks often yielded promotional clips that simultaneously advertised a song, a film, and perhaps a sound track album.

These observations are a necessary contextualization for Laing's (1985a) assertion that the music industry developed video clips in order to gain entry into the domestic audiovisual leisure market. Although some individuals within the music industry saw video as an essential component in its future, most record companies saw no prospects of selling music videotapes directly to the public, and were thus cautious about developing an expensive, solely promotional format.[15] As doubts about music television's long-term future began to fade, and when the long-form tape *The Making of Michael Jackson's "Thriller"* (released in 1983) sold almost half a million copies, the music industry gradually developed a commitment to the production of promotional clips. More recently, home sales and rentals are generating significant income for the record companies, although this remains tiny in comparison with sales of the three established "configurations" (records, cassettes, and CDs).[16] In December 1990 (in time to generate Christmas sales), Warner Bros. (through Warner Reprise Video) released the first mass-selling video single (following a ban imposed by MTV and the BBC), Madonna's JUSTIFY MY LOVE, directed by Jean-Baptiste Mondino, selling 400,000-500,000 copies.[17]

Developments in the music industry itself thus form the final element in my attempt to explain the rise of music television. As Frith (1988b) has shown, music television forms one response to the music industry's crisis of profitability in the 1980s. Through direct sales and rental of tapes and—more significantly—the sale of music and music videos to television companies, record companies began to reorient themselves as "rights exploiters" rather than commodity producers (Frith, 1987a).

These trends do, however, need to be understood in terms of the needs of consumers, for although advertisers ultimately were leading these various trends (that, after all, is the impulse that generated the expansion of broadcast and cable television programming), music televison also needed an audience in order to appeal to them. If we examine the key demographic changes in music consumption, it is clear that music television very precisely addressed two trends in the 1980s: the aging of the rock audience and the growth (at least in the United States) of a youth culture that was *not* centered on music.

The fact that it is not just rock stars but the audience itself that has grown older has been remarked upon by John Qualen (1985):

Recent British and American audience surveys suggest that, for

> the first time in history, the rock audience is getting old. In
> America, for example, the latest RIAA [Recording Industry
> Association of America] survey indicates that in 1982 the 15-24
> age-group accounted for 39% of record and tape sales as against
> 45% in the years 1979-1981. This decline in the purchasing
> power of the industry's key target audience is the joint result of
> recession, which has hit the employment prospects of young
> people dramatically, and the demographic decline in the numbers
> of that age-group. The latter means that even if there is an
> upturn in the economy which creates jobs for this group of
> young people, their reduced numbers will not guarantee a return
> to the heyday of the early seventies. (p. 5)

This generational change has profound consequences for the music industry: it has helped to fracture pop taste, so that there is now a market
for music that is neither completely youth oriented nor part of a prerock
culture—acts such as the Rolling Stones, Tina Turner, Don Henley, Phil
Collins, the Moody Blues, and Steve Winwood are the key artists for this
demographic group.

This audience is reached via out-of-town arena shows rather than
through performances at small, inner-city clubs; it is catered to by publications such as *Q* and *Rolling Stone* rather than the traditional pop press;
it buys its music at carefully designed chain stores, such as the Where-
house (United States) and Our Price (United Kingdom), rather than in
the forbidding youth-oriented environment of the small record store.
Given the demand for performance and visuality to complement the aural experience of music, this older audience (which is seen less frequently
at live performances) is perfectly suited to promotion via television and
video. It is this audience that is targeted for purchase of videocassettes
such as the live concert performance of Paul Simon's *Graceland* album; it
is this audience that underwrites the increasingly frequent tendency in the
United States to finance a major concert tour partly via pay-per-view
television rights; and it is this audience that has its own all-music cable
station, VH-1 (Video Hits 1, established by MTV Networks in January
1985 and aimed at the 25-54-year-old demographic).

But the new role of television in pop culture is not confined to this
older audience. As Lawrence Grossberg (1986) points out:

> Contrary to the common wisdom, the rock and roll generations
> were not the television generations. . . . If youth in the fifties,

sixties and even seventies would have sacrificed anything rather than give up their music, there is increasing evidence that television plays the same role in the life of younger generations. (p. 63)

This is a view clearly shared by the creators of MTV,[18] and it locates yet another pressure on the pop industry to rethink the most profitable site for pop performance today.

So far, I have tried to show that the origins and definition of music video depend on a prior identification of the economic impulses behind the format, and that these determinations depend on an interaction between changes in the processes of music making (and related ideologies about rock music) and developments in the broadcasting industries. This interaction, which created the conditions for the emergence of music television, was then exploited by the music industry, partly in response to changing demographic patterns of music consumption. These points can now be used to establish briefly the context of music video production and, in the final section of this chapter, to ask some theoretical and methodological questions about the nature of commodity production in the study of pop music and promotional video clips.

The Production Context

The production context of music video is rather unusual, and needs some explanation. Most clips are made to promote pop singles and are shot in a very short space of time, sometimes in just two or three days (see Shore, 1985). This occurs partly to minimize the budget, but also because many clips are not made until there is some expectation of chart success, which then necessitates very speedy production in order to catch the relatively brief active sales life of a pop single. But promotional clips are not cheap to make. Estimates of the average cost range from a few thousand pounds to the $2-million price tag on the 17-minute clip, made in 1987, for Michael Jackson's song "Bad," directed by Martin Scorsese.[19]

This makes music video look like extremely expensive television, on a cost per hour basis. But of course the repeatability of promotional clips is much greater than that for broadcast TV programs. Successful music videos also circulate on an international scale that is generally unhindered by language barriers (English being the international language of pop lyrics, which are in any case less important, in the video age, than they ever were). Furthermore, the clips can be consolidated into packages and sold or rented as videocassettes, and may on occasion glean revenue via television distribution. Michael Jackson's BAD was integrated into a thirty-minute television program (*Michael Jackson — The Legend Continues*) and sold around the world as a documentary.[20]

Unlike many cultural products, music video is not primarily a commodity form, but a promotional one. Record companies do get back a small proportion of the costs of music video production through sales to consumers and some payments from the TV and cable stations that carry them,[21] but the costs of music video are largely written off against advertising or promotional budgets. (However, sometimes artists agree to fund video production as a recoupable advance against future record sales, or even from their own pockets.) Ultimately music video is therefore paid for through increased record sales — that is, the success of another product, rather than the success of the video itself.

Figure 2.1 illustrates this cycle, demonstrating that, economically, music video production is dependent on the increased revenues generated by music video promotion, garnered through consumer spending on records, cassettes, and CDs.[22]

The growth of consumer interest in music video has led to an unusual situation, in which media consumers are willing to pay directly for a proportion of the costs of what is essentially promotional material, through cable TV subscriptions and home video sales/rentals. This may eventually lead music television into a new economic relationship with the music industry and a role as a fourth "configuration," but currently direct sales are usually limited to only the most devoted fans of a particular act.[23] This promotional role of clips is also displaced into the conflict between record companies and other media institutions over payment for the right to screen music videos. The TV companies have often argued that they should pay nothing for videos, since they are essentially free advertising. The record companies, on the other hand, point out that consumer demand for music video is such that payment is quite proper — videos do, after all, boost ratings, and in many cases they sustain entire cable stations and large sections of network and broadcast TV programming (see Denisoff, 1988).

Rethinking the Commodified Text

The intersection of cultural production and consumption continues to be

Figure 2.1 The Music Video Cycle

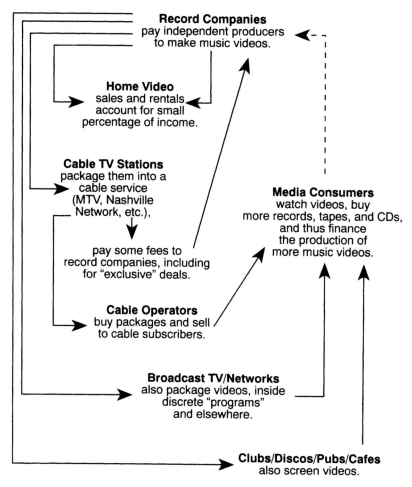

an arena of debate in contemporary cultural studies, and, as I suggested in the previous chapter, the relation between these areas and text analysis needs to be rethought before we can engage with music television. My starting point here is the recent rethinking of cultural consumption in Marxist theory, admirably summarized by Ien Ang (1985):

> Put simply, the current Marxist case is as follows: because the production of culture is subject to the laws of the capitalist economy, cultural products are degraded into commodities to

make as much profit as possible on the market. The exchange value of those products is therefore essential for the producers, leading to a neglect of quality. The capitalist market economy is only interested in the production of surplus value and as such is indifferent to the specific characteristics of the goods: caring only that they are sold and consumed. Mass culture is the extreme embodiment of the subjection of culture to the economy; its most important characteristic is that it provides profit for the producers.

But this is a one-sided presentation of the case. Marx himself stated that "a commodity only has exchange value in so far as it is at the same time a use-value, i.e., as an object of consumption; it ceases to have an exchange value if it ceases to have a use-value." In other words, one cannot succeed in selling a commodity if it does not have a certain usefulness. And it is here that the contradictory character of the capitalist mode of production lies. From the standpoint of production the product only features as a commodity, but from the standpoint of consumption the same product features as a use-value. (p. 18)

It is this line of reasoning that underwrites most post-1970s attempts to reevaluate the nature of the popular and its relation to ideology.

Some developments following this rethinking of the relations of production and consumption generated work that might contribute to a more sophisticated model of ideological process (Ang, 1985; Morley, 1980a). Other work seemed to emphasize the popular and depoliticize pleasure to the point of losing track of the ideological entirely. In other theoretical developments, the Marxist model of ideology was abandoned in favor of a critique of the relations between representations and the "real" and an attempt to explode the connection between economics and cultural symbols (Baudrillard, 1988b).

What all of these areas of work have in common is one fundamental oversight: in a media economy that is increasingly invaded by advertising and new kinds of promotional devices, the use-value of cultural products is rarely something that can be determined solely through study of the media audience. As Dallas Smythe (1977) has suggested, the "chain" of communication in advanced capitalist cultural industries is often one in which the message has been replaced by audiences, who become the "product" to be "delivered"—to advertisers.

The importance of Smythe's thesis is brought home in this comment from the chief executive of MTV Europe, in answer to a query about whether MTV would ever begin making its own video clips: "I don't think so. I don't think you want to compete with your customers." [24] The customers here are unambiguously the record companies themselves, not the television audience. Smythe's essay drew much criticism, and it is surely too simple a model to serve in any general way as a new paradigm for cultural studies. Yet his analysis might serve as a beginning in any attempt to think a way out of the current impasse in cultural studies that has emerged out of the emphasis on the audience.

What is problematic about each of the attempts to rethink the issue of consumption (from Marxist to post-Marxist efforts to do so) is the suppression of the fact that so few cultural texts are today produced as pure commodities. The major broadcasting media (radio and television) throughout the capitalist world function as pure commodities in only exceptional cases — those pay TV and cable TV services that carry no advertising. Newspapers and magazines rely to an enormous extent on advertising revenue, and publishers have now perfected the art of producing the "free" advertising-funded newspaper that defies the commodity production model. It is not necessary to argue, as Smythe does, that advertisers are the "real" consumers here to see that their function as *recipients of use-value* is grossly neglected. We might, however, follow Nicholas Garnham (1979a, 1979b) in an effort to investigate the concrete connections between commodity and meaning in contemporary culture. My aim here is not to attempt to "reduce" the text to its budget sheets; my purpose is simply to open up the question of meaning in music television, with an acknowledgment that the implied *consumer sovereignty* of some recent cultural studies work is also quite inadequate.

First, there are *empirical* problems in seeing music video in these terms. In the field of pop music, the use-value of commodities is undercut in two ways. First, as I have tried to establish, the commodity forms of pop music (records, cassettes, compact discs) seem to deliver insufficient meaning to satisfy consumers, who supplement the meanings offered through the commodity with ancillary texts — live performances, media interviews, photographs, posters, T-shirts, and so forth. Second, as Simon Frith (1987a, 1988b) has noted, the pop music industry in the 1980s has increasingly shifted to a role as rights exploiter rather than commodity manufacturer, and a result of this trend is that the music itself is often a promotional vehicle for other products, services, and corporations.

Thus, in the 1980s, pop music was doubly undermined as a cultural commodity, for it is now not only an incomplete commodity (from the point of view of use-value), requiring essential discourses of promotion (which have themselves become increasingly commodified); since the 1980s, that incomplete commodity increasingly finds its use-value for the music industry itself in its promotional role for advertisers and corporate sponsors. Thus, music television is rarely a pure commodity, but rather functions, as I will show, in this ancillary role — promoting the music itself, which (in its turn) is increasingly mobilized to promote something else (jeans, movies, beer, cosmetics, and so on).

Furthermore, there are broader *conceptual* issues at stake. In light of the observations above, we can now consider the Marxist analyses of contemporary cultural commodities offered by Wolfgang Haug (1986, 1987) and Nicholas Garnham (1979a, 1979b), which, when synthesized with my earlier comments, will illuminate a great deal about the nature of music television.

Haug provides a more complex Marxist analysis of cultural commodities than that of some recent cultural studies research. As he shows, the question of use-value is not simply a matter of identifying the essence of what the consumer consumes after the commodity has been valorized (purchased). While he does share with some recent cultural studies commentators (such as Ien Ang) a rejection of theories of media "manipulation," in favor of stressing *real* use-values, Haug first notes an important nuance in the structure of commodities: that they must offer, in addition to a use-value that may be enjoyed after its purchase, a *seeming* use-value — which is our motive to buy that commodity. The point is echoed, for instance, in accounts of capitalist advertising as a "magic system" that promises those things that cannot, or have not yet been, commodified in the marketplace (Williams, 1980: 170-95). We might also usefully supplement this observation with Garnham's (1983) point about the specifics of *cultural* consumption, that commodities are not usually available for partial consumption, in the manner of a "free sample." When we pay for a new CD, a new cable television channel, or a movie ticket, we must purchase the commodity *before* we know whether or not we want it. By the time we discover the answer to *that* question, it is too late, for the commodity has already been consumed.

It follows from the arguments of both Haug and Garnham that cultural commodities will offer a use-value *ahead of time*, before the actual moment of consumption:

A duality is produced in all commodity production: first, the use-value; second, and additionally, the appearance of use-value. For until the sale, with which the exchange-value standpoint reaches its end, use-value tends to play a role only as semblance. The aesthetic in the broadest sense—sensuous appearance and the sense of the use-value—here detaches itself from the thing. Domination and separate production of this aesthetic turn into a means for the end of money. Thus . . . in the principle of exchange, the tendency toward the technocracy of sensuousness is set up economically. (Haug, 1987: 106)

Clearly, Haug's comments have great pertinence to a cultural form such as music television, whose purpose is precisely that of generating the appearance of use-values for the putative purchaser of pop commodities.

One result of this analysis should be to encourage a shift away from a naive notion of consumer sovereignty in cultural analysis. Another effect, in relation to music television, is to draw our attention to the *real relations that exist between live performance and video clips*. It is not, as is often assumed, that one is a "simulation" of the other (although this may sometimes be true in a limited chronological sense, as I suggested earlier). More important, however, is that they are instances of what Haug calls "semblance." If we follow Haug's line of thinking, it is apparent that both live performance and music television constitute forms of the "technocracy of sensuousness." The spectacular displays of the live performance (lighting effects, smoke, costumes, the decibel level, dancing/ choreography, video and film inserts, and so on) that are mirrored in many music video clips are not reflections of each other, but are the "sensuous stimuli" that promote the commodities of the music industry. They suggest, through overwhelming and sometimes outrageous stimuli, the use-values (excitement, arousal, eroticism) that will be delivered if the consumer purchases the commodity (record, cassette, CD) that they promote. (This point will be detailed in chapters 4 and 5.) The link between a simple consumer sovereignty model of cultural consumption and recent cultural studies emphases on "real" use-values is this: both neglect the fact that the "technocracy of sensuousness" deploys a use-value of another kind—the usefulness of the promotional device as a means of delivering an audience/potential buyer.

This makes the music video text an extremely complex and unusual cultural artifact, for it seems to both *exceed* and *contain* the commodity it advertises. The music video clip almost manages to provide both levels of use-value: on the one hand offering the second level of use-value appearance (as advertising) and on the other providing the actual use-value (the song itself). If this were exactly so, video clips would have replaced other media as the commodity form of popular music. However, promotional videos do not quite encompass the first-level use-values. This is because each contains only one song (as opposed to the album-length experience that is being advertised—in this respect they resemble singles, which now function almost entirely as advertisements for albums); because videos are not as easily accessed as records, cassettes, and CDs (even if we tape them through our VCRs they are not as easily replayed); and because their sound quality is generally significantly poorer than that found in records, cassettes, or CDs.

Finally, it needs to be noted that while Haug is careful to avoid the endorsement of "manipulation" theses about mass culture, he refuses to make the necessary theoretical move of seeking out the *real* use-values inherent in the second-level "appearance of the use-value." Which is to say that in order to understand the meaning of music television texts we need to deploy the insights of *both* Haug and Ang. Music television makes this especially clear: it demonstrates the real use-values of "semblance" through the fact that the audience is willing to devote substantial quantities of time and money to the consumption of advertising.

The political implications of this will be explored further in the final chapter of this book. The question of *how* music television promotes the music itself and establishes its "technocracy of sensuousness" will be addressed via textual analysis in the following chapters.

THREE

A Musicology of the Image

> Kids come to my house all the time with their demos. I put on
> [N.W.A's] *Straight Outta Compton* and tell them to close their eyes
> and tell me you can't see it. Whenever you got a record that you
> can see, that's a fly record.
>
> —Daddy-O, Stetsasonic[1]

In a fascinating effort to consider the sound-image relation in popular
music, John Corbett (1990) suggestively begins the task of applying film
theory to pop through an engagement with the ideas of Laura Mulvey
(1975, 1989). The "problem" that Corbett confronts neatly illustrates my
thesis about the limitations of certain kinds of text analysis, since its core
is the notion that pop music constitutes "a set of objects that produce
their own visual lack," leading to the psychoanalytic observation that "it
is the lack of the visual, endemic to recorded sound, that initiates desire in
relation to the popular music object" (Corbett, 1990: 84). There are two
problems with this starting point. First, it is empirically unsound, in that
the popular music text may contain visual lack only if it has already been
wrenched from its actual contexts of consumption (identified in chapter
2) and analyzed as something that it is not—a discrete, purely aural, text.
Second, the assumptions made by Corbett in this essay (which has some
very plausible and sensible things to say about music television) center on
an *image fetishism* that is pervasive in film theory and psychoanalytic theory alike. It seems reasonable to ask why it is that we should want to use
theories of the visual to understand pop's aural codes (even if they could
be so neatly distinguished). Clearly this presents a challenge to the more
common kinds of psychoanalytic criticism (although see Silverman,
1988, for an exploration of the role of the *voice* in the formation of the

unconscious), but nonetheless I will suggest that it is useful to reverse that expectation and use musicology to illuminate the visual. That last notion, which seems more than appropriate for a cultural form whose visual codes *illustrate* its sounds (and not the other way around), is the task that is begun in this chapter.

I will thus begin the project that is now required to take this account of music television beyond the preceding critiques and contextualizations: that is to say, if music video involves some relation of "semblance" to the commodity itself, we can expect that the music (the object of valorization) will be *imaged*. Therefore, it will be important to engage with the music itself and its relation to promotional video clips. That work involves the essential business of theorizing the relation between sound and vision, which in its turn leads me to suggest a wide variety of ways in which we can mount a *musicological* analysis of visual imagery. I argued in the previous chapters that visuals are a key element in the production of musical meaning before the intervention of video imagery, because of the circulation of visual representations of pop in the music press, in advertisements, and in live performance. However, there is a prior visual moment that demands some investigation: this is the phenomenon of *synaesthesia*, the intrapersonal process whereby sensory impressions are carried over from one sense to another, for instance, when one pictures sounds in one's "mind's eye." [2] This concept is key for understanding music television, since video clips build on the sound track's visual associations. I will sketch in some of the background to the operation of synaesthesia in pop, and proceed to suggest some ways of in which terms drawn from musical analysis may be applied to individual video clips.

Visualizing Music

There is no shortage of empirical evidence suggesting that musicians and audiences alike sometimes visualize music, both before and after its production. The comment from rap artist Daddy-O that heads this chapter is but one example of a musician articulating the centrality of vision in producing "successful" music. The effort to look at music in visual terms is therefore highly appropriate to understanding how pop works; the suggestion that music itself *lacks* a visual component is, however, a symptom of not listening carefully enough. And the question that is often put regarding the *effects* of music videos (Have musicians begun to write songs with the video images in mind?) is also misplaced, since we know that musicians do in any case tend to visualize songs, in both abstract and narrative forms. Bryan Ferry's "Virginia Plain" (recorded in 1972 by Roxy Music) is a famous example of a song inspired by visuals (a billboard advertising a brand of cigarettes) that uses imagery to create a series of puns around the title. And this comment (from guitarist Steve Stevens) is a very typical response to a question about songwriting techniques: "Usually the lyrical idea comes first—that gives you a certain palette to work with. I think of songs as environments, or little movies" (quoted in *Guitar Player*, 1989). References to colors, tone, shades, space, and the musical "palette" are common ways of thinking among the producers of popular music.

Musicians have occasionally speculated in a more abstract way on the question of synaesthesia, as in this conversation between Elvis Costello and Tom Waits:

> TW: I always go for the low end . . . if I'm left to my own devices, I will discover the various shades of brown. And I'm seeing them of course as red and yellow next to each other. . . . I'm also color-blind, which is kind of interesting. I juggle with brown and green and blue and red, and green looks brown, brown looks green, purple looks blue, blue looks purple . . .
>
> EC: Do you see it like that? Because I see it definitely in color. The last record I made before this one, it was red and brown, it was blood and chocolate. That was an actual picture of a room in my head all the way through it, and most of the songs took place in it. (quoted in *Option*, 1989)

What is fascinating here about Costello's comments in particular is the extent to which this visualization of the music finds expresssion in the musical text. In the case of the album *Blood and Chocolate* (Columbia Records, 1986), the mood of the music (which listeners may also associate more abstractly with colors) is also present visually in the settings of the songs' narratives (where Costello's characters are visualized through being physically placed—in rooms, on stairways, on beds, and so forth) and in the album cover itself (the design of which can often influence how we "see" the music).[3]

The importance of album covers in helping to create meaning in the pop text can hardly be overemphasized, since it is here that genre is often established. Just as credit sequences in television and cinema texts have been identified as key components in mass media texts, helping to establish a frame of reference for interpretation, so album sleeves (and related imagery in posters and advertising) suggest the "correct" generic decoding in pop. Album covers have, after all, become sufficiently important to merit collections of record sleeves, for instance, in the works of album cover designer Roger Dean. A related development here is the Talking Heads book *What the Songs Look Like*, in which contemporary artists take a page each to visualize a Talking Heads song (Talking Heads & Olinksy, 1987). It is interesting to note that a number of the artists who contributed to this book subsequently made music video clips and station identification segments for MTV.[4] But perhaps the most striking synaesthetic connection in rock culture is the representation of psychedelia, where certain kinds of sounds (most widely circulated on the Beatles' 1967 LP *Sgt. Pepper's Lonely Hearts Club Band*, EMI) trigger associations with gaudy, colorful, surreal images (which in turn are associated with drugs in general, and the hallucinogenic substance LSD in particular). As late as 1989, this connection was so routine that two albums by contemporary British groups who use "psychedelic" sounds came packaged in psychedelic record covers — XTC's *Oranges and Lemons* (Virgin Records, 1989) and Tears for Fears' *The Seeds of Love* (Polygram, 1989). More recently, groups such as the Soup Dragons, Deee-Lite, and Inspiral Carpets have deployed psychedelic imagery on album cover art and in videos (respectively, I'M FREE, GROOVE IS IN THE HEART, and THIS IS HOW IT FEELS).

Listeners, as well as composers, "see" images when music is heard. I have conducted an informal survey of students' responses to pop songs that, although not constituting systematic audience research, is revealing in many of the connections made between sounds and visions.[5] The students (part of a general education communications class at San Francisco State University) were asked to write down what they "saw" on listening to brief extracts from a selection of pop songs. Responding to an extract of the instrumental track "Moments in Love" (a cut that had no accompanying video, made by the Art of Noise — an act with no significant visual image), students listed visual associations that very clearly broke down into two "clusters" drawn, respectively, from romantic images of nature and from mass-mediated technological associations.[6] The slow pulse of the music and its simple, naive melody suggested "naturalness" to some listeners, who responded thus:

Two old men sitting on a bench in the park watching everyone walk by, but in slow motion. It's summertime and very hot. I think of this *every* time I hear the song.

A lonely person sitting in a park or someone sitting alone thinking.

A glass-walled room at the bottom of the ocean with waves of light flowing rhythmically over it.

Romantic starlit night. Along a river's edge.

Walking in a surrealistic setting, like a tropical island or beach.

At a beach, sunset, two lovers, a sailboat passes in the orange sunset.

Two people walking on a beach, holding hands with the sun going down, warm colors.

Water, summer, relaxing summer day. A natural type of scene, e.g., waterfalls, trees.

Making love to my girlfriend. Walking on a beach.

Rain outside a window, a storm.

Other respondents associated with the mechanistic pulse of the music, perhaps through their knowledge of the Art of Noise as a studio-based high-tech group, often making links with television:

Black clothes, razor blades, drum machines, bleached hair.

Certain TV shows such as *Miami Vice* and *21 Jump Street*.

A *Miami Vice* suspense-building piece.

Reminds me of a certain television commercial for computers.

Reminds me of the interior of a yuppie's apartment.

A blinking computer screen.

Two respondents interestingly combine the two clusters I have identified:

An astronaut dancing in outer space.

Robots in an automated love story.

These readings of just one extract from a song are typical of responses I received when students were asked to listen to twenty song extracts, in that the majority of listeners were able to identify visual imagery, even where the music itself suggested (as in this case) no mass-mediated iconography. It is also noticeable that songs with high media visibility were visualized *to some degree* in terms of their video imagery, and yet also generated many other readings, thus offering further evidence for the refusal of the "fixing" thesis discussed in chapter 1. Indeed, what is clearly happening here, in Volosinov's terms, is the collision of external aural signs and codes at a junction point where they meet the sounds of "inner speech," which are clearly different for each listener, and yet (importantly) socially coded, so that the responses do in fact cluster around two dominant kinds of aural decoding.

Here is a selection of responses to the song "La Bamba," by Los Lobos. The song, originally recorded in 1958 by Ritchie Valens, is well known through the film about his life (also titled *La Bamba*) and for the LA BAMBA video featuring Los Lobos in performance at an amusement park, intercut with extracts from the film.

> Latino people doing the twist with poodle skirts and 501s with loafers. Drinking tequila and Corona in Mexico and getting tatoos with the American eagle on it.
>
> Young white college students from San Diego State [University] drinking Corona in Mexico.
>
> Right away I think about Ritchie Valens and the movie made about him.
>
> Convertibles, saddle shoes, and skirts.
>
> Old Mexican town celebrating someone's birthday, dancing in the streets, eating good food.
>
> The movie. Summer of last year. The video.
>
> Cruising in a pickup truck in San Jose, happy and energetic.
>
> Mexicans dancing at a fiesta.
>
> I see a group of teenagers in the 50s dancing to this song. The women dressed in hoop skirts and the men with their flooded pants.
>
> Spanish music revival, Buddy Holly tragedy.
>
> Los Lobos singing Rich Valens's La Bamba in some amusement park.

Finally, here are some responses to Robert Plant's "Tall Cool One" that similarly mix video imagery and other iconography. TALL COOL ONE was also a video (featuring Plant lip-syncing a performance) and a Coca-Cola television commercial.

> An athletic beer party out in the country.

Vintage cars driving on the freeway.

Hard-core rock group screaming into mikes with guitars and the whole ensemble.

Soft drink commercial, beach, surfing.

People rolling down a popular street with the music loud screaming at girls walking down the street. Long hair.

A teenagers stuck in his room waiting to get out because he is grounded.

Beaches. Ocean.

Summertime. Cruising aimlessly on a hot day in a convertible.

A man strutting around trying to impress a woman that he is very cool.

Asshole jocks blasting this from their cars as they throw something at you and drive away.

I see a group of guys surrounding a woman and singing to her.

A commercial—pretty dumb. A Coke ad.

Pop drink commercial, Top Gun-type movie . . . Coke.

Make-out music. Teenagers cruising in cars.

There are a number of points I wish to draw out from these comments on extracts of "Moments in Love," "La Bamba," and "Tall Cool One." First, it is worth noting that the vast majority of students in this sample were able to note down visual images associated with the musical extract. Second, there is a high degree of consensus on the kinds of iconography associated with each extract. This finding is in line with research by Philip Tagg (1983) on the coding of musical associations (and their relation to the category of "nature") that demonstrates how music encodes feeling, moods—and *images*.

Third, while a variety of mass-mediated imagery is invoked in these accounts, a significant amount of this imagery does *not* derive from music video (at least not in any clear, literal sense), and a good deal of it is clearly triggered by personal memory. This is most obviously the case in the comments on "Moments in Love" by the Art of Noise. But even in the comments on "La Bamba" and "Tall Cool One" (where mass-mediated imagery, including music video, was pervasively available for the song), the students "see" visual imagery deriving from their personal lives, and from American popular cultural myths, that are not present in the mass-mediated iconography actually used in relation to the song.[7] This can be observed in the reference to Buddy Holly in relation to "La Bamba": while Holly is not visually present in the LA BAMBA clip, the source here is either the *La Bamba* movie or a connection made by the student, since Valens and Holly died in the same plane crash (along with the "Big Bopper") in February 1959. More significantly, there are various visual details suggested in relation to "La Bamba" (San Jose, Corona beer, San Diego State University) and "Tall Cool One" (beaches, vintage cars) that are not present in the videos or the movie/television commercial associated with them.

These examples of synaesthesia suggest a number of sources for the iconographies stored in popular cultural memory: (a) personal imagery deriving from the individual memories associated with the song; (b) images associated purely with the music itself (following Tagg's research), which may work through either metaphor or metonymy; (c) images of the musicians/performers; (d) visual signifiers deriving from national-popular iconography, perhaps related to geographical associations prompted by the performers; and (e) deeply anchored popular cultural signs associated with rock music and that often link rock with a mythologized "America" (cars, freeways, beer, beaches, parties).

That these levels of iconography are *already* present in the music itself (albeit partly as a result of a history of mass-mediated pop imagery) is central for any understanding of music television, where so many aspects of these levels are "cashed in" by the directors of promotional video clips. It is not the place of this project to investigate the first of the levels identified above (personal memory). At this point in my argument I want to draw out some correspondences between iconography in music television and its wider application in the consumption of popular music.

Listen Up

As McClary and Walser (1990) have noted, one of the enduring problems in studying pop music derives from the enormous complexity inherent in the "stacking up" of elements of meaning in the pop song. Any moment of music contains a number of phenomena that must be taken into account (timbre, tempo, rhythm, acoustic space, melody, harmony, arrangement, lyrics), and these meanings need to be related both to one another and to the temporal movement of the music. This text is then expressed through and framed by codes of performance found in various sites, including the mass media. Analyzing these elements of the music in relation to music video clips is extraordinarily difficult, not only because it has to be attempted in a conceptual vacuum (leaving us with few critical tools to begin the task), but because the analysis of the music itself remains so undertheorized. There is, for instance, no way of talking about *timbre* in traditional Western musicological terms that even begins to be adequate to its role in establishing musical meaning in pop.[8]

Indeed, it is notable that two central terms used to describe music imply visuality: *timbre* denotes tone color and is often described by musicians in terms of "brightness," "sharpness," "presence," and so on. Acoustic space (the environment in which the recording occurs, or its artificial simulation through electronic devices) actually writes into the recording process itself a synaesthetic process, by aurally representing the physical space within which sounds appear to be recorded.[9] The representation of acoustic space in music is often termed the *stereo image*, and concerns the physical placing of elements in the mix. Peter Laurence (1974) has discussed the stereo imaging of sounds in terms of synaesthesia, limiting his analysis mainly to the question of where we place the sounds in our "mind's eye," rather than the broader questions of visual association developed here. It is clear from even that elementary investigation that issues of visual "realism" are raised by stereo imaging, since it may either reproduce or undermine conventional notions of where sounds come from (see Goodwin, 1991c). Sounds can be placed in the mix so as to represent acoustically the conventions of a "real" performance, or they may be shifted around to create a more artificial image — for instance, a sound may be panned dramatically to one side of the stereo image, or a drum kit may be spread across the stereo field in its discrete elements, and thus deconstructed.[10]

How do these elements of music relate to the study of music television? As J. Walker (1987) writes:

> What the makers of music videos discovered was how to provide visual experiences equivalent to musical ones. For example, a visual "echo" could be achieved by simultaneously multiplying and diminishing the image of a face. Musicians order and manipulate sounds for aesthetic and emotional effects; film and video directors discovered how to do the same with pictures.
> (p. 140)

However, my point is that these visual associations *already* exist. In other words, to return again to Volosinov's terms, video imagery attempts to tap into visual associations that exist prior to the production of the clip itself, in the internal sign systems of the audience.

The "inner speech" of music-visual associations that is triggered in the moment of consumption is one source of video imagery. This process may occur (in Piercian terms) through any combination of three essential relations between signifiers and signifieds. (To be precise, the process is one in which an aural signifier generates *another* signifier, which is visual, *simultaneously* with the mental production of the signified. What is problematic here, in the terms of semiotics/semiology, is the question of *which* signifier attaches to the signified — or whether indeed the sound-image fusion is sometimes so great that the two signifiers are actually one.) A *symbolic* relation exists where a musical convention has been established. This convention may be internal within a musical system; for instance, the heavy metal guitar solo signifies, for many listeners today, machismo or virility, almost regardless of the actual notes played. (The phallic association is displaced in Judas Priest's PAINKILLER, when a male metal fan mimes the guitar solo by "playing" the legs of a woman, in the backseat of a car.) Certain kinds of scales may signify non-Western "otherness" and perhaps suggest quite specific visual signifiers. (Led Zeppelin's "Kashmir" is a famous example that makes the geography of the visual allusion specific in its title.) The symbolic aural signifier may also have its roots in pop's multidiscursivity; for instance, the Prefab Sprout song "Hey Manhattan!" (which is about that city) uses a swirling, Gershwin-like string arrangement that signifies "Manhattan" partly because of the deployment of Gershwin's piece *Rhapsody in Blue* in Woody Allen's movie *Manhattan*.[11] (Unsurprisingly — to close the semiotic circuit — the video clip HEY MANHATTAN! used chromakeyed images of that city.) Similarly, the well-known theme tune from the film *The Big Country* has been reproduced and sampled (for instance, by Yes, on the Richie Havens song "No Opportunity Necessary, No Experience Needed," on the *Time and a Word* album; and on the 808 State/M.C. Tunes dance track "The Only Rhyme That Bites"); in each case the theme suggests familiar iconography deriving from the Hollywood genre of the western.

The sign may also work *iconically*, that is, through *resemblance*. But here the resemblance is not visual (as is usual in semiotics and semiology), but rather one that involves onomatopoeia: guitars emulating police sirens (the Clash, "Police on My Back"), vocal performances that suggest sexual acts (Donna Summer's "Love to Love You Baby"), rhythm sections that emulate a train or drumming that signifies machinery through its timbre and/or rhythms (Heaven 17's "Crushed by the Wheels of Industry"). Sampling has made this form of sound-image relation transparent (conceivably making music more visual still?) because it involves the incorporation of the actual sounds themselves (police sirens, machinery, and so forth) into the music. For instance, on Kraftwerk's song "The Telephone Call" we hear the sound of telephones incorporated as an element in the music. This process may also involve mass-mediated intertextuality, as when Prince samples the Joker (Jack Nicholson) from Tim Burton's *Batman* movie on his song "Batdance"; in the music of Big Audio Dynamite, who sample extensively from cinema ("$E = mc^2$" uses extracts from the films of Nicolas Roeg); or when rap and rock groups sample speeches by Jesse Jackson (Stetsasonic, "A.F.R.I.C.A.") or Malcolm X (Living Colour, "Cult of Personality").

When Chuck D of Public Enemy describes rap as "the television of black America," he refers to the way in which rap lyrics allow the listener to *see* the events and environments described by the rapper—that is the point of Daddy-O's comments on N.W.A.'s *Straight Outta Compton* album.[12] It is also true that the sampling of sounds helps to accomplish this, for instance, where the sampling of gunfire and a police siren (N.W.A's "Fuck tha Police") may produce its visual image. This example also reminds us that sound is recorded in acoustic spaces that have their own associations. Usually the recording process is transparent, or designed to suggest the versimilitude of a "real" performance. On occasion, however, an actual setting is implied by the acoustic space, or shifts of timbre, for instance, in the manipulation of the timbre of the voices in "Fuck tha Police," which is designed to shift the direct address of the main rap and place the dialogues in other settings, such as a courtroom. Another example is Deee-Lite's dance single "Groove Is in the Heart," which acoustically establishes itself as being set "in" a disco by including crowd noise.

Often, the sound-vision link is made *indexically*, where a causal link is "seen" in the "mind's eye"—that is, the musician's movements create the sounds, and that is what we see. (The examples of sampling given earlier, in which the source of the sound bite is widely known, visually speaking, may also be cited under this heading.) A pervasive aspect of this connection is the "scratching" sound incorporated into rap music, where the visual association with a DJ manipulating a record on a turntable is readily made. (I am *not* arguing that it is *always* made. I am following Volosinov in attempting to sketch out some possible kinds of relations between aural signs and inner signification.) This connection is also likely to occur when the aural codes denote a "live" performance, through elements such as acoustic space (a concert hall or club environment rarely sounds like a recording studio), "noise" (unwanted "feedback," interference, etc.), crowd sounds (applause, shouting), and framing (spoken direct-address introductions to the song itself, a "one-two-three-four" count-in).

It would be possible to establish an elaborate system of classification thus, perhaps developing the pioneering ideas of Umberto Eco (1972) in his semiological analysis of the televisual message, and integrating the *linguistic* codes (including metaphor and metonomy) present in pop song lyrics. Here I wish instead to continue to focus on the music-vision relation itself, by exploring the possibilities for understanding music video clips in terms of musical elements. I will discuss five aspects of the music itself (tempo, rhythm, arrangement, harmonic development, and acoustic space) and the role of lyrics in order to mount an exploratory musicology of the video image. Rather than pursuing the prospects for further semiotic cataloging (a practice of which Volosinov is critical),[13] I want to consider the specifics of the possible interrelations between music and image in video clips, for, despite Walker's insight quoted above, this axis of interpretation remains almost entirely neglected.

Synaesthesia in the Video Text

The tempo of popular music (as opposed to its rhythm—a more complex element) is very clearly and directly represented in music video clips. A variety of techniques are used to visualize speed: camera movement, fast editing, movement in the pro-filmic event, and postproduction computer effects. These phenonema are so pervasive that there they hardly need illustration, but I will give brief examples of each in which movement motivated by music helps to explain the apparently nonsensical nature of music television's iconography.

Camera movement is of course a routine element in video clips, and is often motivated by running, dancing, and walking performers. In Bon Jovi's clip LIVING ON A PRAYER, for instance, lead singer Jon Bon Jovi actually gestures to the camera (utilizing a direct mode of address) to join him as he turns away from us to run to the back of the stage. As he moves, so does the camera, and so—by implication—does the viewer. Editing techniques are likewise routinely used to suggest pace—so much so that to give an example would be redundant. The fast cutting that is a feature of the vast majority of clips is clearly used because to cut at the speed of cinema or broadcast television would appear incongruous in relation to the sound track. That is why old clips of rock and pop television shows from the 1960s and 1970s often look "too slow," despite efforts to create the feeling of speed through, for instance, the well-worn cliché of the rapid, repeated zoom shot.[14]

Movement in the pro-filmic event is often signified through images of the musicians in performance, jumping, running, and gesturing. In Peter Wolf's COME AS YOU ARE, Wolf literally bounces his way through the entire video, as he does a childlike pogo through a fictional small-town world in order to arrive at the bandstand, where—at the very end of the clip—he joins his musicians. (This device also involves an intertextual reference to Wolf's role as lead singer in the J. Geils Band, and their clip LOVE STINKS, which similarly features Wolf jumping. Connections *across* videos by the same act are important and will be explored in chapter 5.) Often, computerized effects are added to introduce more movement into the frame: in Asia's HEAT OF THE MOMENT multiple split screen is used, so that the television image is fractured into more than a dozen rapidly changing sections. Something similar happens in John Cougar Mellencamp's JACK AND DIANE, in which images within the discrete frames also mimic the music—in, for instance, the shots of Mellencamp's hands providing a "clap" that illustrates (rather than generates) the sound on the record. And in the Fine Young Cannibals' DON'T LOOK BACK, the performers remain more or less static while fine lines of visual "interference" intersect their images at great speed.

The "visually decentered" nature of watching music television is a result at least partly of the sheer speed of the images. In some of the most extreme examples (Peter Gabriel's SLEDGEHAMMER, Julian Lennon's STICK AROUND, Public Enemy's WELCOME TO THE TERRORDOME) the images move so fast that they are incomprehensible on first viewing. This points to another reason for fast-moving images: by making clips that are difficult to decode on one viewing, those involved hope to produce something that will withstand repeated viewings. Like pop records, and unlike most broadcast television, music television is designed for a high degree of repetition, both within individual clips and across the schedule. As Stephen Johnson, director of *Pee-Wee's Playhouse* and clips for Talking Heads (ROAD TO NOWHERE) and Peter Gabriel (SLEDGEHAMMER and BIG TIME), puts it:

My opinion was that videos should not be like little features —
they should be a different medium entirely. We should make
videos that address different needs — they have to bear up under
repeated viewings and still have something to offer. You see a
feature one time and you're supposed to get it all. . . . there are
many means of cramming the information. It's all what I
consider "thought beats." I try to have a greater number of
thought beats than you often see. (quoted in *Mix*, 1987)

Not all clips use techniques designed to emphasize speed, however. A
few clips have drawn attention to themselves by disturbing the conventions of pace. An example is Godley and Creme's CRY, which uses slow
dissolves between parts of the human face ("morphing") to create "iden-
tikit" faces whose slowly changing elements mirror the tempo of the
song. Malcolm McLaren's MADAME BUTTERFLY also utilizes slow camera
movement and dissolves (or fades), instead of cuts, to illustrate the pace
of the music. The same is true for Sinead O'Connor's NOTHING COMPARES
2 U, which centers on a static close-up of O'Connor's face, culminating
in one piece of "movement" (in both senses of the word) — a tear falling
from one eye. Bruce Springsteen's BRILLIANT DISGUISE is unusual in having
almost no movement within the frame (only Springsteen's lips and arms
move as he mimes the song, with an acoustic guitar, in a kitchen), no
cuts, and (in one long take) extremely slow camera movement (which
shifts over the course of the entire video almost imperceptibly to an extreme close-up of the performer). Here the lack of frenetic visual imagery
underscores not only the relatively slow pace of the song (it is a good deal
faster than the other examples above, but is nonetheless considerably less
overstated than most of Springsteen's rock-oriented singles), but the introspective nature of the lyrics.

Rhythm in music video clips is not generally represented through the
technique of cutting "on the beat" — that is, placing cuts on the third beat
of the bar, a downbeat where a snare drum accent is often found.[15] (Although this sometimes happens; for example, in the opening bars of John
Cougar Mellencamp's SMALL TOWN, almost every cut occurs on the snare
drum accent. Similarly, the final choruses of U2's DESIRE are cut on the
snare drum beat, which works to emphasize the syncopated nature of the
"Bo Diddley" beat used in that song.) Instead, cuts tend to occur around
the beat, with emphasis on the music illustrated by a cut on the beat
when the rythmic emphasis is syncopated — stressing an "up" beat that is

accented in the music. In the Genesis clip TONIGHT, TONIGHT, TONIGHT, lights are used in this way. Snap's THE POWER uses the same technique, with a flashbulb accenting stresses in the rhythm. In Prince's video 1999, a percussive whiplash sound in the music is illustrated by a rapid cut to the drummer hitting a crash cymbal and the glare of a white light. On I WANT A NEW DRUG (Huey Lewis and the News), a three-way split screen is occasionally introduced, cut to the beat of snare drum fills. In George Michael's FREEDOM 90, syncopated beats are emphasized toward the end of the song by shots of an exploding guitar (an image that clearly has metaphorical significance!). In John Cougar Mellencamp's SMALL TOWN, a fast run on the piano (a familiar rock/rhythm and blues aural trope) is cut to a rapid, blurred shot that pans very fast along a wall to create a metaphorical figure that visually implies the pianist's keyboard.

While the rhythm as a whole is not usually rendered into visual iconography, there are examples of the vision track taking up the musical pulse during parts of a clip. In Herbie Hancock's ROCKIT, a famous example of this technique occurs when the aural "scratching" on the sound track is imitated via the video edit suite, as the robots performing in the video are made to seem to move back and forth in time, in correspondence with the manipulation of rhythm in the music. (As I suggested earlier, the aural "scratching" implies a synaesthetic moment; while the music was almost certainly produced with the aid of a sampling computer, it conjures up a visual image of a DJ implementing the effect with the use of record turntables.)[16] In Fleetwood Mac's BIG LOVE, the song ends with a sequence using a prominently mixed snare drum playing rolls that seem to push the music into a faster gear and also hint at a reversed-tape sound. The imagery imitates this sound by running the visual imagery backward, very speedily.

The arrangement of pop songs balances three central elements: the voice, the rhythm, and the backing that supports them both (see Hennion, 1990). Broadly speaking, music video can be seen to mirror the prominence of the voice in pop by foregrounding the singer's face and (less centrally) emphasizing key rhythmic moments. Often there will be a tension in the cutting of images, between the emphasis on the pulse of the music and the imperative to return to the singer's face—a key anchoring motif, as Kaplan (1987) has noted. Most clips resolve this tension in favor of an emphasis on the latter (the reasons for this will be pursued in the next chapter), but there is usually some combination of rhythmic and vocal emphases. In this respect, as in many others, videos stress conventions already established in the lighting of rock concerts, where spotlights highlight singers and instrumentalists at key moments, and where lighting is used to create dramatic effects that punctuate the music in accord with its rhythm.[17] These techniques are so routine that they do not need specific illustration. Two clips that make the connection between video imagery and arrangement very explicit are the Who's YOU BETTER YOU BET, in which the camera moves in and out of focus on the two singers (Roger Daltrey and Pete Townshend) according to which of them is singing, and Eurythmics' SWEET DREAMS (ARE MADE OF THIS), in which we see two (lip-syncing) images of the singer's face (Annie Lennox) at the point in the song when her multitracked vocals divide into two distinct parts.

By the *harmonic development* of a song I refer to key shifts in melody (such as the introduction of the chorus, a solo, or a "middle eight") and to changes in key. Many videos employ imagery that mirrors these shifts within a given song. One well-established ploy is to make some emphatic visual change during the choruses. The Police clip EVERY LITTLE THING SHE DOES IS MAGIC moves from black and white to color during the song's choruses. In Van Halen's HOT FOR TEACHER, the more subdued guitar sections are shot in monochrome, but with the simultaneous arrival of the song's verse and (on the screen) the visual presence of a "sexy" female schoolteacher this is replaced by color imagery. Other clips use changes in mise-en-scène, camera movement, or the pro-filmic event itself to signal an instrumental segment (often the song's bridge). In the Yes clip OWNER OF A LONELY HEART, the guitar solo is illustrated both with a development in the visual narrative (the central protagonist escapes from the clutches of his mysterious captors) and with new movement—the camera runs with him as he escapes. The excitement that is supposed to occur in a rock guitar solo is thus generated visually both in the story line and in its narrative representation.

A more striking example occurs in Michael Jackson's MAN IN THE MIRROR, where an ascending key change is illustrated with a shot of an atomic bomb exploding (cut to the beat, on the word "change," referring to social/personal change). The visual image is subordinated to the music—to its rhythm, which is why the cut is on the beat, and to its musical development, the key change. The shift in imagery also corresponds, at another level, to a move in the song's lyrics, from political-personal protest to nostalgic optimism. Indeed, it is this change in the sentiments of the lyrics that seems to motivate the key change itself—a classic (some might say hackneyed) technique that has a long history in popular song. I use the phrase "seems to" advisedly, however. We do not know whether the lyrics can be said to motivate the ascending musical shift or vice versa. Appeals to Michael Jackson's intention as the song-writer are clearly inadequate—it is no help to speculate on whether the lyrics or the music "came first" in the process of making the song. The problem is a *textual* one and lies in the absence of a hierarchy of discourses in the pop song itself.

Arrangement and harmonic development are jointly illustrated in an early clip from broadcast television for Traffic's song "Glad." (This sequence has frequently been aired on MTV as a "classic" clip.) During the song's verses we see conventional shots of a band in performance, focusing mainly on vocalist/keyboard player Steve Winwood. But during the extended instrumental sequence, documentary conventions are abandoned in favor of abstract, psychedelic images that are clearly intended to evoke the dreamlike, floating feel of the music itself. A video equivalent occurs in Cyndi Lauper's GIRLS JUST WANT TO HAVE FUN, when the instrumental bridge featuring a synthesizer solo is illustrated by breaking up the images of the girls into a more abstract sequence, which uses computer-manipulated imagery of tiny globes whose scale reflects the "small" sound of the keyboard.

Song lyrics are the final element of the musical text that I wish to relate to video imagery. Pop music studies have progressed some way from their initial naive emphasis on the study of words in songs, and I will pursue in the next chapter the question of how to place the lyrics themselves in the narrative of pop.[18] At this stage in the argument it is sufficient to note that lyrics do sometimes play a key role in establishing the *mood* of a song. It is not necessary to view the consumption of songs as primarily articulated through lyrics in order to establish that overall themes, verbal hooks, and recurring phrases play a role in constructing meaning. I want to argue at this point (before moving on to more detailed narrative analyses) that lyrics often work to establish an emotional mood or ambience in songs, much as *timbre* or tempo does in the music, or as a source of metaphor. These verbal clues (which are sometimes, but not necessarily, part of a coherent lyrical story) are then picked up for illustration in the video imagery.

Suzanne Vega's LUKA is a classic example of this technique, in which a tragic story of child abuse is matched with quiet, reflective music based mainly around an acoustic guitar and Vega's voice. The downbeat content of the lyrics not only corresponds to the mood of the music, but is also illustrated in the visual imagery of the LUKA clip, which was shot in monochrome and is presented in blue-tinted tones. The simplest commutation test (imagine the clip in color, or tinted red, purple, or yellow) reveals the contribution of the blue-filtered tinting to the clip's affective intent. Color is used here to suggest the *blues*—a connection that is much more than an iconographic pun.

Another revealing example of this kind of coding is found in the George Lucas film *Captain Eo*, starring Michael Jackson, which can be seen at Disneyland. This short movie, shot in 3-D, features Jackson as a renegade commander in outer space who is eventually able to liberate his evil enemy with *music*. Significantly, Jackson's singing and dancing work to colorize his foes, so that the arrival of his music transforms them from monochrome badness to Technicolor goodness—a feature of *Captain Eo* that may not be lost on the show's sponsors, Kodak.

Shooting clips in monochrome, often with stark, exaggerated shadows, is a typical method for suggesting sadness, melancholy, and loss. (In the academic literature on music television the technique is often related to cinematic codes in film noir or German expressionism—conventions that are surely relevant, but hardly unconnected, to the music on the sound track.) U2's WITH OR WITHOUT YOU, the Police's EVERY BREATH YOU TAKE, and Chris Isaak's WICKED GAME (directed by Herb Ritts) are three examples of this approach. In each clip, black-and-white cinematography, slow dissolves, violent tonal contrasts (created by lighting in the U2 and Police clips), and pervasive shadows are utilized to suggest the emotions of the song—respectively, a maudlin, a vengeful, and a resigned tale of romantic pain.

The process of visualizing lyrical themes needs to be understood, however, through the pervasive use of metaphor in pop and rock lyrics, where the visualizing of these figures has had a sometimes unfortunate history. Many songs work with a central metaphorical or metonymic sign (which is often the song title) or series of figures, the most pertinent of which are built into pop's generic labels—for instance, in "rock 'n' roll" (referring to sex) and soul music (meaning passionate, perhaps spiritual, music). We have only to think of how many songs use the word *heart* metaphorically to see this, and it should be noted also that this figure is then often combined into a further analogy (as in the Human League's song "Heart Like a Wheel").

When music video attempts to make lyrical metaphor visual, it can sometimes produce texts of crushing banality or—worse still—misread the song entirely. An infamous such episode concerns Elvis Costello's song "Shipbuilding," whose metonymic title (more precisely, it is an example of synecdoche, in that the partial motif of shipbuilding stands for the whole purpose to which some vessels are put—i.e., fighting wars) actually alludes to the Falklands War rather than the business of constructing seafaring vessels. Nonetheless, the BBC's *Whistle Test* did once complement the song with one of its in-house visual segments, which centered on imagery of shipbuilding, thus undermining the point of the song. A music video that similarly undermines the lyrical symbolism of the song is the Vapors' TURNING JAPANESE (a racist metonym for masturbation), in which the video sidesteps the sexual reference of the song's hook and settles instead for a familiar iconography of Orientalism.[19]

Some music videos work with lyrical metaphors to better effect. For instance, the Peter Gabriel song "Sledgehammer" has lyrics that play with a series of sexual metaphors, and so in the video clip SLEDGEHAMMER we see a variety of images of reproduction, beginning with the fertilization of an egg and moving through to a concluding image of the night sky, whose mulitiple twinkling stars suggest nothing less than a literally universal image of creation. Another, simpler, example would be the use of a red light in the Police clip ROXANNE, where the "red light" in the lyrics is a metonym for prostitution.

These techniques have become increasingly sophisticated as video technology, using computerized postproduction equipment, has greatly developed the degree of electronic manipulation possible after the recording of the pro-filmic event. Many of them are, however, clearly in evidence in early broadcast television clips, where directors struggled to illustrate pop music for the first time. In programs such as *Ready, Steady, Go!, Top of the Pops, American Bandstand,* and *Soul Train,* directors attempted to mirror the music with lighting effects, in the pace of cutting, and sometimes through camera movement (the rapid zoom shot mentioned earlier). There were also efforts to use mise-en-scène to complement the theme of the song—a strategy that stretches back to the Soundies of the 1940s. Far from representing a new aesthetic or any kind of radical break with television conventions, these techniques are classic examples of light entertainment strategies of signification, as identified by Richard Dyer's (1973) study of the form. This is important for the argument that follows in chapters 4 and 5, because the debate about realism and narrative structure has been conducted to date as though the main conceptual touchstone in the study of music video clips should be cinematic Hollywood "realism." It is clear, on the contrary, that the conventions of the video clip do not differ in any *qualitative* sense from the modes of address and general visual rhetoric of television light entertainment, where the codes of realism are routinely abandoned. This issue will be explored further in chapter 4.

Music and Movement

A further link between sound and image clearly occurs, through the medium of the body, in *dance*. As Angela McRobbie (1984) says of dance: "Of all the areas of popular culture, it remains the least theorised, the least subject to the scrutiny of the social critic" (pp. 130-31). Dance on television and in music video has similarly been neglected, although Fiske and Hartley (1978: 127-41) usefully discuss the role of dance in *Come Dancing* and *Top of the Pops*, and Kobena Mercer (1986) also analyzes dance in Michael Jackson's THRILLER clip.

One way of approaching the analysis of dancing (and it provides merely one way into the topic, which certainly does not fully engage with its meaning) is through its attempt to visualize music. In rock culture, the distinguishing properties of dancing are impossible to define because they are less routinized than in folk, classical, or modern dancing, and blur into the bodily movements that arise in the less formalized contexts of producing and consuming music. Thus, along with the dancing of audience members or professional dancers in music videos, we need also to consider the gestures and movements of the musicians. Classic rock icons such as the Pete Townshend "windmill," the Chuck Berry "duck walk," or the Michael Jackson "moonwalk" are thus a part of "dance" in video clips. More recent examples would be the swaying motion used by Guns N' Roses singer Axl Rose, the twirling dance executed by Depeche Mode's Dave Gahan, and the eccentric gesturing of Public Enemy's Flavor Flav. Sometimes the indexical element of synaesthesia emerges in the movements of the audience—for instance, when rock fans play "air guitar," miming to the guitar part. Dancing of a more formal kind is also an element in the choreography of the musical performance, from the routines of soul groups in the 1960s through to the more recent iconographic function of the Security of the First World dancers (with Public Enemy) and members of contemporary dance/rock groups whose function is mostly nonmusical (for instance, Bez of Happy Mondays).

These various forms of pro-filmic movement—encompassing musicians, nonmusicians, professional dancers, and audience members, and ranging from full-fledged dance routines to all matters concerning gesture and the visual rhetoric of the body—may connect with synaesthesia through their effort to visualize the music itself. Hebdige (1979: 108-9), for instance, has written briefly on the links between the pace of punk rock music and style of pogo dancing that went with it. It is quite obvious that if we move through the musical elements outlined above, each of them can reference dance (broadly defined, in rock and pop terms); indeed, I have already suggested some ways in which movement in the frame (e.g., in Peter Wolf's COME AS YOU ARE, Bon Jovi's LIVING ON A PRAYER) illustrates the music.

The underscoring of tempo through dance and movement hardly needs elaboration, so tight are the links between the two areas: unsurprisingly, we tend to find fast-paced dancing in up-tempo videos (Michael Jackson's THRILLER, Madonna's EXPRESS YOURSELF) and slower movement in slower songs (Malcolm McLaren's MADAME BUTTERFLY, Don Henley's LAST WORTHLESS EVENING). Similarly, rhythm may be emphasized by gestures and movement. For instance, in SHOCK THE MONKEY, Peter Gabriel dramatically crosses his arms in time with an accent on the word "shock," which functions to accentuate the music further. Harmonic development is also illustrated when a dance routine, usually of a fairly exuberant nature, occurs in sync with a middle-eight sequence or instrumental solo. In Pat Benatar's LOVE IS A BATTLEFIELD, the formalized dance routine occurs during the instrumental break and the display of the body involved in the dance thus corresponds to the display of virtuosity implied by the instrumental solo in rock and roll. In Van Halen's HOT FOR TEACHER, the schoolteacher's dancing coincides with, and highlights, the song's choruses.

The lyrics may also be illustrated through dance, and here the connection drawn by McRobbie (1984) between dance and social fantasies of escape (especially for young girls) is clearly relevant. They are crystallized in the videos of Paula Abdul, a singer who began her career as a choreographer (for Janet Jackson, among others), in which the narrative role of dance (for instance, in the COLD HEARTED clip) connects with young girls' fantasies of success and escape through dance-as-career. Dance as an assertive act linked to protofeminist lyrics may also work as "access signs" or "discovery signs" (to use Lisa Lewis's terms; see Lewis, 1987a, 1990), providing for either female appropriation of male movements (Joan Jett,

I LOVE ROCK 'N' ROLL) or a validation of female dancing (Madonna, INTO THE GROOVE; Pat Benatar, LOVE IS A BATTLEFIELD).

These speculations on the music-video connection have, I hope, established two things. First, there are a variety of identifiable techniques — most of them extremely obvious — that demonstrate a close connection between visual and musical/lyrical elements in the music video text, encompassing forms of bodily movement that include dancing. Second, I believe it follows from this that we can buttress the argument made in chapter 2 with some elementary textual evidence: it is precisely because the clips essentially *promote* musical commodities that *illustrative* components can so easily be discovered. It is commonplace to observe that the aural element in music television does *not* work as a *sound track*, as in cinema (Laing, 1985a). Here I have tried to show, with some textual detail, exactly how we might invert the position of film studies, by demonstrating exactly how the visuals *support* the sound track.

It seems to me that this account also helps to explain what is *pleasurable* about watching music television. Visual pleasure is present not so much at the level of narrative, but in the *making musical* of the television image. Television is *musiced*. The process of synaesthesia is toyed with and developed. Television is made to succumb to new rhythms, in the pulses of rock, rap, and dance music. The pleasures of listening (and perhaps of dancing) are heightened through the submission of vision to its sound track. It is as much the case here (if not more so) that music has invaded television as it is true that video has "taken over" music. This is one way of explaining what constitutes a "good" video (a problematic question raised by Frith, 1988a) — it is a clip that responds to the pleasures of music, and in which that music is made visual, either in new ways or in ways that accentuate existing visual associations. Certainly, other criteria are used in assessing the aesthetic quality of video clips, such as "originality," whether the clip opens up/helps establish the meaning of the song, whether it is "faithful" to the act represented, the art of politicizing a song and giving it new meaning. I would speculate, however, that the essential element of pleasure in viewing the clips must involve more than purely visual pleasure (scopophilia, voyeurism), since this in itself provides no incentive to buy the aural commodities that are being promoted. Thus, following Haug's (1986, 1987) argument, discussed earlier, the clips must encompass a delivery of pleasure that relates visuals to the music that is being *sold*, that provides an experience of use-value offering a promise of further use-values in the commodity itself.

However necessary these initial explorations are, my argument so far has been conceptually quite simple and is open to two criticisms in particular, the implications of which I will pursue in the next chapter. First, if the process of synaesthesia operates, as I have argued, in the consumption of pop music, then generalized correspondences between music and image still tell us too little about the production of *meaning*. The effort to illustrate songs with emotive or corporeal elements that are motivated by the mood or rhythm of the music does not reveal much about what that music means. (It should be clear by now, however, that I contend that the dominant project in this field of showing the links between videos and cinematic genre reveals even less.) Second, establishing a connection between music and image on the basis of isolated musicological components only begins the work of linking the two levels. A more thorough exploration of the music–image nexus will involve the construction of video analysis categories that draw on the *formal* properties of popular music. In the next chapter I will therefore explore the relations between the song and its visualization at the level of narrative organization.

FOUR

The Structure of Music Video
Rethinking Narrative Analysis

> There's nothing in it, it's just a video.
> —Peter Buck, R.E.M.[1]

It has become commonplace to note that music video clips tend to defy the familiar regimes of narrative structure that have been an object of criticism in Marxist, psychoanalytic, and film theory for the last twenty years. Those approaches had identified a "classic realist text" (sometimes perhaps more accurately termed "naturalism"; see Williams, 1977a) that was criticized from the point of view of Brechtian Marxism (Garnham, 1972; MacCabe, 1974; McGrath, 1977) and feminist psychoanalytic theory (MacCabe, 1976; Mulvey, 1975, 1989) as carrying formal properties that sustained existing inequalities of social power. This line of thinking became pervasive in the field of media and cultural studies during the 1970s and is most closely associated with the film studies journal *Screen*. Subsequently, these ideas were subjected to a considerable amount of criticism (Caughie, 1980; Gledhill, 1978; Hall, 1978; Harvey, 1978; Lovell, 1980; Modleski, 1988; Morley, 1980b; Rodowick, 1988; Williams, 1977a).[2]

A succinct summary of the critique of this enormous literature runs to just a few telling lines:

> One should not too forcibly generalize, in the analysis of
> collective representations, about the psychic economies and
> responses of actual spectators. . . . Contemporary film theory

has often totalized complex questions of sexual difference and identification within a singular unity which merges the "forms" of spectatorship with the "forms" of the text, or, just as badly, divides identification into two mutually exclusive forms, male and female. Here the question of "the spectator," which hypothesizes the collective in an image of false unity, is of little interest to a historical and materialist criticism. (Rodowick, 1991a: 136-37)

Rodowick references the issue of sexual difference, but his comments hold equally well for the effort to link realism with (bourgeois) class ideologies. However, the narrative analysis of music television has tended to evade the critique of antirealism/naturalism, by suggesting that empirical differences in the music video text require analysis that moves on from the assault on classic "realism." While that is often (although by no means always) empirically correct, it has directed narrative analysis away from the necessary revision of its essential formalism—by which I mean a tendency to equate narrative organization with meaning and reception. In the literature on music television, the break with the formalist tradition is still incomplete in two areas that concern, respectively, the consumption and production of narrative systems.

First, the abandonment of the realism/nonrealism paradigm has been too tentative, and has given up too much ground to formalism. The usual argument (articulated, for instance, by Kaplan, 1987) is that because the *empirical object* eludes the terms of that debate, we need a new paradigm; and this is one—albeit *only* one—determination behind the emergence of postmodernism. (This argument thus parallels the position of Ellis, 1982b, and others, who similarly view television's narrative organization and the context of consumption as running against the grain of film theory.) This allows Kaplan and other writers to reproduce the very position they claim to transcend, except that the new approach no longer searches for realist or avant-garde texts, but instead looks at the formal properties of the postmodern text, *using the very terms drawn from the analysis of realist narratives.* Thus, the postmodernists still persist in seeing "subversive" elements (subversive, that is, of bourgeois subjectivity) in the "break" with realism. But this argument is misguided (and will ultimately lead nowhere, for exactly the same reasons that 1970s film theory found itself in an avant-garde cul-de-sac), because its claim to constitute a break with previous approaches is misleading. Indeed, a good deal of current postmodern criticism precisely fulfills the function of sidestepping the critique of 1970s film theory when it abandons the old terms of the debate (realism), because they are supposed to be outdated, while continuing to employ the *same methods*.

The second area where the narrative investigation of music video remains merely embryonic is in the neglect of any attempt to *explain* (other than through some idealistic notion of a postmodern zeitgeist) the structure of music video clips. Other than in the most general and reductive sense (see Jameson, 1984a, 1984b), the reasons for the emergence of texts that defy the realism/nonrealism debate remain obscure. Therefore, a materialist investigation of music television needs to explore the actual aesthetic, historical, and institutional mechanisms that account for its narrative structures.

In the following analysis of narrative, I will argue that the structural organization of music video clips needs to be seen in the context of the clips' function as promotional items (thus further developing Haug's notion of the "technocracy of sensuousness" cited in chapter 2) and in relation to the sound-vision correspondence (explored in chapter 3), which is expanded upon here to include questions of structure and narrative. I will show how music videos may be simultaneously nonrealist and highly ordered/rational, and how the Marxist musicology of Theodor Adorno remains pertinent to this debate. Before these points can be explored, however, it is important to note some fundamental differences between the structure of the pop song and other mass-mediated and literary narrative systems.

How Songs Are Not Movies

An initial point of difficulty concerns the question of modes of address in video clips. Traditionally, in film theory, it has been assumed that realism/naturalism is characterized by the effacement of narration, through which the process of narrative construction is made invisible to the spectator. The cinematic mechanisms for achieving this have been explored by Christian Metz (1975) and include the use of indirect modes of address, especially in visual coding. To address the spectator directly would alert him or her to the fact of narration (what Brecht advocated as "revealing the machinery") and break the spell of illusionism. Music video scholarship has expended a great deal of time and energy on showing how video clips break with realist modes of address (Kaplan, 1987; Kinder, 1984) and thus transcend the paradigm of realism.

One confusion in work that attempts to consider music video narratives is the almost universal failure to notice that pop music's stories are told by aurally (and, often, visibly) present storytellers. That is to say, the division between the "real author" and the "implied author" (cited, for instance, by Kozloff, 1987) that exists throughout the majority of mass-mediated storytelling does not apply in the case of songs. Whereas the novel may make a distinction between the author of the work and the fictional narrator (a device that is infamously subverted, for example, in Philip Roth's novel *Deception*), and where television and cinema provide an unseen narration via the camera, which is usually isolated from the text's authors,[3] pop songs continue to be addressed to us directly, from the mouths and musical instruments of narrators who are not entirely mass mediated (as is the camera narration in television and cinema).[4] This form of direct address (albeit one that is highly mediated through the technology of the recording studio) is often mistaken for modernism when it is read through the wrong codes — the codes of cinema and the realist novel. In fact, it derives from the nature of the song itself, which requires the physical presence (through, as a bare corporeal minimum, a voice) of a narrator. (This leaves open the interesting possibility that this narrator may turn out to be, like the voice-over in film noir, a fictional invention, a character. I will pursue that line of thinking in the next chapter.)

It follows that the analysis of music television's use of double identity (discussed by Kinder, 1984) needs to be grounded in the context of pop itself, rather than in film or dream theory. As Simon Frith (1988b) has pointed out, one great confusion in the analysis of music television arises from the apparent absence of a hierarchy of discourses (in particular the common use of two "looks" that stem from separate and unprivileged points of textual enunciation) in video clips — a double address that in fact is commonplace in pop songs. When a pop singer tells a first-person narrative in a song, he or she is simultaneously both the character in the song and the storyteller. Often the two positions become confused for audiences. Some artists (such as Bruce Springsteen) are prone to be read autobiographically even when they are speaking through characters; this issue lies at the heart of one debate about obscenity and violence in rap lyrics, where some rappers have defended themselves against charges of glamorizing gang violence by arguing that they are merely acting out characterizations, much as an actor does in a gangster film.[5] Thus, pop singers often complain in interviews that the feelings they put into the mouths of characters in their songs are mistaken for their own. This is not surprising, however, and is explained—through narrative theory—by the conflation of the real/implied authorial voice.

Even where a second- or third-person address is used in lyrics, those words are addressed to us directly, more in the manner (in terms of media codes) of a television news anchor than of an actor. Thus pop lyrics are always about both the content of the words (which may often be less of a story and more a series of slogans or linguistic gestures/poses) and the voice/face/character who is singing. The linguistic address of pop music lyrics is thus quite unlike any other discourse in the mass media. While its directness suggests a television news reader, the level of identification and emotional investment goes quite beyond that directed toward television "personalities" (see Langer, 1981). In that respect, pop singers are more like movie stars. However, this analogy also breaks down immediately, because film actors *become* other characters within a fictional diegesis to an extent that far exceeds the involvement of the singer in the characters in songs. The aural address of the pop singer is thus unique in constituting a direct address to the listener/viewer in which the personality of the storyteller usually overwhelms characterization within the story. (The nearest media equivalents in that respect would be stand-up comedians or talk-show hosts.)

This double address accounts for a good deal of the apparent antirealism in music television. For example, Suzanne Vega's 1987 hit single "Luka" (a song about child abuse) is told in the first person, so that Vega sings: "My name is Luka." No one takes this literally—we know that a story is being told by a pop singer, and yet she does not "become" the character, either, in the manner of an actor. In the promotional clip LUKA, a child acts out visual motifs from the story, providing one strand of the clip's narrative. But the other strand is a series of shots of Vega singing "My name is Luka." There is no hierarchy of visual discourses between the two strands, which seem to contradict each other. But there is no need for such a hierarchy, and there is in fact no contradiction, because in the context of pop's aesthetic it is entirely conventional and thoroughly ordinary for this text to present us with a story and its teller in this manner. The break with a "realist" system of address is not aesthetically radical, it is a *convention* of pop performance. Reading video clips as nonrealist or antirealist thus constitutes one of the most elementary mistakes of media analysis (one that has often been warned against, for instance, in relation to soap opera; see Allen, 1983): that of misreading the generic conventions of the form by applying rules carried over from another (inappropriate) genre or medium. (Indeed, within the established codes of rock music, the act of "revealing the machinery" rarely involves making narration visible, but instead is a *guarantor of authenticity*. That is the significance of the all-pervasive mise-en-scène of the rehearsal room/ warehouse space in music video clips.)

Therefore, if we resituate music video clips within the context of pop music narratives, we can begin to see a different structural logic at work. It is then apparent that the pop song utilizes a direct mode of address, both aurally and (in performance) iconically. It is these conventions that are in play when singers and musicians look into the camera and perform directly for us.

The familiar nature of this form of address can be seen if it is noticed that the codes of television (rather than cinema) upon which music videos draw are those of the highly conventional devices of light entertainment. When musicians look directly into the camera in a music video clip, they do not step out of a fictional diegesis so much as provide a well-established framework within which elements of mininarrative are sometimes acted out. (I have merely reversed the usual terms of reference, but that operation is, I think, significant.) The well-established framework is that of the television "variety" show (see Dyer, 1973) — which in its turn derives from the theatrical conventions of the music hall (see Williams, 1974). Here a televisual host introduces comedians, variety acts (magicians, acrobats, and so on), and singers, some of whom address us directly. (The format is thus quite different from the forms of address used in "factual" programming or drama, in which institutional and aesthetic conventions tightly control who may look into the camera.)[6] Dyer (1973) observes:

> There are few programmes in which performers, particularly in
> introductions and greetings, do not address the camera and
> therefore attempt to address the domestic audience. But few
> performers address the camera in the actual performance of their
> act: they either address no-one or else the unseen studio
> audience, which since it is unseen is for the domestic viewer only
> a kind of enlargement of her or himself. (p. 18)

It is interesting to note that singers more so than other acts *are* likely to address the camera directly—a practice that is no doubt meant to under-score the supposedly more "intimate" nature of songs.[7]

The codes of television "variety," far from being transgressive of re-alism, in fact clearly derive from the ideology of transparency (an aspect of realism, in film theory) in broadcast aesthetics; the direct address is in-tended to mirror the codes of live performance, where singers sing di-rectly to the concert hall audience (a look that is displaced, via camera, onto the television viewer). The development of pop music program-ming on broadcast television (*Top of the Pops, American Bandstand*) tended to imitate these conventions, and it was not unusual for the mise-en-scène and/or additional performers (such as dancers) to visualize aspects of a song while the performers addressed us directly.

Taken together, these two points (concerning modes of address in the pop song and the conventions of television light entertainment) demon-strate why the image of George Michael or Janet Jackson singing directly to us and looking directly into the camera is no more subversive or avant-garde than the fact that singers sing to *us* (the audience) at live concerts and musicians address the camera on *Top of the Pops* or *Saturday Night Live.*

My Spine Is the Baseline: Music, Narrative, Anchorage

If the modes of address deployed in video clips reflect conventional and highly ordered generic conventions, what of the music itself? One sig-nificant effect of the discussion of narrative in music video so far has been to miss the degree of coherence and closure that occurs on the sound track. Promotional video clips have usually been discussed in terms of their anarchic incoherence, their break with "realism," their narrative fracturing. This may seem odd if we consider that Theodor Adorno's fa-mous essay describing popular music as convention bound and highly predictable, written in 1941, is still very pertinent to today's pop. While I do not share Adorno's pessimistic conclusions regarding the reception of pop music (and while some areas of contemporary pop, such as rap and hip-hop, do not entirely fit his description; see Goodwin, 1991c), the essential mechanisms identified in that essay remain pervasive. Most im-portant, popular music uses what Adorno called "part interchangeabil-ity" (described below) to such an extent that most of the songs we hear can be "recognized" through their similarities to other songs. (Unlike Adorno, I am not attaching any pejorative sense to that description; nor do I assume that originality and innovation are therefore absent.) The rationalization of song structure (a function of mass production) also gives pop songs a highly predictable form, and this may be combined with Max Weber's (1958) argument about rationalization in Western music *tout court*, since in that respect pop music is usually very conservative, in terms of its tonal one-dimensionality. Thus, in the consumption of music videos we can find three kinds of closure or coherence that introduce a high degree of stability via the sound track: repetition, structural closure, and harmonic closure.

Repetition occurs at three levels—within songs, between songs, and across media sites.[8] First, pop songs are based on the repetition of elements such as the verse and chorus within any given song, and on the repetition of lyrics, chord progressions, riffs, and rhythms. For instance, in the song "Faith" by George Michael, the structure comprises ten segments, as follows:

1. Instrumental introduction
2. Verse 1
3. Bridge
4. Refrain/chorus
5. Verse 2
6. Bridge
7. Refrain/chorus
8. Guitar solo (over music from verse)
9. Bridge
10. Refrain/chorus

Musically, then, the song consists of just one segment (2-4, 5-7, 8-10, of roughly a minute in length) that is repeated three times. The lyrics for the second verse and the guitar solo represent the only variations on the opening segment. In this, "Faith" is quite typical of pop song structure.

Second, pop songs are also repetitive in their resemblance to other pop songs, drawing on almost identical lyrics, melodies, riffs, rhythms, and styles of performance. I have chosen "Faith" as my example because it demonstrates a classic rhythmic repetition in that its central rhythmic figure (established by the drums, bass, and acoustic guitar) is a beat sometimes known as the "clave" or "Bo Diddley" beat,[9] which listeners will recognize (consciously or not) from songs as diverse as the Buddy Holly/Rolling Stones classic "Not Fade Away," the Who's "Magic Bus," Led Zeppelin's "Custard Pie," David Bowie's "Panic in Detroit," Thomas

Dolby's "Europa and the Pirate Twins," Bow Wow Wow's "I Want Candy," the Clash's "Rudie Can't Fail," Bruce Springsteen's "I Ain't Got You," the Smith's "How Soon Is Now," U2's "Desire," and Soho's "Hippychick." [10]

Third, pop music is also based on a high degree of repetition across media sites, so that any current song can be heard on the radio, on our stereos, on television, and at the cinema—until familiarity breeds either sales or contempt. In the case of "Faith," heavy airplay on the radio was combined with television appearances, a music video, a concert tour, and a television commercial for Coca-Cola.

These aspects of popular music were first identified by Adorno (1941)—and while his interpretation of the phenomenon of part interchangeability has been challenged (most interestingly by Gendron, 1986), few writers have refused the description. [11] These aspects of repetition explain why music television cannot be understood on the basis of one or two viewings of an individual video clip. For most consumers, music television is seen and heard in the context of varying degrees of familiarity with songs, their lyrics, and the pop singers and musicians who perform them.

Most pop songs also feature a high degree of structural and harmonic resolution. By *structural resolution* I mean the organization of songs around classic formulas both within verses and choruses (the use of obvious rhymes, the predictable employment of A/B/A/B/C/A/B structures, and so forth; see Loewenthal, 1983) and across the whole song— most important, the way a song ends with the repetition of a chorus or refrain that "ties up" the song, perhaps as it fades out. This is not quite the same as repetition, for while it involves repetition, the argument about structural closure is that *it explains why repetition does not render the pop text subversive of the alleged effects of realism.*

At first sight, repetition clearly undermines the principles of the classic realist text. It defies progression and—therefore—resolution. (This is true of both the song itself and pop music in general.) Indeed, repetition in pop is sometimes so extreme that it can seem that a whole song might be reduced to one two-to-five-second sound bite, or to a four-bar figure—as in the Bo Diddley rhythm of "Faith," for instance. Pop songs in this respect invert the relation of story (or plot) time to discourse time, identified by narrative theorists (see Chatman, 1981; and the critique of this scheme offered by Hernadi, 1981) in relation to fiction and mass-mediated texts as one in which story time (the time that spans the plot) is condensed in discourse time (the temporal unit that measures the length of time spent consuming the narrative). In pop, we might say that discourse time is actually *longer* than story time, since it involves the multiple reiteration of the same moment. As Paul Willis (1976) puts it:

> The structure of classical music, with its hierarchy of beats in the bar, meant that it existed clearly in a time sequence—some things had to come before others. In subverting the discontinuities of the bar, rock 'n' roll also subverted the sense of order and ordered time—if all the elements of a piece are the same, it does not matter in which order they appear. Rock 'n' roll music can be stopped or started at any time; it can be turned back or forward; it can be suspended here and carried over there; it can be interrupted. (p. 76)

This is an insightful passage that explains a good deal about rock and pop music, and its possible homologies with everyday life. Willis argues that this "timeless" state mirrors the practices and myths of the "motorbike boys" who are so devoted to the music. The relation of narratives to everyday life and reading practices is an issue to which I shall return in chapter 7. Here I want only to add a note of dissent to Willis's argument. Some time after the publication of his book *Profane Culture*, the reggae, hip-hop, and dance scenes generated a mutation of the pop song, in the form of the twelve-inch single, which seems to prove his point. In the twelve-inch single, the "original" (seven-inch, three-minute) version of a song is expanded (often to between six and ten minutes) and radically restructured. This restructuring (some would say *deconstructing*) of the song occurs through changes in the arrangement, acoustic space, and sometimes the timbre. Crucially for Willis's argument, the song structure is also altered, with the original, predictable format chopped up so that the new version is often held together only by the *beat*. The twelve-inch single enjoyed extraordinary and surprising success during the 1980s and is now a central commodity form for the music industry.[12]

The fact that the twelve-inch single has not become the chief mode of promoting albums and acts is, however, deeply significant and demonstrates why Adorno is still relevant. While the audience has developed a taste for longer, remixed versions of pop songs, the music industry bases its *promotional strategy* on the three-minute single, for reasons Adorno would recognize.[13] In the effort to sell a new song, and often a new act, the pop song possesses a structure that *cannot* be tampered with too much—which explains why Adorno's description of prerock, popular jazz hits still applies today, post-rock and roll. The single has increasingly become a vehicle designed to hook the listener.[14] In that respect it has certain properties: the title will usually be contained in the chorus; the chorus and/or bridge will be the most "catchy" part of the song (of course it is the audience who is in fact "caught"); the verse will *lead up* to a chorus (or hook), which generally appears within the first twenty-five seconds of the song;[15] and the chorus (containing the song title—i.e., *the name of the product*) will be repeated at the end of the song.

In Haug's terms, then, the three-minute single is a commodity possessing an additional level of use-value. The pleasure we derive from the hook is a promise that not only delivers (unlike Adorno, I maintain that it *does* make good on its seduction—popular culture is not *only* a tease),[16] it also offers another promise, which is the implication that the use-value of this hook will be found elsewhere in the music of this act, probably in the latest album or on a tour (which is almost always selling an album); indeed, industry terminology speaks of acts touring in "support" of "product."

It is for this reason (because Willis's motorbike boys, like all other consumers, do *not* determine the nature of popular cultural products) that the seven-inch single cannot be stopped and started at random, and cannot be subverted in terms of its formal organization.[17] This is precisely why it is the three-minute version (rather than the twelve-inch remix) that is used as the basis for promotional videos. The three-minute single that forms the structural basis for music video clips is thus both highly repetitive and highly ordered and stable—indeed, it is highly *rationalized*, in both the Weberian and Adornian senses.

We can see in this what it is that is essentially misconceived about the cultural studies appropriation of theories of realism. Having set up a model of the classic realist text and its supposed effects on the audience, cultural studies theorists then match narratives to the ideal and infer effects on the basis of adherence to or subversion of the ideal. The problem here is of course not just that realism may not in fact have the properties ascribed to it by its critics, but that there is a suppressed middle in the logic. For there may be *other* narrative forms that exist outside the paradigm of realism/nonrealism, so that a text (in this case, the pop song) may be nonrealist and at the same time highly conventional and predictable. If, as I argue, pop songs constitute such an example, then this clearly has serious implications for any attempt to use narrative theory—

at least as it has so far been applied to popular culture—in relation to video clips.

Again, Adorno's (in)famous analysis of popular music established this point. It is worth noting here that there is an empirical argument that might be mounted against the charge that song structures employ such a degree of predictability. In recent years pop songs have developed variations upon the classic Tin Pan Alley formula that have ranged from the minor shift of beginning with the refrain/chorus through to the abandonment of verses and choruses altogether, in the dance-floor music hits of M/A/R/R/S and S'Express for instance. Nonetheless, the bulk of successful pop songs do continue to adhere to the classic formula, and it is noticeable that the "second wave" of popular dance music, in the shape of acts such as Black Box, C + C Music Factory, and Soho, exemplifies the process whereby experimentation invents new possibilities that are then transformed in order to fit conventional pop formulas. (I hope it goes without saying by this point in my argument that I do not draw Frankfurt School-style *conclusions* from this *description*, which nonetheless clearly supports much of their cultural theory.)

Finally, in this discussion of the music video sound track, I mean by *harmonic resolution* the organization of the music itself around conventions of tonality and musical arrangement that both ground the music in a system of tonal relations that may be seen as the aural equivalent of the realist systems of "looks" in cinema and often enable it to end with a musical "resolution," which may be seen as the aural equivalent of a realist narrative reaching its conclusion. That is to say, once again the pop song seems to contain elements that mirror the imputed effects of realism in cinema and television, but without adhering literally to the same model.

In classic narrative theory, resolution is reached temporally through the unfolding of conflict resulting from the disturbance of an equilibrium that is thus restored.[18] Because the logic of rock and pop music is not linear, it is often assumed that its timeless state negates the possibility of resolution. And yet even the most amateur of rock musicians ("amateur" in this context of course being a state to which the musician *aspires!*) knows that tension and conflict are central to music and are present as soon as a chord is struck on a guitar or a rhythm is set into motion by bass and drums. Conflict and resolution exist in music, but they are played out simultaneously. Resolution exists, and order is restored in just the way Max Weber (1958) described, through tonal rationalization and harmonic unity. This resolution is often made explicit through an ending that lands on the root note/chord, but it is also achieved through the repetition of the song's hook/chorus, sometimes during a fade-out. In other words, just as a visual narrative may be rooted (through shot-reverse shot) in the process of "suture" (see Heath, 1977-78), which establishes a kind of psychic baseline for the viewer, so popular music generally proceeds through the establishment of a system of relations that roots the music, anchoring it in familiar regimes of tonality and rhythm. Similarly, as the realist narrative ends with all its questions answered, so the pop song tells its musical story in order to finish, to complete itself with a final chord and/or hook.

Before I move on to relate the music further to pop's visual imagery in music television, it is important that I reiterate the point that musical meaning in music television is highly autonomous. It is central to my argument not only that many visual features of music television can be explained by listening to the songs themselves, but also that the music is a discrete and central anchor of meaning in the consumption of music video. Critics of music television have exaggerated the decentered, unstable nature of music television partly by failing to take account of the music itself.

Music video clips thus defy the terms of the debate about the "classic realist text" derived from film studies on two counts. First, the music itself achieves resolution through repetition, rather than linear development. Second, the song lyrics often operate without any temporal development—and even where a story is told in the words from beginning to end, the method of storytelling is certainly entirely different from that found in television or cinema. Consequently, the images of music television (which mirror music, not film or television) avoid the mechanisms of a cinematic system of realist "looks" and (to a lesser extent) the rhetoric of TV editing (discussed and usefully distinguished from cinema by Ellis, 1982b) without necessarily engendering alienation, schizophrenia, or confusion in the audience. The audience, after all, has been listening to pop music all its life.

To sum up the argument so far: both pop music and music television defy certain conventions of the "classic realist text"; in particular, neither quite adheres to the classic sequence of disruption-action-resolution. Despite this, however, it is possible to see an enormous degree of stability and coherence in these texts, since they remain rooted rather than thrown into textual chaos by pop's musical characteristics. Music television makes sense partly because it so closely mirrors these features of pop with which its audiences are extremely familiar.

These features of the pop song itself are not the only anchoring mechanisms in music television, however. If we return again to Adorno, it is clear that video clips may be structured around techniques that derive from the pop song but that, as I will now show, have their roots in the economic organization of the music industry.

Logics of Visual Structure

We can now begin to consider the relation between the elements discussed above (modes of address, codes of entertainment television, and musical structure) and the narrative organization of video clips. So far, I have argued (both in this chapter and in the preceding one) that the visual layers of music video clips can be explained in relation to the music: specifically, synaesthesia and pop's dual modes of address explain a great deal of the textual detail in promotional clips. Yet these features do not fully explain the apparently fractured nature of video clips. As I argued in chapter 2, music television is one among many of pop's multidiscursive promotional forms. Synaesthesia connects with this function of music videos but does not fully explain it. Neither does the narrative structure of the pop song fully account for the narrative structure of pop promos. In trying to give a specific aesthetic and institutional grounding for the narrative analysis of video clips, there is no attempt to reduce them to *only* a visualization of musical elements. (Here I am tending to stress that point in order to redress the balance.) It is clear that music video is relatively autonomous from the music, to a limited degree, in a number of ways:

1. The visualization of a song may go beyond its meaning.

2. The clips seek to provide pleasure (sometimes, but by no means exclusively, of a narrative nature) in order to keep the viewer watching and to encourage repeated viewings.

3. The clips might promote *other* commodities (such as films).

4. The clips might narrativize/display images of stardom that exceed any given individual song—a point taken up in the next chapter.

I want now to discuss the first three of these elements.

Music video clips often appear to display high levels of incoherence when viewed from the perspective of film theory. That they should not in fact be viewed from such a perspective has already been suggested (in chapter 1); here I will explore some possible alternative ways of reading them. One key problem arises from the nature of the popular music text itself. The three codes of popular music (music, lyrics, iconography) do not always constitute a unified address, and this conflict routinely spills over into video clips. A famous example is the Bruce Springsteen song "Glory Days," in which the lyric is apparently undermined by both the music and the performance. The song is a downbeat story of working-class resignation in which the narration (related by Springsteen in the third person) positions characters in the song as essentially defeated, while still living out a fantasy-memory of the "good old days." However, this story is undermined both by the nature of the music itself (the "glory days" refrain, instead of sounding ironic, is sung as if it were celebratory) and by the upbeat style of performance offered both in the recording and in Springsteen's live concerts. As with LUKA, the GLORY DAYS video clip confuses the issue still further by positioning Springsteen as a character within his own diegesis—while leaving ambiguous the question of whether this character could be the *same* person Springsteen depicts as a singer in a small-town bar. In other words, the "real" narration offered in the clip by Springsteen himself (as a singer with his band) may in fact be an implied narration through the character Springsteen portrays. (This question can be made more complex, but is also more easily resolved, if we consider that the actual "Springsteen" is already a character, constructed via the mass media.)

This opening observation should lead us to begin with a slightly more complex concept of how sound-vision relations work in music television than has so far been the case. The debate about whether or not the video image triumphs over the song itself needs to take account of *where the emphasis lies in the visualization* (lyrics, music, or performance iconography) and surely then must engage with the question of whether or not it illustrates, amplifies, or contradicts the meaning of the song. This idea needs to be related to the music, as well as the song's lyrical message, but it should already be clear that visual images do indeed tend to follow a musical logic. Here the argument concerns how the lyrical content is visualized, where it is possible to identify three kinds of relations between songs and videos: illustration, amplification, and disjuncture.

By *illustration* I refer to those clips in which the visual narrative tells the story of the song lyric. In the Jam's THAT'S ENTERTAINMENT, singer Paul Weller provides a bitter account of life as a pop star (the title, clearly, is ironic) while the video (including home video shot by Weller's father, who is also his manager) shows the band going about its business on the road. In Madonna's PAPA DON'T PREACH, one possible reading of the song ("Papa" here is the real, as opposed to the holy, father) is acted out by Madonna and Danny Aiello. Public Enemy's 911 IS A JOKE similarly narrativizes that song's lyrics, as does A-ha's TAKE ON ME. The Pet Shop Boys' OPPORTUNITIES (LET'S MAKE LOTS OF MONEY) illustrates the song (the title is ironic) as an electronic tableau. Aerosmith's DUDE (LOOKS LIKE A LADY) makes its title explicit. David Bowie's DAY IN, DAY OUT takes the song lyrics and constructs a classic realist mininarrative around them. Elvis Costello's VERONICA uses flashback to reveal the point of the song's words. Ice-T's I'M YOUR PUSHER illustrates the words in a manner that makes the lyrics explicit, so that the deliberate ambiguity about the term *pusher* (Ice-T is pushing education, not drugs) is made clear. The Jesus Jones clip RIGHT HERE RIGHT NOW even goes beyond the illustration of the lyrics, to restage the manner in which the song was written—when songwriter Mike Edwards sat down in front the television to watch the news of the fall of the Berlin Wall. Further examples that could be cited here include a huge proportion (perhaps the majority) of music video clips.

As noted in the previous chapter, the business of illustrating songs is fraught with danger—in particular the making too literal of metaphors and tropes. Thus, illustration will often involve the effort to signify a *mood*, as opposed to telling a story. Dance is often illustrative in this way, where a singer tells us he or she is feeling sexy/romantic, and the dancing attempts to visualize this. Examples would be Samantha Fox's TOUCH ME, Janet Jackson's WHEN I THINK OF YOU, Paula Abdul's OPPOSITES ATTRACT, Tone Lōc's WILD THING, Debbie Gibson's SHAKE YOUR LOVE, and George Michael's I WANT YOUR SEX. A similar device (which is prevalent in rap and hip-hop) occurs when the words tell us that the music is going to make us *feel*, or want to dance (often this is also a sexual metaphor), and the enactment of the song shows us the effect the music is supposed to have. Examples of videos that take this approach include C + C Music Factory's GONNA MAKE YOU SWEAT, Run-D.M.C./Aerosmith's WALK THIS WAY, and Mick Jagger and David Bowie's DANCING IN THE STREETS. If we include these kinds of instances as a variation of illustrative narratives, then it is clear that by far the largest proportion of clips do in fact occupy this category.

Amplification occurs when the clip introduces new meanings that do not conflict with the lyrics, but that add layers of meaning—this, for some critics, is the mark of a "good" video. Culture Club's DO YOU RE-

ALLY WANT TO HURT ME? (discussed in chapter 1) is an example. More brazenly, Van Halen's HOT FOR TEACHER takes a lyric in which it is the pupil who is eroticizing his teacher (although a gendered counterreading by young girls and women is presumably just about possible here) and visualizes the fantasy, so that an additional layer (the teacher appears as also wishing to be eroticized, through her dance routines) is added. Philip Hayward's (1991) discussion of Madonna's CHERISH would place that clip in this category, since the mermen introduce into the visual scenario an element unavailable through any reading of the song.

Clips might also (intentionally or not) involve *disjuncture* between lyrics and image. This may be of two kinds. The disjuncture may be one in which the imagery has no apparent bearing on the lyrics.[19] Such cryptic strategies are unusual, and often signal that the act in question is making a claim upon cultural capital. Depeche Mode's recent clips seem to work this way; if there is a connection between the words and images in NEVER LET ME DOWN AGAIN, for example, it is certainly extremely oblique and works to suggest that the band (and its fans) are "serious."

On the other hand, the visual narrative may either flatly contradict the lyrics or perhaps unintentionally undermine them. Michael Jackson's MAN IN THE MIRROR is an example of the latter. The song implores us to begin social change with ourselves—"the man in the mirror"—in a familiar individualistic appeal that suggests we cannot change the world unless we begin with ourselves. The video clip, however, uses the now-familiar device of a news and documentary montage drawing heavily on images from the 1960s (see, for comparison, Billy Joel's WE DIDN'T START THE FIRE), which somewhat contradicts the message of the song by focusing so much on images of *collective* protest—for instance, anti-Vietnam War demonstrators. The question of disjuncture is often at the heart of censorship issues, when a songwriter claims a meaning for a song that broadcast institutions read differently through its video image. A notorious example of this was the BBC's banning of the Police clip INVISIBLE SUN (which featured footage of British soldiers in Northern Ireland)—an action that was justified by the BBC on the following grounds: "The theme of the single is anti-violence, but the presentation film could be said to convey meanings which are not present in the single" (quoted in the *Daily Mirror*, September 23, 1981).

These relations of music, lyrics, and iconography thus reveal one area in which narrative relations are highly complex, since they may also involve the music itself and/or performance iconography. For instance, we also need to think about how the imagery might illustrate the music (cutting on the beat, emphasizing syncopations, responding to the song's arrangement—as discussed in chapter 3), amplify it (setting up its own, complementary, visual pulses and timbres), or create a disjuncture (for instance, when low-budget clips are badly made or, simply through lack of technical resources, fail to respond to the feel of the music itself).

Correspondingly, clips may illustrate an act's already-established iconography. This is obviously another pervasive means of constructing clips—the "performance" video, in which we are offered a pseudodocumentary (the act is mimicking live performance) account of the act's "real" imagery. Even performance videos that contain narrative elements may be placed in this category, since it is often the act's performance iconography that is made into a story, rather than the song itself. Bon Jovi's WANTED: DEAD OR ALIVE conflates both levels, in that the refrain "I'm a space cowboy" seems to reference both a fictional identity (based on the western) and a metaphorical allusion to the musicians as real people (who are, by implication, outlaws). The performance-video relation may also encompass amplification (as in Jon Bon Jovi's BLAZE OF GLORY, which operates along similar lines to WANTED: DEAD OR ALIVE)[20] and disjuncture. A famous example of the latter is New Order's TOUCHED BY THE HAND OF GOD, in which the band appear in heavy metal costumes. (A similar device, albeit one generated by the lyrics themselves, is used in Eurythmics' KING AND QUEEN OF AMERICA.) Less witty instances occur when a new (and therefore relatively powerless) act is forced to dress up and enact inappropriate scenarios; from the point of view of video's promotional role, this clearly constitutes a "mistake." (It is quite a subjective point, but I would place the Rolling Stones clip IT'S ONLY ROCK AND ROLL, in which Mick Jagger is dressed in a sailor's uniform, in this category!)

To illustrate the complexity of these issues, we could look at the GLORY DAYS video as one that contains disjuncture in relation to the song's lyrics (the downbeat framing of the narrative is arguably undermined by the bar scenes), while clearly operating through illustration of Bruce Springsteen and the E Street Band's performance iconography and their music, since the band is known to make unpublicized "surprise" appearances in small clubs on the New Jersey shore.

There are two reasons for wanting to make these arguments. First, we can see that any research that wishes to deal with the question of how music video frames audience responses to songs must take account of the complex relations between the video clip and the three elements of the song (lyrics, music, performance). Second, it should become increasingly clear that although the mechanisms of intertextuality and multidiscursivity make the structural analysis of any clip quite complex, nonetheless there is every reason to emphasize coherence and aesthetic logic in this task. If we assume, as I do, that the music television audience is both highly knowledgeable and quite sophisticated with regard to both music and popular culture, then there is good reason to speculate that in the act of decoding, the tight relations between the song text and the video text are already "known." While the audience would not generally use my terms, I believe I am describing the processes that explain how video clips make sense to the audience. Another way of saying this is to note that for pop fans, concertgoers, radio listeners, and music video spectators, the points I have just made are probably rather obvious. Hence, we need to invert the process criticized by Hernadi (1981) when he suggests that literary and film studies scholars often have *too much* knowledge, through studying texts too carefully and in such a way (for instance, using freeze-frame to dissect a single shot in a movie) that actual reading formations cannot be understood. Analysts of music video narrative have been all too eager to freeze the moment and study videos shot by shot, but here the problem is that this generates not too much but too little knowledge, because the individual narrative is highly intertextual. In the task of knowing how to *describe* music video narratives, it is often the educators who need the most education.

I turn now to my second point: the question of how music video narratives are determined by a desire to inscribe the text with pleasure in ways that might exceed the business of underscoring the song text itself. The analysis presented in chapter 3 leaves open the question of whether or not video clips might have structural corespondences with the pop song. I want to identify two elements of the video text that suggest this structural link with music. The first is the presence of visual hooks.

We know that a pop song is organized around the repetition of a hook (or chorus, refrain) that is designed to compel the listener to want to hear the song again and again.

Do videos use a similar device? Burns (1983) argues that clips do possess hooks, without being very clear on their nature or their roots in music and advertising. I want to develop that notion further and suggest that three different kinds of visual hooks are present in promotional music videos. First, there are the routine close-ups of pop stars' faces, which are often repeated during a song's chorus or refrain. Peter Gabriel's SHOCK

THE MONKEY offers a classic example of this, in which the camera repeatedly returns to close-ups of Gabriel's face (often in tandem with a rhythmic emphasis), which undergoes a series of transformations (echoing Gabriel's own penchant for using costumes and taking on fictional identities, which stretches back to his time with Genesis). We are unsure how Gabriel will look each time he reappears, and the delivery on this hook occurs when his costuming is mixed up: wearing a Western business suit, he appears in "primitive" face paint.

This is the kind of hook emphasized in the discourses of stardom promoted, for instance, by MTV: in its trailers for its daily slots (*Classic MTV*, for instance) and special programming (*Rewind, Decade*, etc.), the station promotes the programs by screening key images from video clips. For example, *Classic MTV* is previewed with a sequence that runs quickly through a montage of very familiar close-up shots. Each image is intended effectively to "remind" us of the specific videos and the era from which they come, and it is significant that MTV has chosen close-ups of stars (as opposed to the various other hooks that might be chosen) to trigger these memories. Such hooks are pervasive in the mass media, for instance, in the celebrity faces used on music magazine covers.

A striking example of this phenomenon occurs in the clip VOICES THAT CARE—a song featuring various American pop stars and media personalities (Fresh Prince, Hammer, Mark Knopfler, Jani Lane, Dudley Moore, Whoopi Goldberg, Kevin Costner, Meryl Streep) that was made to announce support for the U.S. forces fighting in the Gulf War of 1991. The clip uses the familiar device (since 1985's Live Aid video DO THEY KNOW IT'S CHRISTMAS?) of cutting from a chorus of well-known music and media stars to individual close-ups. This form is now so well established that it constitutes a subgenre in itself, so that both pro- and antiwar (the Peace Choir's GIVE PEACE A CHANCE) videos used exactly the same format.[21] The shot of Dire Straits guitarist Mark Knopfler, which occurs during his guitar solo, is embellished via postproduction effects with abstract colored lines that recall the use of that same technique in Dire Straits' MONEY FOR NOTHING. In other words, it is as though some elements of music video function much like Adorno's concept of "pseudoindividualization," in which part interchangeability is overcome through gimmicks that make each performer seem unique. Just as the music itself is punctuated with signs that function as "trademarks" to signify "Michael Jackson" (his little yelp), "Chris Isaak" (his overwrought crooning), "Scritti Politti" (ultraclean acoustic space), "Genesis" (the big Phil Collins drum sound), "Johnny Rotten" (out of key, sneering vocals), or "Morrissey" (deadpan delivery), so there are now video equivalents. The jet-set iconography of Duran Duran (RIO, HUNGRY LIKE THE WOLF), the hyperbusy computer effects for Peter Gabriel clips (SLEDGEHAMMER, BIG TIME), the clocks and watches ("We know what *time* it is") and trademark black-man-in-the-crosshairs of a gun sight of Public Enemy (FIGHT THE POWER, NIGHT OF THE LIVING BASEHEADS, DON'T BELIEVE THE HYPE), the downbeat, monochrome enigmas of Depeche Mode (NEVER LET ME DOWN AGAIN, PERSONAL JESUS, POLICY OF TRUTH), and the female mannequins of Robert Palmer (ADDICTED TO LOVE, SIMPLY IRRESISTIBLE) are examples of cases in which video clips (usually temporarily) establish visual trademarks for acts.

A second type of hook employs the scopophilic male gaze identified by Mulvey (1975). Here, images of women that employ the classic techniques of objectification, fragmentation, and (occasionally) violation (see Myers, 1982) are placed throughout the clips in order to encourage viewers to keep watching. This device is used in Whitesnake's HERE I GO AGAIN and STILL OF THE NIGHT, ZZ Top's LEGS, GIMME ALL YOUR LOVIN', and SHARP DRESSED MAN, Robert Palmer's ADDICTED TO LOVE and SIMPLY IRRESISTIBLE, Too Short's SHORT BUT FUNKY, the Beastie Boys' SHE'S ON IT, Van Halen's HOT FOR TEACHER and FINISH WHAT YA STARTED, David Lee Roth's CALIFORNIA GIRLS, the Rolling Stones' SHE WAS HOT, George Michael's I WANT YOUR SEX and FATHER FIGURE, Ice-T's HIGH ROLLERS, the J. Geils Band's CENTERFOLD, Dire Straits' MONEY FOR NOTHING, Warrant's CHERRY PIE, and Mötley Crüe's GIRLS, GIRLS, GIRLS.

Sometimes the two appeals outlined above are combined — for instance, in many of the clips by female musicians, such as Madonna (MATERIAL GIRL, CHERISH, VOGUE, JUSTIFY MY LOVE), Debbie Harry/Blondie (DREAMING), Eurythmics (LOVE IS A STRANGER, BEETHOVEN — I LOVE TO LISTEN TO), Bananarama (I HEARD A RUMOUR), Tina Turner (WHAT'S LOVE GOT TO DO WITH IT, THE BEST), Wilson Phillips (YOU'RE IN LOVE), the Divinyls (I TOUCH MYSELF), and the Bangles/Susanna Hoffs (IF SHE KNEW WHAT SHE WANTS, WALK LIKE AN EGYPTIAN, MY SIDE OF THE BED). Here, however, the system of looks operative in classic Hollywood cinema is broken up by the introduction of a direct mode of address from the female musician(s).

With greater or lesser degrees of narrative integration, images of women are mobilized in these clips in ways that are not merely classically scopophilic, but organized structurally so as to display them briefly and strategically throughout the clip. The link with musicology is this: just as we wait for the repetition of the chorus, which is offered early in the song and then repeated throughout until the final series of refrains, so these scopophilic hooks are designed to offer a visual incentive to keep watching. Responding to criticism of the clip CHERRY PIE, which was considered sexist by many critics for its lyrics ("She's my cherry pie") and its (scopophilic) display of a female model, Warrant's lead vocalist Jani Lane made the motivation quite explicit:

> I'm pushing 30, and as an artist I want to communicate with people my age who are thinking along the same lines that I am. But we've also got a pretty large following of kids, and we have to be visual to appeal to them. So I've got to split the difference somewhere. . . . Maybe five years down the road, we'll get to the point where people will automatically sit down and pay attention to anything we do, but right now we've still got to grab people's attention. (quoted in *Pulse!*, December 1990: 108)

Indeed, this aspect of music video cannot be underestimated, given its essentially promotional form. Haug's terms of reference are useful here, since music video deploys the classic rhetoric of advertising in its effort to attach the song to sensual/erotic experiences. Sometimes this is combined with a metatextual appeal to "controversy," as Kevin Godley, co-director of Duran Duran's clip GIRLS ON FILM, has revealed:

> People are always accusing that tape of sexism, and of course they're right. Look, we just did our job; we were very explicitly told by Duran Duran's management to make a very sensational, erotic piece that would be for clubs, where it could get shown uncensored, just to make people take notice and talk about it. (quoted in Shore, 1985: 86)

It is impossible here not to think of other examples, the most famous of which is surely Madonna's JUSTIFY MY LOVE, in which the erotic imagery acted not only to tease the audience into repeated viewings (it is hard to tell exactly who is doing what to whom on just one viewing) but also to generate a media event that helped promote the single. Other instances that could be cited are Frankie Goes to Hollywood's RELAX,[22] the Tubes' MONDO BONDAGE, Duran Duran's THE CHAUFFEUR, Cheap Trick's UP THE CREEK, and David Bowie's CHINA GIRL (for accounts of some of these clips, see Gross, 1984a, 1984b).

A third kind of hook is more deeply rooted in the music itself, but is harder to explain. Here a visual image seems to carry an emotive charge or set of associations that connects with a musical motif, and it is repeated throughout the clip in parallel with its musical partner. An example of this kind of hook is the use of the armadillo in the Clash clip ROCK THE CASBAH.[23] In this clip, the band stands in front of oil drilling equipment to lip-sync the song while a fictional comic narrative is acted out about Middle East politics. At certain moments in the clip we see an armadillo trundling along—at a poolside, across the desert sands where the Clash are performing, and so on. This image occurs only when the song's unmistakable minor chord piano pattern is being repeated.

Finally, I want to mention a more fundamental structural correspondence between images and song form. I have already noted McClary and Walser's (1990) important argument about the "stacking up" of elements in the pop song—a phenomenon that creates a multilayered text that can be heard in a variety of ways, depending on where we place our aural attention (with the rhythm, the voice, the backing, the lyrics, and so on). This structure implies a separation of elements common to Brechtian aesthetics, rather than the hierarchy of discourses identified as central in the classic realist text (see MacCabe, 1974). The visual structure of video clips arguably reproduces this arrangement, which helps to explain the apparently fragmented nature of its organization: some visual elements illustrate lyrics and others represent the voice, the rhythm, and the various aspects of the music discussed earlier in this chapter. In other words, a musicology of music video images can address not only specific instances of visualizing music and lyrics, but the possible correspondences between aural and visual narrative organization. As I have already suggested, however, the separation of elements apparent here does not imply the effects attributed to it by the antirealists.

Another issue worthy of discussion here is the much-neglected one of the intrusion of other texts and forms of commodity promotion into the video clip—a practice that clearly dovetails with the business of "product placement."[24] I suggested above that particular video effects are associated with an act and sometimes function as a kind of trademark, usually for a limited period only (see Haug, 1987: 110-11). However, as Corbett (1990) has pointed out, a more transparent aspect of the structure of music videos that parallels advertising even more closely is the use of logos and graphic designs that directly promote the acts. Indeed, the BOHEMIAN RHAPSODY clip so often cited as the "first" music video actually deploys imagery that closely (and, clearly, quite deliberately) matches the art-work on Queen's second album, *Queen II*. This tactic has been used frequently, and clearly connects with Haug's assertion about the role of the trademark in "commodity aesthetics": here a logo is made familiar (either an image that suggests the act in general or one that promotes the most recent album). ZZ Top have repeatedly used a logo both on album covers and in the form of a magic key (which performs exactly as Vladimir Propp's "magical agent")[25] in a series of video clips (GIMME ALL YOUR LOVIN', LEGS, SHARP DRESSED MAN). In ENJOY THE SILENCE, CLEAN, and WORLD IN MY EYES, Depeche Mode use the image that adorns the cover of the album (*Violator*) from which the singles are taken (a long-stemmed red rose) and this was also present in a back-projected film sequence on the world tour that also promoted *Violator*. Public Enemy's logo is also frequently seen in their video clips and throughout the long-form collection *Fight the Power—Live* (CBS Music Video Enterprises, 1989).

Ambiguity is a further factor in promoting music, determined by the need to address a divergent mass audience. In fact, a striking element in music video is not its sense of narrative closure, but the very opposite process—its pervasive ambiguity. According to Frith (1984), the producers of Bronski Beat's 1984 video SMALLTOWN BOY were told to make a clip that would be read as explicitly gay in the United Kingdom and utterly straight in the United States! It is certainly true that the advertising function of music video leads to a structured ambiguity that is designed to cater to an increasingly heterogeneous audience. Hence, we have Moody Blues tapes that offer both modernity and nostalgia, ZZ Top clips that critique sexism while offering scopophilic pleasures, ABC promos that sell the band to teenyboppers and poststructuralist postgraduates, and Bruce Springsteen tapes that offer political sentiments designed to please everyone.

The Moody Blues clip YOUR WILDEST DREAMS offers a case study in this kind of multiple encoding. Made to promote an album that attempted to relaunch their career in the mid-1980s, it offers an ingenious solution to that band's evident distance from youth culture. It has as its central character a disillusioned, middle-aged housewife, daydreaming about her 1960s youth; we see young people dancing to 1980s Moody Blues music. The Moody Blues' early career is alluded to and acted out by young lookalikes, while the housewife pines for the excitement of her youth, when (it is revealed) she was romantically involved with singer Justin Hayward. The clip thus promotes the band as a modern act that appeals to young people while combining this with a nostalgic address that is heightened by the narrative resolution: the housewife is inspired to attend a modern-day Moody Blues concert (which is predictably, if implausibly, full of young people), but fails to meet Justin Hayward backstage, as he is whisked away by an entourage of media personnel and "minders" (thus reestablishing the band's superstardom). YOUR WILDEST DREAMS is thus designed to sell the new Moody Blues to older fans of the group and to a new generation of listeners, through this double address.

There is another feature in the structuring of video clips that arises from their economic role: through increasing tie-ins between entities within the media corporations that own the music business, there are now many opportunities for cross-promotion, especially between the music and film industries. Thus clips that use songs that have been either written especially for or incorporated after the fact into movies will often feature clips from those films. Examples are Billy Ocean's WHEN THE GOING GETS TOUGH, Duran Duran's A TIME TO KILL, Los Lobos' LA BAMBA, and Dusty Springfield's NOTHING HAS BEEN PROVED.

I have tried to show in this chapter that the question of narrative structure is one that has to be rethought in more than just its empirical detail. It is clear that the formal arrangements of pop (and music television) defy certain conventions of classic realism, yet the form may still contrive to forge reading positions of great stability and coherence. Pop music and music television develop through time, and through predictable formulas without offering quite the kind of narrative resolution expected of the literary or cinematic realist text, and both forms also work through a multiplicity of address that often defies the ordering of a hierarchy of discourses.

The argument so far addresses two issues. First is the question of reading formations. I do not have empirical evidence on actual modes of consumption (the analysis shares that much with film theory and postmodern criticism), but I do believe that text analysis shows us some key ways in which music videos can be read beyond the paradigm of the realism debate. Second, this analysis reveals something about the concrete determinations that operate upon narrative construction. I have tried to demonstrate how the fractured, "nonrealist" structure of video clips can be explained (whether or not it is appropriate to find broader, more generalized explanations in terms of a late capitalist postmodern aesthetic) in more prosaic terms: as an effect of both the structure of the pop song and the industry that seeks to promote its commodities.

I have thus moved from very detailed examples of the visualization of the music itself (undertaken in chapter 3) to the slightly broader question of overall structure. However, this text analysis requires one further shift, to take account of the role of stardom and characterization beyond the borders of any individual clip. The visibility of the storyteller raises the question of where to locate the analysis of character in pop music — in the story or in its teller. Music television is also made stable by the central presence of the singer and by metanarratives of characterization and star personas. These issues will be raised in the next chapter.

FIVE

Metanarratives of Stardom and Identity

Sometimes I just wish you could put records out anonymously.
—Lou Reed[1]

Having identified the narrator of the pop song as a crucial site of fictional construction, I now wish to document and delineate some of the ways in which star-texts intersect with video clips. The argument here is not so much cumulative as a series of parallel explorations in how the audience objectifies, and identifies with, star identities. Having established the centrality of understanding the star's persona(s) as an element in reading video clips, I will look at a variety of ways (by no means exhaustive in scope) in which music television is expressive both of a common rock and pop aesthetic (Romanticism) and of the interests of the music industry. The latter point entails a reengagement with the neglected and much-assailed notion of "manipulation" in popular culture.

The Material Girl and the Serious Boys

My starting point in the analysis of star-texts concerns the ways in which a Romantic aesthetic underpins both the promotion and the reception of popular music, so that the discrete fictional diegesis of song narrative is perpetually overwhelmed by a kind of popular *auteurism*. I will begin by investigating two examples—a much-discussed video clip by Madonna and a live performance by the Pet Shop Boys.

In the Madonna clip MATERIAL GIRL we encounter a striking case of the dominance of star-text over narrative. This clip has received a great deal of attention from scholars (see Brown & Fiske, 1987; Fiske, 1987: 273-283; Kaplan, 1987: 116-126; Lewis, 1990: 129-135), and my intention in going over such familiar ground is to show how much simpler analysis of MATERIAL GIRL is when narrative and star identity are considered in the manner I am suggesting.

This clip has been discussed as if it were extremely complex. In fact, the visual narrative of MATERIAL GIRL is quite uncomplicated. An initial situation is established, in which a movie producer (played by Keith Carradine) desires a film star (Madonna) who is performing (in rushes) a musical song-and-dance routine (the song "Material Girl," visualized via Marilyn Monroe's rendition of "Diamonds Are a Girl's Best Friend" in the film *Gentlemen Prefer Blondes*). As rehearsals/filming continue (segments that are addressed directly to the video spectator, following the direct-address conventions of the song, elaborated in chapter 4), the producer discovers that the movie actress is in fact not a "material girl" and so he pretends to poverty—for instance, giving her a bunch of daisies instead of an expensive present. The denouement resolves the simple conflict of this plot, when the producer deceives the actress further, by paying a studio hand for the use of an old truck. He and Madonna leave in the truck, and the final shot is of them kissing, through the none-too-subtle metonymic moisture of a rain-washed windshield.

MATERIAL GIRL is thus a highly conventional narrative that moves through an initial lack, via action, to (romantic) resolution. Before looking at the function of stardom in this clip, I want first to comment on the question of gendered and ideologically oriented counterreadings. In the rush to appropriate Madonna for feminist counterreadings (a drive that Madonna has not been slow to exploit) two things have been missed about this clip, and both points suggest that there are ways of reading MATERIAL GIRL that run counter to the main themes of the feminist appropriation of Madonna.[2] First, the visual narrative provides a point of male identification (the film director) whose gaze is directed at Madonna in classic scopophilic/voyeuristic terms (as Kaplan notes). I am not, however, merely making a formalist argument here. This is significant in that it reveals the importance of thinking about how some male viewers decode Madonna—a neglected topic, which suggests that the feminist counterreading of Madonna is not just one of many plausible interpretations, but the most optimistic one that is conceivable. Second, given this problem in feminist-oriented cultural studies, it is no surprise to discover that not a single critic has noted that the movie actress character played by Madonna in MATERIAL GIRL is an object (in both senses of the word) of a successful male deception/seduction. This is especially important given that one of the few pieces of empirical evidence that we have on the reception of Madonna categorically challenges the neofeminist interpretation provided by Madonna herself and by her devotees. Brown and Schulze (1990) have shown, in an audience study related to the OPEN YOUR HEART and PAPA DON'T PREACH clips, that the former in particular is read through the codes of soft pornography—I am not criticizing this, merely noting its distance from a popular feminism. One male viewer of OPEN YOUR HEART mainly recalled "Madonna's shapely and oh so tasty figure"; he especially liked "the way her breasts shake" (Brown & Schulze, 1990: 98).

However, the misreading of MATERIAL GIRL is not merely a matter of wishful textual thinking. In MATERIAL GIRL neither Madonna nor the character she plays is a "material girl." The Material Girl in the visual narrative (and additional dialogue) is the character played by the character whom Madonna portrays. The persona taken on by Madonna in this clip is that of an actress who sings the song "Material Girl," but who is, in fact, not one herself. Why, then, do academic readings of the clip and popular cultural framings of Madonna insist that she is the Material Girl? The answer is obvious. It is Madonna's star identity that has been constructed as that of Material Girl, and this clip was precisely designed to help establish it, because, as Lewis (1990: 131) notes, it served the function of shifting Madonna's image from that of disco-bimbo to "authentic" star. Indeed, MTV's *Rockumentary* special about Madonna (screened in April 1991) set up her career in precisely these terms, as a shift from struggling dancer/musician through to disco singer and then pop star, faltering only in her largely unsuccessful attempt to establish herself as a film star, and culminating in a maturing change of gear when she became a controversial "artist."

Politically speaking, this discourse is both potentially empowering of young girls and also quite reactionary; it is easily reappropriated by men and boys as Madonna-as-slut/whore, and by girls as a form of what Kaplan (in another context; see Kaplan, 1987: 216) refers to as "bourgeois feminism"—that is to say, it represents the emergence of a promotional line that Madonna has exploited ever since, through the notion that extraordinary individual economic success by one woman, achieved within the terms of a competitive capitalist marketplace, represents a victory for all women.[3]

This approach to MATERIAL GIRL reveals the fallacy of interpreting video clips as if they were fictional narratives: we should not do this, because fiction, narrative, and identity in music television are generally located at the level of the star-text, not within the discursive world of the fiction acted out by the pop star. MATERIAL GIRL has thus been read as if its central motif (the femme fatale who uses men to gain wealth and power) is co-terminous with Madonna herself precisely because this is one of many images Madonna has portrayed in the promotion of her music.

The sites of this character construction are media interviews and imagery (including music video clips), onstage performance iconography and direct address to the audience, and critical commentary — rock critics have been eager, following the initial disparagement of Madonna, to hail her strength and risk taking as an authentic contribution to rock culture. Thus, Madonna-as-musician has been constructed (by her media relations organizations, and through compliant pop culture journalists and critics) as a woman making it in a man's world, on her own terms. This image of Madonna became increasingly important in the latter part of the 1980s, replacing the idea that Madonna was a chameleonlike figure whose identity remained unstable (see Kowalski, 1986). This new discourse became so dominant that JUSTIFY MY LOVE (which years earlier would have been read as yet another example of sexploitation through objectification) was widely hailed as a blow for cultural freedom and feminism.[4] The release of the movie *Truth or Dare* in the spring of 1991 further developed, and exploited, Madonna's new image.

My second example is drawn not from music video, but from a live performance of pop music that is at least symptomatic of some post-New Pop trends (see chapter 2) and perhaps prescient with regard to the future of live music. On their 1991 world tour, the Pet Shop Boys presented a live performance (based mainly on computerized music) that took to new extremes the effort to make pop and rock music theatrical. I mean by this that the attempt to portray songs in character (rather than through the medium of the songwriter, singer, or musician) was taken further in these shows than at any time in pop history.[5] The Pet Shop Boys' performance eschewed the conventions of the rock concert by having the duo act out scenarios that illustrated or complemented the songs, with keyboardist Chris Lowe spending almost no time actually producing live sound. Instead, he and vocalist Neil Tennant performed among dancers in a show designed and choreographed by David Allen and David Field-ing (who had previously worked with the English National Opera);[6] at times, backing singers performed the music while Lowe and Tennant re-moved themselves from the stage or performed a purely iconographic function—often, significantly, as *onlookers*.

Previously, Madonna had also abandoned the presentation of an au-thorial voice in concert; on the Who's That Girl? and Blond Ambition tours of 1987 and 1990, she acted out her videos. But Madonna nonethe-less spoke to her audience, albeit briefly, and thus established some direct contact between narrator and audience. In the Pet Shop Boys' 1991 per-formances hardly a word was said to the audience until the penultimate song, and the visualizations of the songs, rather than being based on video clips, introduced new imagery. Thus the Pet Shop Boys under-scored the task of decoding visual imagery in live performance and asked us to take the songs, rather than their narrators, as the main focus of the show, just as in opera or modern dance we are expected to concentrate on the diegetic space rather than the performers or the composer. As in film, television, and theater, this performance seemed to demand that we in-habit the fictional world of the text, as opposed to the conventions of pop, where we are supposed to inhabit the emotions of the performers.[7]

However, despite this effort to close off the usual channels of commu-nication between pop stars and their audience, the Pet Shop Boys found that their fans expected them to *step out of the diegesis of the songs* and ad-dress them directly. When Neil Tennant sang, "If I was you, if I was you / I wouldn't treat me the way you do" (on "I'm Not Scared"), he wagged a finger in the direction of the audience, and the fans waved back, want-ing to be pointed at by Neil. When Chris Lowe used binoculars as a prop, scanning the audience, fans waved at him, hoping to be looked at by Chris. But this inverted scopophilia (the desire to be looked at) was not the only way in which we—the fans—wanted to be recognized. We wanted Neil Tennant to talk to *us* (and we cheered when he did), and some people wanted to be touched—not figuratively, but literally. Dur-ing the final song ("Always on My Mind"), fans in front of the stage stretched out to reach their idols. During the first night of the San Fran-cisco shows, a fan jumped up onto the stage during the final song to cud-dle Chris Lowe. Thus, even in the context of a show that reduced the function of the narrator to an absolute minimum (and that parodied and exposed the pretensions of stardom, on "How Can You Expect to Be Taken Seriously?"), the pop audience demanded something more (and something less): that the storytellers become the object of the text, the (barely obscured) objects of desire.

I mention these performances in detail because they demonstrate something important about the role of stardom in pop and rock music. They enable us to see that characterization, fiction, and perhaps even narrative itself exist in popular music at the point of narration, outside the diegesis of individual songs, live performances, or video clips, through the persona of the pop star. The significance of this is twofold. First, the creation of character identities for pop stars provides a point of identification for the listener-spectator—a necessary one, given the lack of characterization or narrative depth in song lyrics. As Fred and Judy Vermorel (1985) have shown, the star-texts can have extremely varied meanings for pop fans. Second, the construction of star identities is central to the economics of the music industry. It has been an article of faith in the record business for forty years now that career longevity can be achieved only by *stars*—that is to say, artists whose identities guarantee massive sales, or at least the media exposure that makes this a possibility.[8] Thus, stardom, while it may have varied meanings for the consumer, is always functional from the perspective of the music industry.

Along with generic stability, star loyalty is a key element in the music industry's effort to rationalize the impossible task of predicting public taste. The music industry already knows what cultural studies scholars have only recently begun to focus on: that the audience has its own sense of what it likes and does not like, and cannot be manipulated into spending money on goods and services that lack sufficient use-value. However, cultural studies theorists need to remember that the media industries know this so that they can pay better attention to the mechanisms used to overcome the "problem" of taste. The construction and maintenance of star-texts is one such strategy. Only a very few acts have ever attempted to sustain careers in popular music without establishing some kind of metatextual identity: the Residents remain to this day the most striking example, since they are a band whose identities are secret— although that in itself is perhaps a sales gimmick of a kind.[9] In recent years the dependence of record companies upon star acts has become more marked than ever. The deals signed by the Jacksons (Janet Jackson with Virgin Records, Michael Jackson with Sony)[10] in the spring of 1991 represent a further shift in this direction: in both cases, the advances and percentages promised the artists mean that an entire record company is dependent on the success of each release by these two stars. Should either career founder, Virgin or Sony could lose historically unprecedented sums of money.

This point reveals something important about the aesthetics of rock and pop, which remain thus locked into an essentially Romantic discourse of self-expression, even where mimesis, truth, and faithfulness to "reality" are stressed (in rock's classical/realist appeal) or where manipulation, self-consciousness, and artifice are trumpeted (the modernist, or postmodernist, address). Whether we take the first case (Bruce Springsteen, the Clash, U2, Ice Cube) or the second (Madonna, Sigue Sigue Sputnik, Scritti Politti, De La Soul), what is really at stake for pop fans and critics is related to a Romantic aesthetic concerning suppositions about intentions, feelings, and sincerity. M. H. Abrams's (1953) discussion of Romanticism is instructive here:

> Through most of the nineteenth century, the poet's invention and imagination were made thoroughly dependent for their materials
> . . . on the external universe and the literary models the poet had to imitate; while the persistent stress laid on his need for judgement and art . . . held the poet strictly responsible to the audience for whose pleasure he exerted his creative ability. Gradually, however, the stress was shifted more and more to the poet's natural genius, creative imagination, and emotional spontaneity, at the expense of the opposing attributes of judgement, learning, and artful restraints. As a result the audience gradually receded into the background, giving place to the poet himself, and his own mental powers and emotional needs, as the predominant cause and even the end and test of art. (p. 21)

Robert Pattison (1987) has shown that this Romanticism is a dominant strand in the rock aesthetic, and while it does not explain the totality of rock music (let alone the more mainstream forms of pop), this approach is very revealing as an explanation at one level (the aesthetic) for the centrality of the narrator in pop music.

This argument has implications for the analysis of apparently modernist or postmodernist pop music also. Thus, it becomes meaningful to ask questions such as these: Was Sigue Sigue Sputnik's "insincerity" (like the Sex Pistols' pretense that they could not play) a fake (see Reynolds, 1990: 111)? Does the Pet Shop Boys' truthfulness about media manipulation make them *more* authentic than Springsteen?[11] These questions can be addressed only by considering the issue of personas and characterization, through which pop meanings are made that are more important than the meanings of the songs themselves. And they reveal the continuing centrality of a Romantic aesthetic (identified also by Frith, 1986; Stratton, 1983) for an understanding of music video clips.

Forging Identities

Recent work in cultural studies has made a valuable contribution to our understanding of popular culture through its rejection of theories of manipulation: the assumption that audiences are, in Stuart Hall's (1989) words, "cultural dupes." One does not, however, have to agree that manipulation is always successful, or believe that it cannot be subverted or resisted, to see that it is attempted, routinely. Thus, in coming to terms with the construction of star images in music television it is impossible to avoid the conclusion that theories of manipulation should not be abandoned altogether.

Stardom and persona are the mechanisms through which record companies seek out career longevity for their investments. David Buxton (1990) suggests that this process of selling stars was fundamental to the development of consumer capitalism:

> Rock stars, as agents of consumer discipline, help to define the norms and limits of the existing sociohistorical consumer, and thus individual possibilities. They anchor a chaotic aesthetico-ideological discourse and represent it in a "humanized" form by investing the human body itself. Thus the record managed to achieve an enhanced social usefulness far exceeding the mere "need" for recorded music. (p. 434)

Certainly the process of attaching additional meanings to a piece of music through the personas of the performers delivered further use-values to the consumer — a point that directly parallels the arguments of Wolfgang Haug in his discussion of second-level use-values. I have already suggested, however, that the personalization of the pop song is somewhat inherent in the form of musical performance. Needless to say, this process occurs quite differently when it is mass mediated than in the context of folk music. (But we should remember that folk music can also be mass produced, and with mass production will come the construction of mass-mediated identities. An example would be Robert Johnson; see Marcus,

1976.) The content of any given persona may or may not be "true" (i.e., actually built on the real-life circumstances of the performer); the point is that it involves a massive degree of manipulation on the part of the culture industries (not just the music business, but also the media commentators and critics who collude in these constructions). This suggests less a parallel with drama (self-evident fictions) or documentary (mimetic reflections) than with the only area of contemporary culture that is thoroughly legitimated (for reasons having to do with economic power) in its deliberate confusion of the two—advertising (that is, fictions presented as if they were mimetic reflection).

These mechanisms inevitably involve a certain degree of manipulation. For instance, rap artist Vanilla Ice was exposed in 1991 as the object of a forged persona when it was revealed that his record company biography lied about his upbringing—significantly, to structure him as from a lower class position than he comes from (see Handelman, 1991). Another device (often used in promotional videos) is to underscore an incipient stardom so that it will snowball (working on the theory that pop fans and media gatekeepers are attracted to success), or to create the appearance that emerging artists are more successful than they are in actuality. This mechanism has operated in cinema (the Beatles, *A Hard Day's Night*; Prince, *Purple Rain*) and is reproduced, for instance, in video clips such as Sigue Sigue Sputnik's LOVE MISSILE F-1 11, where a new and almost unknown group are chauffered around in limousines and stalked by fans and photographers.

Likewise, the Guns N' Roses clip PARADISE CITY presents the band performing live before tens of thousands of fans at the Giants Stadium in New York. This clip was released early in the band's career as a nationally known act, and it seemed extraordinary at the time that they had made the leap to playing stadiums of this capacity so quickly, on the basis of just one album (*Appetite for Destruction*). In fact, Guns N' Roses were playing in Giants Stadium as a support act (to Aerosmith), and the illusion that the crowd was present expressly to see them was consciously deployed in the clip, according to Nigel Dick, Phonogram's head of video production:

> They said, we're supporting Aerosmith at Giants Stadium in
> New York in front of 60,000 kids. Now Guns N' Roses,
> however big they are, are not going to be headlining stadiums of
> that size for three or four years. But it gives the impression to

the viewer that they can pull that number of people. So let's get them wandering around New York for a couple of days, then let's get them on Concorde going to play Castle Donington. (quoted in Q, May 1989, p. 32)

It has often been suggested that a major weakness in manipulation theories such as the work of the Frankfurt School lies in their assumption that intentions can be read off as results. As Robert Dunn (1986) notes: "The well-known pessimism of the Frankfurt School is but one manifestation of this tendency to identify the intentions of an administered commodity society with the everyday lived results" (p. 49). However, while this is broadly true, it does not mean (as some cultural theorists now assume) that intentions never produce results. I offer the PARADISE CITY clip as an example of cultural manipulation that is typical, and will surely have worked for most viewers—certainly for those who, like me, are unfamiliar with the day-to-day touring activities of hard rock groups—and I offer myself here as one of the "duped." (Theories of manipulation are not necessarily "elitist.")

PARADISE CITY points up one lacuna in the analysis of music video clips, which lies in the failure to notice that performance imagery is far from an innocent realist representation of the music itself. (Too many analyses of music video clips assume that "performance" clips do not intervene in the construction of meaning in any significant way.) In concert, the visual representation of rock music presents a generalized discourse of stardom-as-otherness (through the use of backlighting, which renders the performers' images mysterious and glamorous) and specific hierarchies of fame—through the use of spotlights, costumes, and the position of players on the stage.

Furthermore, music video clips (including performance clips) often seem to be concerned with establishing a sense of community within a group of musicians (following the tradition of the Beatles' films such as A Hard Day's Night and Help!) or between the musicians and their fans. U2's videos work in this way, and indeed the clip WHERE THE STREETS HAVE NO NAME references the Beatles' rooftop rendition of "Get Back" in the movie Let It Be. (Billy Joel also attempts something similar in A MATTER OF TRUST.) A similar sense of exuberance, fun, and community is portrayed in the Crowded House video clips SOMETHING SO STRONG and DON'T DREAM IT'S OVER. What has been missed here is the extent to which music videos function like the kind of pseudodocumentaries regularly produced by advertising agencies, in which televisual and cinematic discourses associated with factual appeals (cinema verité, the TV interview) are used to promote idealized fantasies about the music industry itself. For instance, life as a working musician is not all fun, as press interviews often reveal. Often, members of established acts see each other only in order to perform and promote their music, through tours and videos. In video clips, however, pop groups are invariably presented as having fun (in the studio, on tour, on the video shoot itself), even where (in the case of many heavy metal clips) the emphasis is on their hard work. Similarly, an act is nearly always presented as comprising a group of friends, rather than workers,[12] thus offering a point of identification for the audience.

These points concerning the pseudodocumentary status of music video clips help explain the apparent disjuncture between the content of lyrics and video representations. Elg and Roe (1986), in a content study of music television in Sweden, found that the largest category in terms of "video style" was the "rockumentary" (29 percent of all clips were classified thus). They comment:

> The oft-remarked upon discrepancy between the aural and visual contents of music videos was clearly evident in the videos studied. A comparison of the lyrics of the songs with the themes expressed in the videos revealed that, while love/courtship accounted for 50% of the song lyrics, only 16% of the videos dealt with this as their main theme. Conversely, the rockumentary ("the artist at work") and nostalgia, were both overrepresented in the videos compared with song lyrics. (p. 18)

The explanation here is of course that the essential narrative component of the music video lies not in the song lyrics, but in the star-text that frames it.

Resurrection Shuffle

This leads to an interesting encounter between aesthetic theory and marketing ideology. Cultural studies has over the last twenty years progressively eroded the status of the artist as auteur (see Caughie, 1981), most notably in the essays by Roland Barthes (1977a) and Michel Foucault (1977) that proclaimed the death of authorship as a viable social or cultural category. On the other hand, popular culture itself continues to celebrate authorship and to promote cultural products through the parallel discourses of stardom and auteurism, sometimes (for instance, in the cases of David Lynch, Bruce Springsteen, and Prince) combining the two.

What are the implications of this for cultural analysis, and for the specific areas of popular music and music television? The answer must be that the abandonment of any interest in authorship is at minimum premature, for as long as this remains a central element in the promotion of popular music it needs at least to be critiqued. More so than any area of popular culture, pop and rock music is explicitly involved in the consumption of an auteurism, through the foregrounding of the artist/ singer.

Sometimes this involves an attempt to adopt a fictional characterization (David Bowie's "Aladdin Sane," Elvis Costello's perpetual identity crisis), but most performances by pop stars as "characters" are overdetermined by our knowledge that this is a pop musician and of the discourses of stardom that surround him or her. The interesting question then becomes the investigation of narratives at the level of stardom itself, an area that has been explored in film studies (see, for example, Dyer, 1979), but hardly at all in pop.

Stars in music television are both more and less than characters in cinema or television fiction. Characterization is absent, on one level, in the brief, flimsy, and sometimes nonexistent narratives of a three-minute promotional clip. But characterization is also overwhelmingly present, if we accept the "documentary" status of music television, in that star images are to a large degree its central visual signs. These images correspond to the key role of the voice in pop music. As Antoine Hennion (1990) observes:

> Having a "voice" in pop music terms does not mean possessing
> a vocal technique or systematically mastering one's vocal
> capacities. Instead, a voice is an indication of one's personality.
> . . . it is not the voice for its own sake that matters but its
> expressive power. (p. 199)

Similarly, in music television it is posing, rather than acting, that counts, while the centrality of the voice in pop music is expressed visually by the close-up, often used to degrees that seem extreme according to the conventions of television "grammar." As E. Ann Kaplan (1987) notes, music television is anchored visually by the continual return to close-ups of pop star faces. Simon Frith (1985) makes the link differently, suggesting that the display of the body in video clips actually works to *displace* the centrality of the voice. (This point, however revealing, is also open to the charge that it overgeneralizes and in doing so misses something essential about the sound track; in other words, the power and quality of the voice, as well as its position in the mix, constitute a key element here. In Chris Isaak's WICKED GAME, the images of the body are striking, and yet the voice is too compelling to be *replaced* by the images. A less interesting singer might, however, have to submit to the images. I would place Robert Palmer's video clips, such as ADDICTED TO LOVE and SIMPLY IRRESISTIBLE, in this category.)

These star images then work in a variety of ways that need a great deal of further investigation. For now, I want just to note the level of "characterization" that exists outside any individual video clip, in the metanarratives of stardom set up within the music industry. These narratives can work in a number of ways. Sometimes a pop star takes on a persona to the extent of appearing to "become" that character. Bruce Springsteen is the master of this deception, and it is not without relevance that he has enjoyed an uneasy relation with promotional videos. Springsteen's video clips have often eschewed lip-syncing entirely (ATLANTIC CITY, WAR, FIRE) or opted for extreme simplicity of filmic technique: the clip for BRILLIANT DISGUISE comprises a single shot of Springsteen lip-syncing, with camera movement restricted to a slow zoom from close-up to extreme close-up. The nearest Springsteen has come to characterization within a video is in GLORY DAYS, where he is seen as the all-American dad playing baseball with a young boy, intercut with shots of his band playing in a bar. Even this degree of characterization is based on star image beyond the fictional diegesis, since it refers to the continuing theme of Springsteen's music (how to be an American man) and alludes to the occasional appearances that Bruce and the E Street Band once made at the Stone Pony music club in Asbury Park, where their career began.

Other stars adopt a consistent image without necessarily embracing one of down-to-earth "honesty"—Brian Ferry, Grace Jones, and the Pet Shop Boys have built up "characters" based on sophistication and a degree of intelligent decadence. Stars may also adopt consistent but less prominent character positions; the Pretenders' singer-songwriter Chrissie Hynde always embodied aspects of the "tomboy" and leather-clad sex symbol most famously crystallized in the Emma Peel character (played by Diana Rigg) in *The Avengers* television series. In the 1986 video for DON'T GET ME WRONG this was made explicit when Hynde portrayed the

Emma Peel character in homage to that television series. The reason this was so much more convincing than other attempts to act out television scenarios (such as Ozzy Osbourne's performance as J. R. Ewing from *Dallas*, in THE ULTIMATE SIN) has less to do with acting talent than with the fact that it builds on characterization already established in a star-text.

At the other pole, there are those stars who continually adopt new personas, often making radical changes in appearance and dress. David Bowie is the most well-known exponent of this strategy; in the 1970s he adopted the personas of "Ziggy Stardust," "Aladdin Sane," and "the Thin White Duke," and rock critics appeared to be confused by his decision in the 1980s to be content with his portrayal of an "ordinary" self, culminating in an appearance at the 1985 Live Aid concert in which theatrical characterization was completely absent. Bowie's FAME 90 video clip (featuring footage from his 1990 Sound and Vision tour, during which elaborate staging and characterization were deployed once more) is unusual in being a video that defies the convention that a given song/video tends to be tied to the image being promoted at that time. In FAME 90 Bowie's performance is framed by images from throughout his career, providing a commentary on his own position as an object of fame. (To that extent, the clip classically attempts to illustrate the song, which is about stardom.)

Peter Gabriel has undergone a similar transformation, albeit to a lesser degree, from the arty-boffin of his days with Genesis (when Gabriel would dress up in strange costumes on stage, especially on the *Lamb Lies Down on Broadway* tour, and tell surreal stories between songs) to a more serious persona as liberal spokesperson for a variety of good causes (Amnesty International, for instance) and promoter of World Music (through his work with WOMAD). More recently, Madonna has toyed with a variety of star images (virgin, Marilyn Monroe/sex symbol, whore, working-class teenager, "feminist" entrepreneur) that have left rock critics confused about the "real" Madonna. The point is that in both cases, the artists' music has been read partly through perceptions of their public personae. For instance, following release of the controversial video clip JUSTIFY MY LOVE and the documentary *Truth or Dare*, commentary on Madonna began to focus on whether or not she could "top" the outrageous nature of these texts. Thus, the focus of attention for the next Madonna video is firmly located in Madonna-as-auteur (of her career imagery, regardless of the authorship of her next song/clip), rather than in the content of the clip itself.

In between these poles there are various ways of combining the two attitudes toward character. Michael Jackson, for instance, appears to be straddling these alternatives, mixing the continuing and contradictory personas of fantastic otherworldiness (*Captain Eo*, THRILLER; see Mercer, 1986) and streetwise homeboy (BEAT IT, BAD). In Jackson's case this is all confused by his media image of eccentric, extravagant rock star, which the video clips from his 1986 *Bad* (Epic) LP seem designed to defuse. BAD and THE WAY YOU MAKE ME FEEL display Jackson dealing with the tough life out on "the street"; DIRTY DIANA portrays a "live" performance in a small club; MAN IN THE MIRROR is Jackson showing us his social concern for the less fortunate; LEAVE ME ALONE is supposed to indicate that Jackson has a sense of humor. In 1991, the fanastic and socially aware themes were again combined, in BLACK AND WHITE, the first clip from Jackson's album *Dangerous*.

Characterization is not limited to individual pop stars. It is worth noting that rock groups can have metanarratives, too. One obvious story is that of the rags-to-riches struggle of the pop group against all odds, which involves a degree of "dues paying" out "on the road"—a theme that has been raided for numerous clips of the rock-star-as-Jack-Kerouac. Other more elaborate (and more interesting) tales have been woven around bands—the mythology surrounding Led Zeppelin is one such example (see Davis, 1985). In the survey discussed in chapter 3, one respondent, on hearing ex-Led Zeppelin singer Robert Plant performing "Tall Cool One," "saw" a hard rock group and a "strutting singer." It is likely that the mind's eye here conjured up, if not a direct literal image of Plant's previous band Led Zeppelin in performance, at least a similar image triggered by that association. Such images are pervasive in the pop press, and in music television in the United States.[13]

Furthermore, some characterizations have been carried over from artist to artist, in classic examples of Adorno's concept of part interchangeability—for instance, the Ziggy Stardust/David Bowie imagery evident in David Sylvian/Japan, Bauhaus/Pete Murphy/Love and Rockets, the Blow Monkeys, the Psychedelic Furs, and Gary Numan; or the Robert Plant/Led Zepellin sound/iconography utilized by Whitesnake (most blatantly in the clip STILL OF THE NIGHT), Guns N' Roses, Aerosmith, and Kingdom Come.[14]

It should also be noted that many musicians are not associated with stardom or characterization. While these are often the faceless figures of anonymous rhythm sections, some acts have "stars" who have been successful without engaging in the construction of personas. This was especially true for "progressive rock" bands in the 1970s, and is still true today for progressive rock acts such as Pink Floyd and Yes, for instrumentalists such as Joe Satriani and Jeff Beck, and for some New Wave/"alternative" acts, such as New Order and Depeche Mode. In these instances there is little attempt to build characterization into music video clips, since the bands are being sold first and foremost as musicians rather than characters. Here the star is being sold as an *artist*. Where musicianship is the main selling point of the act, there are generally two alternative strategies in music video imagery. One emphasizes virtuosity through frequent close-ups of performance—more often than not, a lead guitarist's fingers flying up and down a fret board. (Van Halen's early videos are interesting here because they were unusual in being an act who appealed via both the larger-than-life cartoon persona of David Lee Roth and the musical virtuosity of guitarist Eddie Van Halen.) The other strategy is to adopt a minimal visual presence, replacing images of performance with "artistic" images that often plunder the visual arts—this is used, significantly, by both Pink Floyd (LEARNING TO FLY) and New Order (BLUE MONDAY, TRUE FAITH). And once again video clips often draw on appropriate images from pop culture, so that Pink Floyd videos recall their Hipgnosis album covers, and New Order's clips suggest the minimalist designs of Peter Saville, from their album sleeves.

Depeche Mode are an interesting case in point here, having successfully made the transition from pop group with teen appeal (the first half of the 1980s) to art-rock act, where the emphasis is less on musicianship (Depeche Mode make most of their music using computers, which is a process that has so far eluded visualization as a form of star image) and more on oblique nonnarrative video clips directed by Anton Corbijn. In *Strange* (Mute Film, 1988) and *Strange Too* (Mute Film, 1990), Depeche Mode's image as a "serious" act is built up partly through the use of 16mm film stock, grainy black-and-white images (on *Strange*) and Corbijn's oblique, apparently nonpromotional, stagings for the songs. Of course it is the fact that the clips often appear nonpromotional that constitutes the promotional appeal—in this case, to Depeche Mode fans who consider the group to be superior to "pop."

Indeed, the star-text is so prevalent in making pop meanings that its very absence signifies. A group such as New Order or Pink Floyd is sold through its nonimage (a public rejection of image makers and star-making machinery is a notoriously effective way of establishing an image, as the career of Led Zeppelin reveals). This technique has also been used by Bruce Springsteen (ATLANTIC CITY) and George Michael (FREEDOM 90).

Career Opportunities

The kinds of images of persona and stardom presented in music video clips very clearly relate to career structure. Because it is the storyteller, rather than the story itself, that is the central fiction in popular music, the construction of personality and identity around pop musicians is fundamental to success. Understanding the importance of star image is so central to the meaning of pop music (and, therefore, music television) that careers have foundered on confusion about it. Some musicians have found themselves trapped within particular characterizations. Thomas Dolby, for instance, established an image as a vaguely eccentric professor/mad scientist in the clip SHE BLINDED ME WITH SCIENCE and could generate another hit only when he repeated the image (and lyrical allusions equating science and madness) in HYPERACTIVE. Until he finds a new persona, Dolby is likely to be stuck with that one. Consider this comment from Bob Geldof, made after his rise to international fame in the mid-1980s as the organizer of Live Aid:

> I was afraid—still am afraid—that people might not accept me as a pop singer anymore. . . . That people will think it's silly that I want to do pop music at all. And I won't be able to behave like these pop stars on TV . . . because people know me too well. (quoted in *Creem*, May 1987: 39)

Conversely, television stars who make pop records (and video clips), such as Bruce Willis and Don Johnson, offer similar confusions and are defeated not only by a lack of musical talent (the Monkees, after all, did make some records that still made sense when the television set was off)[15] but by a different confusion about their personas. Don Johnson's HEARTBEAT clip builds on his *Miami Vice* character (such as it is), and therefore cannot offer us any credible expressive power—not because his television characterization of Sonny is minimal, but because we do not know who Don Johnson is. An exception is Cher, whose videos indicate that this is mainly done, in terms of imaging, through a scopophilic appeal that clearly embodies more than a suggestion of Oedipal desire.[16] (The most brazen example is IF I COULD TURN BACK TIME, in which Cher appears half naked on the deck of a U.S. battleship, surrounded by blatantly phallic gun turrets and cheering sailors.)

Sometimes promotional clips are used explicitly to present a star narrative that confuses the relations of drama and documentary. In the Richard Marx video DON'T MEAN NOTHIN', made early in his career (in 1987), the narrative presents this rising star as a struggling musician who learns to be cynical about the problems of selling his music to record company executives who do not understand him. The clip thus uses a fictional plot to establish the real Richard Marx as a young musician who has "paid his dues." [17] In DON'T MEAN NOTHIN' Marx plays a young songwriter who makes demos in his Los Angeles apartment, attempting unsuccessfully to get the attention of various music industry gatekeepers. In a subplot, Marx sees a hopeful female starlet arrive at the apartment building. Subsequently, it is implied that she is approached by her landlord for sexual favors. The starlet leaves, to be replaced by another, as Marx stays put and looks on knowingly. DON'T MEAN NOTHIN' is interesting not only because it so explictly demonstrates the opportunities for using video clips to build new star-texts, but also because it shows how the (Romantic) tension perceived by fans and musicians (and, according to Stratton, 1983, media gatekeepers) concerning creativity versus commerce is addressed in video clips. The "artistic" critique of the music business forms an important theme in the construction of star-texts, and is often used to establish new artists—for instance, in Paula Abdul's COLD HEARTED, which portrays record company executives as out of touch with a popular culture that only Paula Abdul and her musicians and dancers (of course) understand.

In the case of Richard Marx, subsequent clips emphasized his role as a "real," touring musician, for example in HOLD ONTO THE NIGHTS, in which onstage footage is intercut with black-and-white still photographs of adoring fans. The 1990 clip TOO LATE TO SAY GOODBYE pointed up the metatext of stardom by portraying Marx now as a *successful* star, and including characters in flashbacks from previous videos whom Marx is shown to have left behind, literally, by the roadside, as he drives on to his concert performance.

Mighty Real

As the Richard Marx clips illustrate, one of pop's most important (Romantic) myths is the notion that its musicians come from "the street," and this remains a major theme in promotional clips. Central here are the urban fantasies of "street knowledge" (alluded to by Frith, 1988b) that are played out in rock and rap lyrics, on album covers, in press interviews, in stage patter—and in video clips such as DAY IN, DAY OUT (David Bowie), TONIGHT, TONIGHT, TONIGHT (Genesis), THE OTHER SIDE OF LIFE (Moody Blues), SMUGGLER'S BLUES (Glenn Frey), WELCOME TO THE JUNGLE (Guns N' Roses), I STILL HAVEN'T FOUND WHAT I'M LOOKING FOR (U2), BEAT IT (Michael Jackson), BAD (Michael Jackson), UNDERCOVER OF THE NIGHT (Rolling Stones), WAITING ON A FRIEND (Rolling Stones), THE GHETTO (Too Short), 911 IS A JOKE (Public Enemy), LOVE IS A BATTLEFIELD (Pat Benatar), GIRLS JUST WANNA HAVE FUN (Cyndi Lauper), INTO THE GROOVE (Madonna), and DON'T WANT TO FALL IN LOVE (Jane Child).[18] It is also surely the notion of "streetwise bad boys" that underwrites a dominant motif in rock culture—that of the hard-living, ravaged vocalist/guitarist duo, first established by Keith Richards (usually pictured with a cigarette dangling from his mouth) and Mick Jagger. The "Glimmer Twins," as Richards and Jagger were known, have been widely imitated by other male-bonding pairings—Robert Plant and Jimmy Page of Led Zeppelin, Steve Tyler and Joe Perry of Aerosmith (the "Toxic Twins"), Billy Idol and Steve Stevens, Ian Astbury and Billy Duffy of the Cult, and Axl Rose and Slash of Guns N' Roses. Even in the New Pop this fantasy of male bonding was played out by Wham!, both generally and very specifically (in the clip BAD BOYS). It forms a key element in my argument that these images are not only present in video clips, but are visual anchors that may be triggered (for some listeners) by the music itself.

Another important, and connected, myth lies in the "authenticity" bestowed on rock music by its roots in black culture (see Frith & Horne, 1987; Pattison, 1987). Music television clips often use black musicians and audiences to "authenticate" white rock music and/or help it sell in the dance-floor markets whose indices are the charts for black music in the United States. A startling use of this occurs in the CONTENDERS clip for the all-white British group Heaven 17, which features lead singer Glenn Gregory and a cast of black dancers, so that the racial identity of the act is confused. The Police clip for EVERYTHING SHE DOES IS MAGIC, John Cougar Mellencamp's PAPER IN FIRE, Madonna's LIKE A PRAYER, and the Black Crowes' HARD TO HANDLE all typify the invocation of black pleasure as a sign of authenticity.

Similarly, images of extremely successful acts playing small venues that they may in fact have long ago outgrown serve to remind the audience that superstars also struggled once upon a time and remain (crucially, for rock ideology) close to their audience. Springsteen's GLORY DAYS is a classic example of this, as are Phil Collins's SUSSUDIO, Wham!'s I'M YOUR MAN and Michael Jackson's DIRTY DIANA.

Father Figure: A Case Study

Pop star George Michael is someone who is capable of his own interesting and perceptive reflections upon stardom. During the 1989 MTV Video Music Awards program, he echoed Richard Dyer's (1979, 1986) and John Ellis's (1982a) more scholarly researches on stardom when he observed: "It's not the something extra that makes a star—it's the something that's missing." Michael's star-text, which was initially constructed as one half of the duo Wham!, has exemplified the extent to which star imagery builds on vulnerability and ordinariness to establish points of identification for the audience. John Ellis (1982a) has usefully unpacked some of these questions in relation to stars in cinema, noting that many of these arguments apply equally well to the rock music industry:

> There is always a temptation to think of a "star image" as some kind of fixed repertory of fixed meanings (Joan Crawford = tough, independent, ruthless, threatening, sexy, etc.). However, this seems to me to simplify the process, and to mis-state the role of the star in producing meanings in films and beyond films. Star images are paradoxical. They are composed, like narrative images, of elements which do not cohere, of contradictory tendencies. They are composed, like narrative images, of clues rather than complete meanings, of representations that are less complete, less stunning, than those offered by cinema. The star image is an *incoherent* image. It shows the star both as an ordinary person and as an extraordinary person. It is also an *incomplete* image. It offers only the face, only the voice, only the still photo, where cinema offers the synthesis of voice, body and motion. The star image is paradoxical and incomplete so it functions as an invitation to cinema, like the narrative image. It proposes cinema as the completion of its lack, the synthesis of its separate fragments. (pp. 2-3)

Ellis goes on to suggest that in rock music the live performance completes the star-text in much the same way.[19]

As Richard Dyer (1986) has observed, "Star images have histories" (p. 3). Therefore, before exploring some of these ideas in relation to George Michael's clip FATHER FIGURE, it is necessary to place this particular manifestation of the star-text in context. Michael became globally famous during his years with the British pop group Wham!, where, alongside childhood friend Andrew Ridgeley, he forged an identity that initially foregrounded fun and pleasure. The group's first release, "Wham Rap!" was an ironic commentary on unemployment that became a hit in Britain only after its rerelease (in February 1983) following the success of "Young Guns (Go for It)" in October 1982. It is worth pointing out that in their early days Wham!'s image as young innocents confronting a sometimes harsh parental world was mirrored in the real-life drama of major conflicts with their record company, Innervision Records, with whom they had signed a contract that was exploitative to a degree that has become somewhat legendary (although it was by no means unique) in the music industry (see Garfield, 1986: 159-70; Parsons, 1991).

Wham! established themselves as fun-loving teen idols, with a string of hit singles over the next two years ("Bad Boys," "Club Tropicana," "Wake Me Up Before You Go-Go," "I'm Your Man," "Last Christmas") that emphasized their appeal to young women. "A Day in Life of George Michael," published in the *Smash Hits Yearbook 1984* (Tennant, 1984), encapsulates this fantastic junction point of ordinariness and glamour:

> I usually get up by about the fifth or sixth time that my mum has come in to wake me up. . . . I'll go downstairs, rewind the Ansaphone . . . my manager, the record company. I don't get quite so many calls now but before we had a manager I was bombarded by phone calls all the time. . . . By about twelve, I normally have to go out of the house to do something, maybe a photo session. . . . Then we've either got interviews to do or more business to see to so we'll quite often go to CBS or Innervision. . . . I usually eat at about two or three in the afternoon. . . . the easiest thing to do is to go to a MacDonalds or some other hamburger place. . . . Two or three nights in the week I'll stay in, the other nights I'll go up to London to different clubs. . . . I never go to sleep as soon as I get in, I read a magazine. . . . very often I'll put some headphones on and

listen to my favourite record—"Avalon" again. . . . My cat, Rover, sleeps with me. (p. 35)

In a 1984 interview, Michael presented fame as an especially pleasurable kind of work: "Suddenly you're in a position where you have as much money as you need, you feel secure, and you have no one to answer to. It's absolutely brilliant! What better job could you have than that?" (quoted in Tennant, 1984; 195).[20] Wham!'s video clips tended to stress happy-go-lucky themes and to present George and Andrew as star-objects, rather than as musicians or people. Their manager, Simon Napier-Bell, summed up one aspect of Wham!'s appeal thus:

> The thing that will continue to sell Wham! is the relationship between them. A public look at a private affair. Their sort of homo-erotic image has never been used in pop. It's that extraordinary relationship like Butch Cassidy and the Sundance Kid that has been done so many times in movies but never before in pop music. They're obviously straight and virile, but they're still more interested in each other than anyone else. At the end of the movie one's got the girl and the other's married, but they still ride off together. (quoted in Snow, 1988: 49-50)

I am not taking this comment at its face value. Napier-Bell is an astute manager and has his own responsibilities to manipulate the press. However, his comment is important in highlighting one aspect of Wham!'s appeal that has carried over into George Michael's solo career.

The issue of Michael as a solo artist was emphasized early in Wham!'s career, when it became apparent that band-mate Ridgeley actually contributed very little to the music. Before Wham! split up, in June 1986, Michael had already released two solo singles—"Careless Whisper" (which earned him considerable critical respect) and "A Different Corner." Both songs are brooding, introspective ballads, and they highlighted both Michael's songwriting talent and the beginnings of an emerging start-text that became the vehicle for the subsequent marketing of George Michael-as-auteur.

The solo trajectory begun by George Michael during his career with Wham! is visually present in the clips themselves. The group's early videos were set either in everyday British locations (mum and dad's living room, the High Street, etc.) or in exotic places. CARELESS WHISPER is a transitional video-text, in that the colorful, romantic settings where we see the narrator's ex-lover contrast with the bleak, less colorful mise-en-scène where George Michael sings to us (backstage, on his own, surrounded by dangling ropes). Just as the singer is marked out from his more carefree past here, so is George Michael, pop star, isolated from the imagery of Wham! Indeed, the fact that CARELESS WHISPER was released as a solo project is revealing about the importance of the star-text in marketing music. Years later, Michael put it like this: "We both had a definite attitude toward what a Wham! record should be about. Right up to "Go-Go," they'd all been young and optimistic. It didn't seem right to abandon it for this one ballad" (quoted in Fricke, 1986: 85). The promotional clip highlights that calculation and underscores the importance of star imagery as a site of fictional construction. (Similarly, the video for Wham!'s final single, THE EDGE OF HEAVEN, includes extracts and multiple back-projection of excerpts from the previous videos—"GOODBYE" runs across the bottom of the screen—and the line "one day you'll wake up on your own" is thus unavoidably a comment on the fracturing star-text as well as a part of a romantic lyric.)

The bridge for the formal shift from Wham! to a solo career was a record George Michael made with Aretha Franklin ("I Knew You Were Waiting") in 1987. Simultaneously linking him with the authenticating power of classicism and soul (and indirectly with the word *respect*), this song foreshadowed his solo career, which was launched with the album *Faith* (Columbia Records) in the spring of 1987. I KNEW YOU WERE WAITING also broke with the homoerotic appeal of the Wham! duo, being a romantic song whose heterosexual interpretation is buttressed through its performance by a male-female duo—a convention that has often been used in video clips.

The first single from *Faith* was the controversial song "I Want Your Sex," which Michael was forced to defend as an ode to monogamy—the video clip had a closing shot added to it in which Michael writes "EXPLORE MONOGAMY" on his lover's back, in lipstick, following criticism that the song and video promoted permissive (and, by implication, dangerous) sexual behavior. "Father Figure" was released in February 1988. In May, *Faith* became the first release by a white artist to top *Billboard*'s Black Album chart. Michael also received an award as best soul/rhythm and blues act of the year at the American Music Awards (organized by the Recording Industry Association of America).

The context for the FATHER FIGURE video was thus one in which George Michael's image was undergoing considerable change, as he was established as a heterosexual solo artist (a key component of success in

the United States) and as his music was increasingly associated with notions of authenticity, as opposed to the discourses of irony (the first three
singles) and triviality (most of the subsequent releases) that dominated
the music of Wham![21] The shift is apparent, for instance, if we compare
two widely circulated long-form videos: *Wham! in China: Foreign Skies*
(CBS/Fox Video, 1986, directed by Lindsay Anderson) and *George
Michael* (distributed in video stores by CBS Music Video and made by
London Weekend Television for *The South Bank Show* in 1990). Where
the tone of the first documentary is partly that of a travelogue, with a
commentary about Wham! as "ambassadors" for British pop and perhaps
even Western youth culture (material that is also deployed in the clip
FREEDOM, which includes extracts from the film),[22] the film offers an un-
critical celebration of stardom that inevitably reverberates with the numerous clips in which Wham! appeared as young jet-setting pleasure
seekers (CLUB TROPICANA, LAST CHRISTMAS). *George Michael*, on the other
hand, utilizes the conventions of the art documentary in its mostly reverential delineation of his artistic development, which is elaborated in an
interview with Melvyn Bragg, and offers the star's own self-consciousness thoughts about stardom and his distance (as he sees it) from the
world of Madonna and Prince.

"Father Figure" is a ballad, but with a dance beat. The use of synthesizers and a drum machine "hand clap" sound (with a very prominent
delay line used to produce an "echo" that is an essential part of the rhythmic pulse of the song) establish this as a "modern" pop song, as generi-
cally part of a body of work that includes Madonna and Prince, rather
than the more conventional acoustic environments used on ballads by,
say, Chicago or Julio Iglesias. The song's choruses feature multilayered
backing vocals that allude to the conventions of gospel singing (thus linking with Michael's newly established "authenticity" and validating him
through musical codes of ethnicity), which are also used in a traditional
"call-and-response" figure during the verses. (In concert, on his 1991
Cover-to-Cover Tour Michael brought a full gospel choir on stage just
for the *chorus* of this one song.) During the choruses, backing vocalists
sing the main lines while George Michael intones over the top of this singing, whispering, sighing, and almost speaking, in a manner that is sometimes extremely intimate and sometimes more public, in that it is appropriately (for the lyrics) reminiscent of a preacher responding to a congregation.

The structure of the song is (like "Faith") highly conventional:
   1. Instrumental introduction

2. Verse 1
3. Verse 2
4. Chorus
5. Verse 3
6. Chorus
7. Bridge
8. Solo (Spanish guitar)
9. Bridge
10. Chorus
11. Chorus
12. Instrumental coda

As I will show, this format is important, because it is illustrated in the organization of images and provides both the song and the video clip with a highly ordered and predictable structure.

The lyrics of "Father Figure" are a first-person address that constitutes a plea to a lover (who is not gender specific) to be taken seriously, and a promise that he will love this person forever—"till the end of time," as the closing words put it. The central theme of the lyric is that the singer will nurture the addressee—"I will be your father figure / Put your tiny hand in mine," and so forth. The vocal performance is seductive, and eroticized, but also plaintive, pleading. The lyrics are reproduced below, but I would caution against too "close" a reading of them, since only the most devoted George Michael fans will have attempted to dissect them. In pop music, it is the overall mood of the lyrics and the "hook" in the chorus that establish what the song is (lyrically speaking) "about."

Lyrics and shots for FATHER FIGURE break down as outlined below. The character identified as "model" is the unnamed female lead. POV refers to the camera's point of view, and C/U, M/S, and L/S refer to close-ups, mid-shots, and long-shots, respectively.

Sound	Vision
1. [Instrumental Introduction]	1.1 City street at dawn
	1.2 M/S model arriving at train/bus station
	1.3 M/S model
[First "hand clap"]	1.4 "TAXI" sign lights up
	1.5 M/S model looking for cab, walking to curb
	1.6 Moving yellow cab, driven by GM

1.7 Glamour photos of models pinned on wall (by GM)

1.8 Model gets into cab

1.9 Repeat 1.7—we see that model is in photos

2. That's all I wanted
something special
something sacred
in your eyes

2.1 C/U GM driving cab

For just one moment

2.2 M/S model in back of cab

2.3 C/U GM driving, smoking

To be warm
and naked
at your side

2.3 C/U model

2.4 Cab driving through the city at night, into tunnel

Sometimes I think
that you'll never
understand me
maybe this time
it's forever
say it can be

2.5 M/S GM driving cab

2.6 GM's POV, through windshield of cab

2.7 GM at home, smoking, clipping glamour photos

3. That's all you wanted
something special
someone sacred

3.1 C/U legs of model in black stockings (camera begins pan up body, almost to her shoulders)

In your life

3.2 Three other models are seen at work, one looks out of frame, the next walks into the foreground, expressionless, the third looks at her

Just for one moment
To be warm
and naked
at my side

Sometimes I think
that you'll never
understand me

3.3 C/U model looking at herself, in makeup mirror, dejected, frustrated

But something tells me
together
we'll be happy

3.4 First of three models again (3.2) looking out of frame

3.5 Fade to black

4. I will be your
father figure

4.1 C/U GM aggressively kissing model

put your tiny hand
in mine
I will be your   4.2   M/S rear view of models
preacher teacher   parading on runway
anything you have is mine
I will be your   4.3   C/U GM-model kissing
father figure
I have had enough   4.4   Camera pans audience at
                                               fashion show
Of crying   4.5   C/U GM-model kissing
I will be the one   4.6   M/S model on runway
who loves you
till the end of time

                                        4.7   Camera pans across a
                                               doorway to reveal L/S of
                                               models in dressing room,
                                               then GM standing outside,
                                               lighting cigarette
                                        4.8   Fade to black

5. That's all I wanted   5.1   L/S busy city street
    but sometimes love
    can be mistaken   5.2   M/S model in cab
    for a crime

    that all I wanted   5.3   Reflections of city
                                               lights on windshield
    Just to see   5.4   C/U GM driving cab
    my baby's   5.5   Cab in street
    blue eyes shine   5.6   C/U model posing at
                                               photo session

    This time I think   5.7   L/S model posing for
    that my lover   photographer, who then
    understands me   adjusts her hair
                                        5.8   C/U model looking at
                                               photographer, smiling
    If we have faith   5.9   L/S doorway, revealing
    in each other   GM looking on
    then we can be   5.10   C/U model,
                                               photographer kisses her on
    strong   forehead (paternally?)

6. I will be your   6.1   Model on bed, in lingerie,
    father figure   with GM

put your tiny hand
in mine
I will be your

preacher teacher
anything you have is mine
I will be your
father figure
I have had enough of crying
I will be the one
who loves you
till the end of time

7. If you are the desert
I'll be the sea
if you ever hunger
hunger for me
whatever you ask for
that's what I'll be

So when you remember
ones who have lied
who said that they cared
but then left
as you cried
beautiful darling
don't think of me
because all I ever wanted

8. [*Spanish guitar solo begins*]

Is in your eyes
baby

And love can't lie

9. Baby with the eyes
of a child

My love is always
telling me so

6.2 C/U model posing
6.3 Model–GM on bed
6.4 M/S photographer giving
     instructions
6.5 C/U model posing
6.6 Model–GM on bed
6.7 L/S model posing
6.8 C/U model posing
6.9 L/S model posing
6.10 C/U model posing, she
     turns to see GM in doorway
6.11 GM turns to walk away

7.1 C/U model, distressed
7.2 L/S of GM and model,
     standing against wall, half
     undressed — camera zooms
     in slowly as they kiss

7.3 C/U model, smiling, in
     bed, looking up (at GM)
7.4 M/S GM–model in bed,
     GM asleep, model looking
     pensive
7.5 C/U model, as 7.4

8.1 Public phone, GM
     dialing
8.2 C/U GM with phone
8.3 L/S up at window,
     model is holding phone,
     puzzled
8.4 C/U GM, hangs up

9.1 Model in back of cab,
     kissing photographer
     (GM's POV from rearview
     mirror?) Model turns to
     look into camera
9.2 Cab driving through
     tunnel at night

heaven is a kiss
and smile
just hold on, hold on
and I won't let you go
my baby

10. I will be your

Father figure
put your tiny hand

in mine
I will be your
preacher teacher
everything you have is mine

I will be your

Father figure

I have had enough of crying

So I will be the one
who loves you

till the end of time

11. I will be your

father

I will be your
preacher

I will be your
father

I will be the one
who loves you

9.3 Model and GM in back of
cab kissing

9.4 C/U GM in cab
9.5 Fade to black

10.1 C/U model
10.2 M/S model hits GM

10.3 GM kisses model
10.4 C/U kiss
10.5 C/U model in studio
10.6 Model pushes
photographer away
10.7 C/U model in makeup
mirror, mimes "fuck it"
10.8 C/U photographer
distraught at camera
10.9 C/U model as 10.7

10.10 Zoom in on GM lying
asleep in bed
10.11 C/U model as 10.7,
hangs head in despair
10.12 M/S model on
runway

11.1 Model's POV on runway,
audience applauds her
11.2 Flashbulb burst reveals
model, as 10.12
11.3 "TAXI" sign, as 1.4
11.4 C/U GM in bed, eyes
open
11.5 Shot 11.2 continues
11.6 GM-model kiss, as 10.3
11.7 11.1 continues
11.8 11.5 continues
11.9 GM-model kiss in cab,
as 9.3
11.10 M/S model on runway

till the end of time	11.11 L/S GM watching fashion show
	11.12 Fade to black
12. [*Instrumental coda*]	12.1 GM pins photo of model on wall, as 1.7

Structurally, FATHER FIGURE is both complex and extremely simple in terms of narrative organization. The complexities arise from its confusion of time frames and because of uncertainty about the point of enunciation in some segments. For instance, in shots 1.7 and 1.9 we see George Michael pinning up a photograph of the model *before* he has met her. Since this is also the last shot, it seems reasonable to speculate that these images occur (in "story time") later than they appear (in "discourse time"). It also remains unclear whether in fact he has had an affair with the model, or whether some parts of the narrative might be taking place in his imagination, a parallel with the pop fan's real-life obsession. Since Michael is seen by the model when they are not alone (for instance, in shot 6.10) it becomes clear that the events really occurred, but that the time frame has been mixed up in ordering the narrative.

Rather than attempting to make sense of this narrative definitively in immanent terms, however, it is more appropriate to consider its relation to the sound track (as suggested in chapter 3), the song (as argued in chapter 4), and the star-text. Visually, an important element running throughout FATHER FIGURE is the prevalence of slow-motion imagery, and the use of dissolves to link most of the shots gives the clip a languid mood, underlining its subtle eroticism and illustrating the music itself, which is slow and understated. Structurally, the video text offers a complete, self-contained televisual "segment," one that illustrates Ellis's (1982a) approach to broadcast television narrative as well as my argument about the image and its relation to a three-minute song. The music itself returns to a moment of completion in its final chorus and coda, and the clip climaxes through two devices: first, sections 10 and 11 have more frequent cutting (during the choruses) and then, via a fade to black (shot 11.12), settle (like the music) on a single, final image (of the model). Second, the last sections are more repetitive than the rest of the clip, reviewing the plot and returning the George Michael character to where he began.

The most striking aspect of song-video linkage concerns the choruses.

"Father Figure" takes some considerable time to reach its "hook," following an instrumental introduction and two relatively long verses. The tension of this anticipation is played out in the visual narrative also, where we wait until the first chorus to see George Michael and the model together. The explosive quality of this moment (which is designed, of course, to sell the song by investing its hook with great dramatic impact) is heightened by the fade to black (shot 3.5) that occurs for the first time immediately before the first chorus. Subsequently, the fade to black again precedes the chorus (shot 9.5).

FATHER FIGURE does not, however, merely illustrate its song. The clip executes a circuit of loneliness that takes its meaning beyond that of the music and lyrics. "Father Figure" eventually establishes a celebratory mood and offers no hint that the narrator will fail in his mission to become a father figure to his lover. The video clip, however, contradicts the song text by leaving its protagonist alone again at the conclusion. The equilibrium in this clip (George Michael as a lonely worker) is disrupted by the arrival of a beautiful woman (the model), who is then taken away by a more glamorous lover (the photographer), leaving the taxi driver alone once again, as he retraces the journey to the bus/train station where the model arrived. While characterization is absolutely minimal (we do not even know the model's *name*), the structure is classic "realism," albeit rather obliquely relayed.

However, as I have been arguing throughout this chapter, the narrative to which FATHER FIGURE refers is also star centered and relates to the story of George Michael and his persona. The new meanings that the video clip introduces into the lyrics are in fact a development of the metanarrative that runs throughout George Michael's career, and this explains why it is plausible (indeed, it was highly predictable) for the visualization of the song to offer a downbeat reading. Paradigmatically, in relation to star-text, this offsets Michael's Wham! persona and helps establish him as a "serious" personality.

As Ellis argues in the passage quoted earlier, star-texts are refashioned every time they are used. However, there is also always an element of continuity. FATHER FIGURE cashes in two symbols that have run from the earliest days of George Michael's career. The first is the black leather jacket—a familiar sign of rock rebellion that was originally worn with some irony (WHAM! RAP, BAD BOYS) and then became an integral part of Michael's iconography as a solo star. The BSA jacket, with its "REVENGE" insignia, is the key visual *motif* of FAITH, and in a later clip

(FREEDOM 90) it is this jacket that bursts into flames. Second, there is George Michael's beard — often worn as low-level stubble, a trendy version of "five o'clock shadow" first popularized by Don Johnson on *Miami Vice*. Again, this symbol made an earlier appearance in the days of Wham! (A DIFFERENT CORNER), but in the context of a bright, lively mise-en-scène that is quite different from the dark, almost monochrome tones of FATHER FIGURE. It is the new, brooding image of an unshaven Michael (often in dark glasses) that adorns the sleeve of *Faith* and is used repeatedly for advertising imagery and press photographs.

Taken together, the leather jacket and the stubble (along with the dark glasses and cigarettes) are not just character appropriate for a Hollywood version of a taxi driver; more important, they established "classic rock" imagery for George Michael at a time when he was seeking mass acceptance in the United States. In fact, it would be more truthful to say that the characterization offered in FATHER FIGURE is secondary to these aspects of the star-text — it was probably chosen for that reason, not the other way around. The fictional diegesis of the video text is thus a reflection of the star-text.

The setting of FATHER FIGURE is the city, mostly seen at night. This is in marked contrast to the locations used for Wham! clips, for which exotic scenes were often chosen (CLUB TROPICANA, LAST CHRISTMAS, FREEDOM) or upbeat color schemes and costumes underscored Wham!'s collective persona (WAKE ME UP BEFORE YOU GO-GO). FATHER FIGURE seeks to establish a new George Michael image (albeit on the basis of some components taken from his Wham! days), in particular through its intertextual play on Robert De Niro's role in Martin Scorsese's film *Taxi Driver*. Wham!'s video clips were set either in Britain (WHAM! RAP, BAD BOYS, I'M YOUR MAN) or on exotic locations abroad. FATHER FIGURE, however, is set in an American city (shots 1.0 and 8.1), and Michael has taken on at least the appearance of being American (he drives a yellow cab).

The shifts in star image are dramatic and indicate an attempt to build a new persona that will appeal to American rock fans. Importantly, in this respect, the narrative offers plentiful opportunities for classic scopophilic objectification that will appeal to the MTV audience while enabling a suppression of the potential for a nonheterosexual reading of the song-text.[23] (As noted in chapter 4, the voyeuristic shots of women are dispersed around the clip in order to maintain the attention of some sections of the audience.) No less important, however, is the degree to which FATHER FIGURE plays on previously established aspects of George Michael's persona that stretch back to songs, video clips, and media interviews from his career in Wham! Michael is still the rejected lover (LAST CHRISTMAS, CARELESS WHISPER, A DIFFERENT CORNER, FREEDOM) who cannot escape from the ordinary world and into a life of glamour.

This reading of FATHER FIGURE illustrates many of the ideas discussed in this chapter and the previous three. While the clip does not adhere to the conventions of the cinematic classic realist text, it can be read as quite conventional from within the dual conventions of the pop song and television "segment." The three-minute visual drama played out here is, however, incomplete unless we consider the relation between the images and the music and the ways in which its narrative elements are intertextual—specifically through the simultaneous deployment and development of George Michael's star image. Thus, in the final section of this chapter, I have tried to show how analysis of a single clip can take account of these features.

Ultimately, this text analysis needs to be related to audience interpretation and reader competence. In terms of competence, it is possible to identify two extremes here, one of total naïveté (in which the viewer is unfamiliar with George Michael and his music and has a relatively "innocent" reaction to the clip) and another in which the pop fan is aware of many of the arguments made in this chapter (and may thus take account of, and possibly criticize, the construction of persona in FATHER FIGURE). I have tried to show that these reading positions can be understood, however, only by taking account of the metanarratives of star identity.

SIX

A Televisual Context: MTV

Turn on the radio or the TV—you don't see anything that inspires you or makes you think about anything.

—Sinead O'Connor[1]

So far, I have been concerned with developing an understanding of the promotional video clips themselves, by locating them in the context of the pop music industry and its aesthetic forms. In order to complete a textual analysis, however, it is important to consider the distribution of the clips via broadcast and cable television. I have already discussed (in chapter 2) some of the elements that contributed to a rapprochement between rock music and television. Here I want to consider the important contextualizing elements of television itself and probe further some of the issues touched on in chapters 3, 4, and 5, concerning links between pop music aesthetics and music television.

The argument presented here also begins a reengagement with postmodern theory, through a critique of such accounts of MTV. Here I am concerned with the televisual context itself, rather than individual video clips. MTV and postmodernism are connected in this respect, according to exponents of the latter, through a number of properties, chiefly because MTV's abandonment of the traditional schedule is thought to constitute a text that lacks boundaries, and that is therefore held to disrupt bourgeois subjectivity.

The main focus of this chapter is on the world's first twenty-four-hour all-music television service, MTV. This is the most developed televisual site for music video clips; it has served as a model for many other services (for instance, Europe's Music Box and MTV Europe) and in addition exports packages of MTV programming to broadcasters in Australia, Japan, and Mexico (see *Los Angeles Times*, 1988). Many of the arguments necessary for an understanding of MTV apply also to other cable and broadcast music television services. Where there are significant differences, I address these in the main body of my argument about MTV.

Historicizing MTV

Unlike the journalistic accounts of MTV, academic writing has usually described MTV as though it were an unchanging form, significant only for its differences from network television. The development of its schedule (which has been considerable indeed) has been almost universally neglected by media scholars. This is thoroughly unmaterialist, because changes in the MTV text result from institutional factors such as shifting personnel and changes in ownership patterns, each of which is intimately connected to the economic and social forces at work in the broadcasting, advertising, and music industries.

Furthermore, to miss the development of MTV's schedule is to miss a central Romantic imperative, for MTV, like pop music, needs to display its creativity, its ability to change, its refusal to stop moving. It is not just that MTV must be seen as hip and irreverent, but that it must seem always to be hip and irreverent in *new* ways. Former MTV president Robert Pittman has summed up the problem:

> One of the interesting things is that for all the "issues" that have been raised about MTV, no one has ever touched on the real issue of MTV, which is: How do you keep the creativity going? How do you convince the creative people to give up a great idea and move on to a new idea? If there is one thing we worry about day after day, it is that issue. (quoted in Hilburn, 1986)

The imperative is not just to change, but to be seen to keep changing. It is an ideology drawn directly from rock culture that should encourage us to consider the historical development of MTV.

It is possible to identify three stages in MTV's history, each relating to its increasingly successful efforts to ally itself simultaneously with the major record companies and national advertisers. In the first phase (roughly 1981-1983), the need for visually evocative clips led to an emphasis on promotional videos made in Britain. The dominant pop form at that time was the "New Pop"—music whose stress on style and artifice perfectly suited marketing through video, and whose production practices perfectly suited the promotional techniques of music video, as I argued in chapter 2. As a consequence, MTV in this period was identified heavily with the so-called second British Invasion of synth-pop acts (such as Duran Duran, ABC, the Thompson Twins, Culture Club, Thomas Dolby, and the Human League).[2] Although more conventional forms of AOR (album-oriented rock) were in fact dominant in the playlist at this time,[3] it was the distinctive look of the New Pop that gave MTV its "cutting edge" kudos and established its visuals as nonnarrative, or antirealist, in the eyes of many cultural critics.

Both AOR music and the New Pop were dominated by white musicians. During its first seventeen months MTV was accused, time and time again, of racism in its programming policy (see, for instance, Levy, 1983). Stories abound of its exclusionary attitude to black music,[4] but the explanation was quite logical, however unfortunate. MTV followed the music industry in defining "rock" in essentially racist terms, as a form of music that excluded blacks. It based its playlist on the "narrowcasting" principle of American radio that viewed rock and "urban contemporary" (i.e., dance music, often produced by black artists) as incompatible. Consequently, blacks were largely excluded from its screens (with the exception of black VJ J. J. Jackson) on grounds of music policy. MTV denied racism, sincerely perhaps, but it nonetheless followed the rules of the rock business—which were the consequence of a long history of racism.[5]

In its early years MTV was concerned to mark itself out from conventional television. It needed to establish itself as a unique, new cultural service. In September 1981 Robert Pittman, then vice president of programming, put it like this:

> We're now seeing the TV become a component of the stereo system. It's ridiculous to think that you have two forms of entertainment—your stereo and your TV—which have nothing to do with one another. What we're doing is marrying those two forms so that they work together in unison. We're the first channel on cable that pioneers this. . . . I think that what we've been doing up to now in cable has been dealing with forms that have already had some success on TV. MTV is the first attempt to make TV a new form, other than video games and data channels. We're talking about creating a new form using existing technologies. (quoted in *Videography*, September 1981)

MTV's only discrete programs at this time were "concert specials" and other occasional special programming (such as interviews and music-related movies). MTV was, as Frith (1988a, 1988b) has noted, a form of visual radio, using the format of continuous flow associated with all-music radio stations. As Blaine Allan (1990) notes:

> In music television, videos are analogously linked to the unfolding of programming; their beginnings often remain imprecise and they frequently do not quite end. As disc jockeys cross-fade music with similar beats to make a sound transition as nearly seamless as possible, so broadcasters use visual and sound techniques to bridge the end of one video into the start of the next. (p. 6)

This initial phase represents the peak of the postmodern claim on MTV, for two reasons. First, it is the period when the MTV schedule most closely dovetailed with the arguments advanced by academics. There were only a few discrete programs during this phase of MTV history, and the relatively small number of video clips available led to a high degree of repetition. For that reason, incidentally, MTV was also postmodern in another sense, because the mixing up of clips in continuous "flow" blurred the categories of art-rock and pop, thus contributing toward a conflation of popular and high-cultural discourses (see Goodwin, 1991b).

Second, the video clips themselves, generated in large part by the British music industry, tended toward the abandonment of narrative, and the New Pop groups of this era eschewed the bland realism of performance videos (partly because many of them did not perform, in any traditional sense). Typical of the genre are clips such as ABC's POISON ARROW and THE LOOK OF LOVE, Duran Duran's GIRLS ON FILM, RIO, and HUNGRY LIKE THE WOLF, Visage's FADE TO GREY and THE MIND OF A TOY, Ultravox's VIENNA, the Human League's DON'T YOU WANT ME, and the very first MTV clip—Buggles' VIDEO KILLED THE RADIO STAR. Other key clips by older British acts who nonetheless played with nonnarrative form include David Bowie's ASHES TO ASHES, XTC's MAKING PLANS FOR NIGEL, Peter Gabriel's SHOCK THE MONKEY, and Elvis Costello's ACCIDENTS WILL HAPPEN. Post-1982 clips in a similar New Pop/nonrealist vein are Thomas Dolby's SHE BLINDED ME WITH SCIENCE, Culture Club's KARMA CHAMELEON, Cabaret Voltaire's SENSORIA, and Eurythmics' SWEET DREAMS (ARE MADE OF THIS) and LOVE IS A STRANGER.[6]

However, these points have to be qualified with three observations. In the first place, it needs to be said that even in this period, there were separate program slots (interview-based programming and concert specials) that demanded some acknowledgment—something that most scholars failed to provide. Second, while the visual aspect of the early videos was often nonnarrative and nonrealist, a full account of these texts involves a discussion of the lyrics and music. As I have shown in chapter 4, while narrative and realism might yet appear to be absent at these levels, there are certainly extraordinary degrees of repetition and stability at the aural level. No one has argued that these videos are as subversive aurally as they are visually. (Instead, it is either asserted or implied that the visual is dominant, as I pointed out in chapter 1.) Furthermore, while the impact of British-based New Pop videos is important, MTV even in this innovative period devoted more airtime to the firmly established format of AOR, whose videos were often extremely conventional in being either minimal realist narratives or performance clips.

Third, it must be noted that this initial phase of MTV, which forms the basis of much scholarly writing about music television, was the least significant historically. MTV's impact on the audience and the industry during its opening seventeen months was negligible, and—as Denisoff (1988) reports—many MTV insiders see January 1983 as the true beginning of the new service, partly because this is the point when it became available in the crucial media gatekeeper markets of Manhattan and Los Angeles.

Following this "second launch," the next phase of MTV (1983-1985) saw a shift in both music and programming policy that severely undermines postmodern arguments. The New Pop had gone out of fashion and, in any case, as MTV expanded from the main urban centers of the United States on the coasts into midwestern cities and towns, it needed to reach out with music that appealed to the rockist tastes of its new demographics. Furthermore, the network was no longer dependent on a relatively small number of clips originating in Europe. These factors colluded to generate MTV's embrace of heavy metal music.

In this phase MTV programmed heavy metal with a vengeance, and in doing so keyed into one of the evergreen forms of American popular culture. This was a make-or-break phase for MTV, in which it fought off network and cable competitors (including Ted Turner's Cable Music Channel), an antitrust suit from the Discovery Music Network, and criticism from both liberals (charging sexism and racism) and conservatives (the National Coalition on Television Violence).[7] Most important, MTV counterattacked its rivals economically by signing exclusivity deals with six major record companies (Viera, 1987). Programming policy during this period saw the beginnings of a shift away from continuous "flow" and toward the use of discrete program slots (such as *The Basement Tapes* and *MTV Countdown*, which programmed tapes from new, unsigned acts and the Top 20 clips, respectively).

The most significant developments here, for cultural studies theorists, are the increasing use of discrete program slots and the ascendancy of the "performance" clip. The latter was a direct result of the need for heavy metal acts to establish an "authentic" (i.e., documentary rather than fictional) set of images and to display musical competence. Thus, "on the road" pseudodocumentaries and the use of close-ups to emphasize musical virtuosity became the main staples of the promotional clips. Unlike the New Pop artists, metal acts had no interest in playing with artifice or in displaying their ironic modernism. Between the edits of fingers buzzing up and down fret boards, denim-clad musicians getting on and off tour buses, and the fans sweating and swaying in the stadiums of North America, antinarratives and antirealism quickly faded into MTV history.

In August 1985, the Warner-Amex consortium, which created MTV, sold off its controlling interest in MTV Networks (MTVN) to Viacom International. This development is absolutely central for any materialist engagement with the MTV text. As Denisoff (1988) reports, chief executive Robert Pittman had attempted a leveraged buy-out of MTVN along with some colleagues, and when this effort lost out to Viacom, Pittman's ascendancy at MTV was bound to end. With it went two of MTV's conceptual building blocks—narrowcasting and flow.

MTV's third phase (since 1986) thus represents a widening musical scope and an accelerated movement toward a more traditional televisual schedule. In February 1985 MTV had announced a cutback in commitment to heavy metal clips, but this led to a period of falling ratings and crisis at the network, as MTV was viewed by insiders and critics alike as bland and outdated. For a service that was dependent on viewer perception that it was on the "cutting edge" of pop culture, this was potentially disastrous. The ratings share fell from a peak of 1.2 in the fourth quarter of 1983 (during the screening of *The Making of Michael Jackson's "Thriller"*) to a 0.6 share in that same period of 1985 (Dannen, 1987).[8]

The third phase was born out of this crisis; it involved a return to heavy metal (which became especially marked in 1987), the shift of some middle-of-the-road artists to VH-1 (a twenty-four-hour music video station aimed at twenty-five- to fifty-four-year-olds launched by MTV Networks in January 1985), the departure of chief executive Robert Pittman in August 1986, and two trends associated with his absence—the decline of narrowcasting and the development of more discrete program slots, many of them abandoning the staple diet of promotional clips.

While heavy metal acts are still prevalent, MTV now screens a wider variety of rock and pop music than ever before. The question of racism has been resolved by two developments: the emergence of rap crossover music that combines black and white musical forms (the Beastie Boys, Run-D.M.C./Aerosmith's WALK THIS WAY, Public Enemy/Anthrax's BRING THA NOISE, Fat Boys/Beach Boys' WIPE OUT)[9] and the success of black heavy metal act Living Colour, who were featured heavily throughout 1989. (J. J. Jackson left MTV in 1986, but black Briton Julie Brown has been appearing as a VJ since then, coming to MTV from Europe's Music Box network.) Along with heavy metal, rap music was the success story in American music in the 1980s, and was afforded its own show on MTV—*Yo! MTV Raps*. Other kinds of music were also given distinct slots (*Club MTV*, *Headbanger's Ball*, and *120 Minutes*, programming dance music, hard rock, and "alternative" music, respectively). MTV's new traditionalism was displayed in its use of broadcast television formats, such as its Beatles cartoons (first aired on the networks) and *The Tube* (which came from Tyne-Tees Television in Britain). And MTV increasingly came to rely on nonmusic programming (comedy, a game show, a phone-in show, a movie news/review magazine, interview programming), some of it derived directly from broadcast television (*Monty Python's Flying Circus*, *The Young Ones*).[10] A key development was the success of its reruns of *The Monkees*, first begun in February 1986.

The post-Pittman sea change was very successful for MTV—which is one reason (among many) that it is a mistake to conceptualize Robert Pittman as MTV's "author." Ratings began to pick up in mid-1986, and by the third quarter of 1988 Viacom was reporting a 44 percent gain in earnings from MTV Networks (as reported in *Billboard*, November 19, 1988), and its Nielsen ratings made it the second-highest-rated basic cable service in the United States.

By 1989 the progress was less dramatic, but MTV Networks was nonetheless in an extraordinary period of expansion. In the summer of 1987 it had launched MTV Europe (in association with British Telecom and Robert Maxwell's Mirror Group Newspapers—the latter partner subsequently dropped out) and was syndicating MTV packages to broadcasting systems in Japan, Mexico, and Australia. It had established an MTV Record Club, selling music, videos, and merchandising items such as T-shirts. MTVN became extensively involved in concert sponsorship and scored a coup in 1989 when it contributed to the sponsorship of the long-awaited 1989-1990 Rolling Stones tour of North America. In September 1989 an MTV comedienne (star of *Just Say Julie!* and also, confusingly, named Julie Brown) debuted on network television with a CBS pilot program titled *Julie Brown: The Show* (she also starred in and co-scripted the Julien Temple movie *Earth Girls Are Easy*). That same year, a weekly version of the MTV game show *Remote Control* went into national syndication in the United States.

In its first decade MTV has thus moved from an almost exclusive focus upon the promotion of specific areas of pop music (New Pop, heavy metal) to a role as an all-encompassing mediator of rock culture — a televisual *Rolling Stone* (or Q magazine) that seeks to keep its viewers up to date with all current forms of music, with developments in popular culture generally (TV, cinema, sports, celebrity news), and occasional "hard news" stories (abortion, the environment, political news). The network has used its involvement in concert sponsorship to gain exclusive rights to announce tour dates and screen brief television premieres of live "in concert" footage. MTV News is reminding its viewers of the costs of *not* watching when it concludes with the portentous voice-over: "MTV News — You hear it first."

These developments render highly problematic statements such as this: "Important tools of sense making like sequence and priority are constantly rejected on MTV. . . . MTV has no boundaries. . . . It delivers random, uniform flow at all times" (Tetzlaff, 1986: 82). This was not true when that analysis was written, since MTV already had a number of programs organized thematically and sequentially. Since then, the growth of genre-based slots and new features such as "Rock Blocks" (four clips from one artist) have further eroded the credibility of such pronouncements. Furthermore, the use of these slots tends to compartmentalize the "popular" (*Club MTV, MTV Top 20 Videos*) from rock's "high-cultural" forms (*120 Minutes, Post Modern MTV*), thus preserving a distinction that music television was supposed to destroy. These trends are important in terms of both the *structure* of MTV's schedule and the *content* of the programming. It is to those questions that I now turn, beginning with some remarks on the role of the VJs who guide us through the MTV schedule and the sets and locations they inhabit.

Talk, Talk, Talk

One reason film theory remains inappropriate for the analysis of music television lies not in the specific musical properties of the videos, but in the more general importance of *sound* in *television*. The detailed account of broadcast television forms presented by John Ellis (1982b) is instructive here:

> The broadcast images depend upon sound to a rather greater degree than cinema's images. . . . In psychoanalytic terms, when compared to cinema, TV demonstrates a displacement from the invocatory drive of scopophilia (looking) to the closest related of the invocatory drives, that of hearing. (pp. 112, 137)

The explanation for this lies in the conditions of exhibition that govern television viewing, where the set is left on for long periods of time while it is not necessarily being looked at. In an important essay on television sound, Rick Altman (1987) directs our attention to the central importance of this aspect in the consumption of television and develops Raymond Williams's concept of "flow." Altman suggests that the sound portion of the television text is designed primarily to interrupt the "household flow" of everyday life and push our attention toward the television screen. This aspect of MTV remains neglected after nearly a decade on the air. Clearly, it would require an engagement with the music itself; here I am concerned with the other central aspect of MTV's sound track—the on-screen VJs and what they say.

The voices of the VJs offer a variety of appeals, from information and gossip concerning the video clips and their stars (VJ Adam Curry and news presenter Kurt Loder), through endorsement of particular acts (China Kantner and Julie Brown), to humorous and sometimes satirical comments on the world of rock culture (of the current MTV VJs, Kevin Seal is the nearest to the rock-critic-as-cynic).[11] Both visually and aurally, the VJs thus *anchor* the MTV text, using the familiar conventions of the radio DJ and the news presenter. Just as close-ups of rock stars' faces ground the visual component of video clips, so the VJs help to forge a path through the fast pace and sometimes oblique imagery of MTV, undertaking the role identified by Altman—that of linking televisual and household flow. Thus the VJs routinely trail upcoming segments, with comments such as "coming up in the next hour, Madonna, Def Leppard, and the new video from the Jeff Healey Band."

But the VJs do more than this. In Altman's (1987: 578-79) terms, the VJ presents the "sound advance," in which talk is used to redirect the viewer's attention toward the screen by previewing the images that are about to be screened — a vital function for a televisual form that is especially open to distracted, sporadic viewing. As Allan (1990) observes:

> Along with sports broadcasting, it [music television] is
> technically one of the most innovative and adventurous visual
> forms available on television. Yet it is also the one that permits
> you *not* to watch, but to listen continuously until, to put it
> paradoxically, you hear what you want to watch. (p. 9)

The VJs also offer a girl/boy-next-door point of identification for MTV viewers that is mirrored in the gossipy, humorous scripts, in the mise-en-scène of the MTV set (an adolescent's "den," a dance club) and in the VJs' interactions with viewers during phone-ins, contests, and outside broadcasts (such as *Amuck in America* and MTV's spring break and Super Bowl specials). The identification point established by the VJs is, unsurprisingly, a conscious MTV strategy:

> There were no specifics except that we wanted to create a human
> status for MTV. We wanted those individuals who would get up
> and wouldn't try to become stars, that wouldn't try to become
> entertainers. . . . For that reason we didn't look for celebrities,
> we looked for those people who wouldn't be overbearing or
> overpowering. (John Sykes, MTV's vice president of
> programming, quoted in Denisoff, 1988: 47)

Or, as Robert Pittman put it, the VJs should be "guides who could sublimate their egos, be *human faces you could relate to*" (quoted in Levy, 1983; emphasis added).

This anchoring identification point is one that has generally been missed in accounts of MTV as an unstable text. Importantly, during the long periods of time that the camera focuses exclusively on the VJs, it usually remains stationary, in a mid- to close-up shot that typifies the framing of television presenters and personalities. Often there will be distracting moving images in the background, but the VJ will usually remain motionless and, generally speaking, so does the camera. In contrast, then, to the aurally motivated camera movement in the video clips, the framing of the VJs gives us a single point of view from which to position ourselves, utilizing a direct mode of address that is a routine broadcast TV code. Thus, just as I showed in chapter 4 (in relation to the music video clips themselves), MTV mobilizes televisual strategies of signification that are remarkable only for their traditional adherence to fifty years of television convention. Where the videos themselves draw on techniques established in television light entertainment (and in the pro-televisual presentation of rock concerts), the MTV text presents its VJs using the standard features of news and documentary programming.

My account of the VJs' function echoes John Langer's (1981) analysis of television "personalities," and suggests the operation of a *hierarchy of identification* in MTV (and perhaps in television more generally). The VJs represent the ordinary, and the rock stars in the video clips represent the glamorous. The hierarchy of identification goes beyond this fairly obvious point, however, in ways that help to illustrate the stable nature of the MTV text. Langer's opposition of cinema and television works surprisingly well for rock music and television also. For instance, Langer notes that while cinema represents a world that is somehow "out there," television remains intimate, domestic, and always available. This is exactly the relation between pop stars and the VJs. The VJs have little media life outside MTV. They are thus (like news anchors and talk-show hosts) conduits who give us, the television viewers, access to pop star celebrities who enjoy fame beyond the confines of the small screen.

This anchoring function of the VJs is partly achieved through the appearance of "live" transmission. This occurs in two ways. First, the prerecorded VJ introductions are scripted and presented as though the VJs were (like radio DJs) playing the clips to us live from the television studio, in real time. (In fact, the taped VJ segments are being edited live into video clips and advertisements by an engineer).[12] Second, the VJs, unlike the pop stars, are actually speaking. Since most of the musicians who appear on MTV are lip-syncing, the VJs inevitably enjoy a more direct channel of communication. Again, this is an important part of the MTV text that has generally gone unnoticed. The contribution of the VJs can be understood better if MTV is compared with those music television services that have no mediating direct address (the Video Jukebox Network) or that use disembodied announcers on sound only (superstation WTBS's *Night Tracks*, for instance), where their absence blocks the possibility of constructing an ambience linked to a station identity, or with the use of celebrity guest VJs (on NBC's *Friday Night Videos*, for instance). In that respect, MTV is very much like *Top of the Pops*, where broadcast media "personalities" contextualize individual segments of "real" stardom.

Importantly, Robert Pittman was initially anxious about the stiffness of VJ presentation, and soon the VJs were encouraged to take a casual attitude to fluffed lines and on-air mistakes, which are often broadcast despite the fact that these segments are recorded and could thus be corrected before transmission. Here, the VJ portion of the MTV text is clearly drawing on rock and roll, rather than televisual, conventions, in which "feel" is more important than accuracy. There are two correlations here between MTV and rock culture. First, MTV seeks to present itself as a "rock" alternative to the prerock culture of network television, hence the emphasis on the construction of spontaneity, which has primacy over competence—a fundamental tenet of rock musicology. Second, the VJ presentation calls attention to itself (through the inclusion of "mistakes," and through the VJ's references to other, off-camera, studio personnel) and thus echoes the nonnaturalistic nature of pop performance. Far from being anarchic, VJ talk is therefore absolutely conventional when read in the light of a rock aesthetic. Therefore, while it is true that music television's mode of representation breaks with the classic realist text of Hollywood cinema, it nonetheless continues to use processes of identification (the rock star and the TV personality) that are fundamental sources of textual stability, not to mention key elements in the aesthetics of pop music.

And Now for Something Completely Familiar

The VJs help us to negotiate a schedule that has become increasingly complex. As MTV has incorporated more nonmusic programming and established regular slots for different kinds of music, it has moved away from the format of twenty-four-hour all-music radio, with its exclusive dependence on one musical genre, and evolved a schedule that is often extremely traditional.

In 1988 MTV turned to two classic audience-building techniques of broadcast media scheduling: "dayparting" and "stripping." Both are designed to make the schedule more predictable and to encourage consumers to tune in at the same time each day. Dayparting is the practice of scheduling different kinds of music during separate blocks of each day's programming. (It thus represents a formal break with the narrowcasting music policy of MTV's early history.) Stripping is a practice derived from independent (i.e., nonaffiliated) TV stations in the United States, in which episodes of the same TV series are screened at the same time each day of the week. Thus, MTV's twenty-four-hour "flow" is increasingly punctuated by regular slots organized around a predictable weekly schedule. As the nonmusic programming increases, it is becoming harder to distinguish MTV from other entertainment-led developments in the U.S. cable industry.

The result is that MTV's schedule on a typical day in March 1991 looked like this:

7:00 A.M.	*Awake on the Wild Side*
9:00 A.M.	Music videos (Daisy Fuentes)
12:00 M.	Music videos (Andrew Daddo)
3:00 P.M.	*Spring Break '91*
4:00 P.M.	*Yo! MTV Raps*
4:30 P.M.	*Totally Pauly*
6:00 P.M.	*Dial MTV*
7:00 P.M.	*MTV's Half Hour Comedy Hour*
7:30 P.M.	*Hot Seat*
8:00 P.M.	*Prime with Martha Quinn*
10:00 P.M.	*House of Style*
11:30 P.M.	*Bootleg MTV*
12:00 P.M.	*120 Minutes*

Other slots not included here are *The Week In Rock, Headbanger's Ball, MTV Unplugged, Club MTV, Idiot Box, The Big Picture, MTV's Big Show, Top 20 Video Countdown*, and the *MTV Rockumentary*. Set out in a *TV Guide* or daily newspaper grid, MTV often has *more* individual program slots than the network broadcasters or its cable rivals (CNN, for instance). Of course, we need to take account of the extensive repetition of segments and programs. This degree of repetition differentiates MTV (and most cable services) from the practices of network television. However, it is now presented in a framework that is very far indeed from seamless, unbounded flow.

In fact, the music television service that most closely resembles the wall-to-wall flow model discussed by so many critics is not MTV at all, but a newer service called the Video Jukebox Network, whose chief executive, Les Garland, used to work for MTV. The Video Jukebox Network has no formal programming; it simply screens video clips, on request, which are selected (via telephone) by the viewers in each area. The service has no on-screen VJs, preferring to communicate with its audience via a disembodied, robotic voice that does indeed seem to emanate from some kind of postmodern televisual cyberspace. The Video Jukebox Network has been aggressive in campaigning against MTV, characterizing its rival as old-fashioned and less liberatory than its own audience-programmed format.

This leads me to comment on the supposedly "timeless" experience of watching MTV. Clearly, the passing of time on MTV *does* work differently from the narrative-based practices of network television. In particular (as chapter 4 demonstrated), the degree of narrativity in the video clips themselves is fairly limited, and the absence of a simple beginning-middle-end structure of storytelling in pop lyrics is mirrored at the visual level in most video clips. This combines with the fact that musical narratives do not work through the classic realist formula of equilibrium-action-resolution, thus producing a sense of timelessness in the clips. The absence of narrative development is further exaggerated by the degree of repetition involved in both the heavy rotation of the same clips and the rebroadcast of the same slots. Music television thus mirrors both rock music itself and the broadcasting practices of all-music radio.

However, critics have hitherto missed some extremely important ways in which the passing of time *is* experienced in music television. First, there is the role of both program identification and VJ talk in locating the clips historically. It is not just that some videos are presented as "oldies" (on *Closet Classic Capsule, Classic MTV,* or *Prime with Martha Quinn,* for instance), but that some clips are presented as "new." Both in the "Hip Clip of the Week" and in the pervasive screening of "MTV Exclusives," the viewer is placed in a relation to the clip that implies a sense of time. We are aware (if we follow pop music, as most MTV viewers do) that we are seeing a mix of very new, current, older, and "historic" clips, and this may well temper the apparently timeless nature of the MTV experience. (When Yahoo Serious hosted *MTV's Big Show* in August 1989, the Australian comedian rooted the opening half of the program in a critique of pop culture's obsession with revivals and historical repetition.)

Indeed, in 1988 MTV became historically self-conscious, airing *Deja Video* (which soon became *Classic MTV* and was then superseded by *Prime with Martha Quinn*). This show featured video clips from the early 1980s and was hosted by original MTV VJ Martha Quinn. "Now you can relive those carefree days of youth," said a voice-over on a trailer for this show, as we watched a shot of a baby. In the summer of 1989, MTV frequently screened "Woodstock Minutes"—segments of footage from the 1969 Woodstock festival, some of it never previously aired (a strategy derived from its sister channel VH-1, which pioneered the use of extremely short "Milestones" featuring archive documentary footage of political events from the 1960s). Unlike *Deja Video/Classic MTV*, these clips did not explicitly frame the video clips themselves, but they certainly did work (alongside MTV News items about Woodstock) to contextualize the development of rock, and they suggest the possibility of a movement toward a "classic rock" format for some sections of MTV programming. This all-too-firmly *historicizing* perspective had already been used on VH-1, where 1960s pop star Peter Noone (of Herman's Hermits) hosted a daily program titled *My Generation*, and which now promotes itself as "VH-1: The Greatest Hits of Music Video."

Second, many MTV slots (such as the *MTV Countdown* and *MTV's Most Wanted*) depend on a temporal experience for the delivery of pleasure. The most obvious example is chart-based programming, which utilizes the narrative enigma of "Which clip will be number one this week?" The process of guessing which videos will be on the chart (and therefore which will be screened) exactly reproduces the narrative element of classic broadcast music programming such as *American Bandstand* and the BBC's *Top of the Pops*.

Third, there are MTV's special broadcasts (often scheduled on weekends), which increasingly mirror the networks' cyclical organization of television "seasons." While MTV, in common with much cable and independent television in the United States, has not generally observed the conventions of the TV season, its year-round flow is organized around various annual events, such as the *MTV Video Music Awards* show, the New Year's Eve special, and outside broadcasts built around national rituals and holidays such as spring break, the Super Bowl, Independence Day, Labor Day, and so on. By the fall of 1989, viewers could watch trailers advertising "MTV's new fall season."

Clearly, these observations raise empirical questions about the validity of postmodern and psychoanalytic accounts that stress the importance of the lack of boundaries in MTV programming, its timeless, ahistorical quality, and its refusal to offer a fixed point of identification for the viewer. Whether the purpose is to establish a correlation with dreams (Kinder) or aspects of postmodernism (Tetzlaff, Kaplan), the analysis must break down, at least partially, if the most dreamlike or postmodern experience in music television moves increasingly toward the establishment and maintenance of programming boundaries within its overall flow. Kaplan (1987) typifies the postmodern *oeuvre*, when she writes that "MTV simply takes over the history of rock and roll, flattening out all the distinct types into one continuous present" (p. 29). Once again, that statement was inaccurate when it was written; ironically enough, it has been rendered even less credible with the passing of time.

MTV's increasingly conventional format can be illustrated through a brief consideration of three recent shows: *Club MTV, Remote Control,* and *The Week in Rock.*

Club MTV needs only a brief comment, but it is interesting because it reproduces a format used in network/broadcast television. Using a set that represents a discotheque, the show plays current dance music hits and features video clips, lip-syncing, and "live" performances by current hit makers and a large portion of audience participation—its anchoring shots are those of audience members dancing, and it includes interviews with audience members, some of whom then introduce the clips. *Club MTV* is hosted by the channel's only black VJ, Julie Brown. In other words, *Club MTV* is a straightforward copy of the syndicated television show *Soul Train,* which first aired in the early 1970s. While *Soul Train* is its most obvious antecedent, *Club MTV* also resembles such chart shows as *American Bandstand, Solid Gold,* and the BBC's *Top of the Pops.* It is important for my argument because, like *Monty Python* and many other MTV programs, *Club MTV* represents a move back to traditional broadcast television formats.

The game show *Remote Control* first aired on MTV in December 1987 and has been its most successful venture into nonmusic programming. Unlike *Club MTV, Remote Control* combines a broadcast television format (the game show) with MTV's trademark sense of satire and lampoon. The hosts are deliberately obnoxious; the show's segments are punctuated with cheesy organ music that parodies game show conventions; while the prizes are displayed, an irksome voice-over underscores game-show consumer greed with a sleazy parody of the genre; the questions are universally lacking in substance (dealing almost exclusively in the minutiae of television trivia); and the contestants are treated with joking scorn—as losing players are eliminated, they are physically thrown from the studio floor, ejected via the back wall of the set while strapped into their seats.

In a typical *Remote Control* exchange, host Ken Ober asks a contestant where he works. The answer, that he is an employee of the greeting card manufacturer Hallmark, provokes this (sarcastic) response: "Well, that's great, you know, because Hallmark says the things that *I can't say.*" This joke, an improvization on a continuing MTV attitude that lampoons aspects of "straight," parental culture finds an echo in such network television talk shows as *Late Night with David.Letterman* and *The Arsenio Hall Show*.

Remote Control is interesting for two reasons. First, in its title and content the program reveals the deep-seated alliance that television and pop music culture have consolidated in the years since punk rock. Its assumption is that knowledge of pop music and knowledge of television go hand in hand. Second, *Remote Control*'s parodies key into *the promotion of satire* that is a marked feature of MTV in its third phase (when *The Monkees, The Young Ones,* and *Monty Python* first aired). The problem here, for postmodernism, is that parody and satire, unlike pastiche, clearly articulate a point of view. Furthermore, in the case of MTV, that point of view has a very clear generational basis (the class politics of *Monty Python* are probably lost on some portions of the American audience), which suggests not postmodernity so much as a more familiar discourse of youthful rebellion.

MTV's program *The Week in Rock* reveals a concrete connection with its *Rolling Stone*-like ambitions, since it is presented by *Rolling Stone* journalist Kurt Loder, who also anchors MTV News bulletins throughout its general programming. It is no surprise to discover, then, that *The Week in Rock* is the MTV show that most clearly displays its commitment to a traditional, Romantic rock aesthetic. By this I mean the construction of an ideology around rock music that sets itself up in opposition to selected elements in the commercialization of music, which establishes an opposition between youth and parental cultures, and which maintains a vaguely oppositional left/liberal political agenda. (For instance, introducing the clip for Paula Abdul's COLD HEARTED, VJ Adam Curry refers to record executives portrayed in its opening sequence as "geeks and goons." He thus emphasizes an us/them paradigm built around musicians and their various gatekeepers that is employed in numerous other clips, such as Neil Young's THIS NOTE'S FOR YOU,[13] John Mellencamp's POP SINGER, Richard Marx's DON'T MEAN NOTHING, Depeche Mode's EVERYTHING COUNTS, Quiet Riot's THE WILD AND THE YOUNG, and the Clash's THIS IS RADIO CLASH.)

It is certainly arguable that this Romantic agenda is collapsing throughout the field of pop culture, and MTV is an element in that process (as is *Rolling Stone*), as the supposed contradiction between art and commerce looks increasingly artificial. Indeed, it is possible to see much postmodernist commentary on MTV as a displaced account of this phenomenon. However, what has generally been neglected is the extent to which MTV insists on *maintaining* elements of this ideology. No doubt this is largely a cynical operation, but it remains a key factor in the production of meaning in rock culture.

For instance, in the edition of *The Week in Rock* broadcast on July 8, 1989, a countercultural sense of rock culture was frequently invoked. This edition of *The Week in Rock* began with an item about the U.S. Supreme Court's decision to allow states to restrict abortion rights. Like most of MTV's hard news items, it was presented with the authoritative gestures and intonation of network news. These news items, like MTV's antidrug and anti–drunk driving ads, indicate that it *is* prepared to suggest that some things *are* worth taking seriously. Regardless of their overt politics, they thus represent a break with the "nothing-matters-and-what-if-it-does?" worldview often attributed to MTV. Furthermore, the coverage of the Supreme Court's abortion decision revealed clear liberal intentions in its 4:1 ratio of interviewees opposed to and in favor of the decision.

The second portion of the show began with news footage of Oliver North, captioned with the word "FREE." As James Brown's song "(I Feel Like a) Sex Machine" played on the sound track, Brown's image then appeared next to North's (using split screen) and the caption "NOT FREE" appeared under *his* photograph. The references were to the then-current decision in North's trial (acquitting him on all but three charges and forgoing a jail sentence) and to the jailing of James Brown for drug and assault offenses some months earlier, with a sentence that many commentators and activists found overly punitive. This political montage went without comment when presenter Loder reappeared, but the message could hardly be missed.

Formally, this might appear to be a typical case of the primacy of the image—the articulation of political argument via visual snapshots. And yet the sequence defies two of the key elements identified in recent postmodern discussions of the image. First, while it is (like all images) polysemic, its use of montage contains a compelling preferred reading. Second, that reading implies a clear sociopolitical stance. In other words, the segments takes a position (using, incidentally, the classic *modernist* device of montage).

In other segments of MTV News the cable channel has offered favorable coverage of the Black Rock Coalition (an activist group designed to promote black musicians working in the hard rock genre), numerous positive accounts of the development of glasnost in the Soviet Union during the late 1980s, sympathetic stories on the AIDS crisis, and a sardonic, liberal account of the furor over flag burning that occurred in the United States in the summer of 1989.

These are admittedly fairly mild instances of countercultural struggle. Judged by the heady days of the 1960s, or the punk era, they are feeble indeed. To that extent MTV absolutely typifies the political trajectory of rock and pop in the 1980s[14] — a shift that MTV itself satirized in its end-of-the-decade documentary *Decade*, which used interviews, news segments, songs, and video clips to mount a liberal critique of the Reagan years. It is important to stress this kind of discourse, just as it is necessary to emphasize the continuing commitment to some kind of liberal/ progressive politics in the music and videos of acts such as Living Colour, U2, Peter Gabriel, Bruce Springsteen, Public Enemy, KRS-One, Madonna, Lou Reed, Don Henley, and Metallica (all of whom were featured heavily in MTV playlists in the late 1980s and early 1990s) in order to redress the imbalance of the postmodern hermeneutic, whose emphasis on MTV's supposed nihilism and/or assault upon the realm of the Symbolic (after Lacan) seriously overstates the importance of such readings.

More than Zero

Postmodern writers have had a field day with the question of MTV's supposedly ahistorical, apolitical, asocial, amoral aesthetic: "MTV denies the existence of all but the moment, and that moment exists only on the screen. . . . There aren't any problems on MTV," writes David Tetzlaff (1986: 89). John Fiske (1986) concurs: "The flashing crashing image-sounds ARE energy, speed, illusion, the hyperreal themselves: they simulate nothing, neither the reality nor the social machine" (p. 79). E. Ann Kaplan (1987) observes that "MTV is part of a contemporary discourse that has written out history as a possible discourse" (p. 146). This is a vivid gloss on Baudrillard, but it is difficult to sustain empirically in relation to MTV.

In one of its most revealing sequences (initially developed by MTV Europe as "One Planet-One Music"), an MTV station ID segment culminates in the legend: "One World, One Image, One Channel." But in fact, there are *two* MTVs. One MTV discourse is the nihilistic, pastiching, essentially pointless playfulness that is invoked in postmodernist accounts of MTV. The other is responsible, socially consciousness, satire and parody based, vaguely liberal—and almost invisible in academic accounts of MTV.

The MTV logo itself exemplifies the devil-may-care discourse, which is constructed in part in explicit (and quite conscious) opposition to network television, in that the logo is both inconsistent and irreverent—it takes many different forms and is often presented through visual jokes. Many of its slogans clearly promote just the kind of discourse the postmodernists analyze: "MTV: We're Making It Up as We Go Along" and "MTV: Better Sorry than Safe" are two such examples. Something similar occurs when the slogan "The Whole World Is Watching" is used in conjunction with images of cows chewing the cud in a field. (Given the roots of *that* slogan in the student demonstrations at the 1968 Democratic convention in Chicago, the Frankfurt school notion of "incorporation" would be every bit as appropriate as postmodern theory here.) Many of the filmed minifictions inserted between clips also fall into this category. The sometimes pointless (but extremely funny) humor of Gilbert Godfrey, who performs stand-up comedic blips between videos from time to time, is a good example. Trailing MTV's *Half-Hour Comedy Hour*, Godfrey asks, "If it's half ours, who does the other half belong to?"

However, there is another cluster of discourses at play within MTV programming and presentation material—a grouping of quasi-political, volunteerist, socially responsible, and sometimes countercultural appeals that the postmodernists have chosen to ignore. What, for instance, are we to make of this statement, from former MTVN president Robert Pittman? In an interview in *Channels* magazine, Pittman appears to return to a classic Romantic rock ideology when he says, "You have to be careful that you stay this side of the line of being perceived by the consumer as a sellout" (quoted in Robins, 1989). MTV's sales pitch has to be seen in relation to this ideology of rock as well as postmodernism. The complicating factor here is the transformation, in the 1980s, of rock's countercultural ideology into a discourse that combines traditional notions of rebellion and Romantic rejection of everyday life with a new sense of social responsibility and philanthropic concern. Thus, at the same time that

MTV has kept its tongue firmly in its cheek, it also had to come to terms with cause-rock events such as Live Aid, Amnesty International's Conspiracy of Hope tour, and the Smile Jamaica benefit concert.

MTV has run frequent promotional clips for the Rock Against Drugs and Make a Difference antidrug campaigns, and in June 1989 banned N.W.A.'s STRAIGHT OUTTA COMPTON on the grounds that it might seem to glorify crime associated with gang membership. Its screening of the antiapartheid video SUN CITY was, as George Lipsitz (1987) notes, reverential and serious. During its broadcast of the Make a Difference rock concert in the Soviet Union in August 1989, it repeatedly used the slogan "Cool Music, Not Cold War." Even its humor sometimes has a point. A July 1989 episode of *Just Say Julie* that appeared to be an irreverent look at the portrayal of animals in music video clips ended with a caption giving the address of People for the Ethical Treatment of Animals. During the screening of the anti-Soviet ABC miniseries *Amerika* in February 1987, MTV labeled itself "MTV-ski" (using the slogan "MTV: Music Television for the Re-educated") and pointedly screened the red-baiting 1956 Department of Defense film *Red Nightmare*. In November 1990 MTV ran special "Rock the Vote" programming in prime time, in which American rock stars (including Madonna) made brief spots designed to encourage young people to vote. These slots, and the VJ talk that surrounded them, highlighted the importance of voting as a tactic to block right-wing censorship campaigns and policies.[15]

The politics of MTV (both its possibilities for radicalism and its limits) were starkly revealed during the Gulf War of 1991. At noon on January 15, MTV responded to the approaching United Nations deadline for Iraqi withdrawal from Kuwait by superimposing a peace sign on the bottom right-hand corner of the screen. It also began airing GIVE PEACE A CHANCE, a remake of the John Lennon song made by the Peace Choir, which featured, among others, Sean Lennon, Lenny Kravitz, Iggy Pop, LL Cool J, Adam Ant, Peter Gabriel, Yoko Ono, Randy Newman, M.C. Hammer, and Cyndi Lauper. At various times of the day and night, the peace sign reappeared on the screen, and the network followed many of its news breaks with other relevant clips—Michael Jackson's MAN IN THE MIRROR, John Lennon's IMAGINE, and Bruce Springsteen's cover of Edwin Starr's hit WAR. GIVE PEACE A CHANCE was at one point screened back-to-back, in long, uninterrupted blocks.

Once the American bombing of Baghdad started, however, the peace sign disappeared from the screen. (An MTV Networks spokesperson said that this was because the network "didn't like the way it looked.")[16] However, GIVE PEACE A CHANCE continued to air, and MTV provided critical coverage of the war, in a special *Week in Rock* report (January 19, 1991) and in an MTV News item ("War Sells," February 25, 1991) devoted to the commercial exploitation of the Gulf War. In the former program, Springsteen's cover of "War" was used to introduce the show ("War—What is it good for? Absolutely nothing!") and the focus of the program was on antiwar protests of various kinds. George Bush's January 15 deadline was referred to as a "threat," his position was summed up as a "war policy," and the initiation of bombing was reported as "Wednesday night's attack." This language was in marked contrast to that found on network news programs, as was the proportionately large amount of time given to interviewees who articulated the position that the war was motivated by oil rather than morality. Marvin Gaye's social protest song "What's Goin On?" was then used as a bridge into a series of sound bites from rock, pop, and rap stars, including a comment from radical rap artist Ice Cube, who stated a position that widened the agenda still further: "I don't think any black kids need to be over there. I don't think any poor white kids need to be over there. I don't think any Hispanic kids need to be over there. I think they need to send the rich over there, and let them die." A following segment on the making of GIVE PEACE A CHANCE was summed up by Kurt Loder with these words: "Still very much a song for our time."

Loder then reported on the Rock and Roll Hall of Fame awards (which took place just as the bombing began) and made frequent reference to the absence of antiwar protest, in a tone of voice that sounded almost incredulous at times. Over a shot of Bruce Springsteen and assorted rock idols playing in the traditional end-of-show jam session, Loder commented: "But in the end, the evening, overshadowed as it was by the war raging half a world away, had a strangely anticlimactic feel to it. Even more strangely, for an event honoring the history of rock and roll . . . not a single antiwar protest song had been sung by anyone." The comment is revealing in its assumptions about what is normal and what is strange in terms of rock's social role, and illustrates an important theme in MTV's liberal/socially conscious interpretation of the rock aesthetic.

This brings me to the question of MTV's political stance. Analyzing one area of MTV's nonmusic programming (its brief, often humorous, fictional clips), Lawrence Grossberg (1988) presents a view of postmodernity that has become a standard interpretation:

MTV offers us a series of ads promoting Randee (the imaginary leader of an imaginary rock group, Randee and the Redwoods), for president. His entire media campaign is composed of clichéd paradoxes: eg, Randee at a press conference says that he was misunderstood when he said that "First there is a mountain, then there is no mountain, then there is." He points out that he did not mean to say that there is no mountain. "There is one," he says to thunderous applause. "And after I'm elected there will be one." Feeling something, anything, is better than feeling nothing. (p. 44)

Grossberg's analysis is worthwhile and suggestive, because he goes on to show that this postmodern structure of feeling is not merely nihilistic. Grossberg's category of "ironic inauthenticity" is a useful addition to our understanding of the formations of readership that inform the reception of MTV and contemporary pop music. (But even this complex category is double-edged, for what is the slogan "One World, One Image, One Channel" but an Orwellian effort to pursue MTV's global intentions and retain countercultural credibility by owning up to the intent? In other words, as with Isuzu's infamous "Joe Isuzu" television commercials, it is the *incorporation* of ironic inauthenticity.)

However, we can also provide an alternative concluding sentence for this passage. I would like to rewrite Grossberg's gloss thus:

MTV offers us a series of ads promoting Randee (the imaginary leader of an imaginary rock group, Randee and the Redwoods) for president. His entire media campaign is composed of clichéd paradoxes: e.g., Randee at a press conference says that he was misunderstood when he said that "first there is a mountain, then there is no mountain, then there is." He points out that he did not mean to say that there is no mountain. "There is one," he says to thunderous applause. "And after I'm elected there will be one." Thus parody is used to establish a critique of campaigning strategies in the U.S. political system.

This, in my view, is the *other* MTV. It is the MTV that organized voter registration drives in 1984. And it is the MTV that is neglected in nearly all the published research on music television.

None of this is to deny MTV's innovations, or its potential for a postmodern reading. As Pfeil (1988) and Grossberg (1988) suggest, work on postmodernism as a condition of reception can be extremely fruitful. But in the analysis of music television as a postmodern *text*, scholars need to pay much greater heed to the empirical data and to the contradictions within MTV, which cannot be seamlessly reduced to a single aesthetic category. These contradictions are mutually supportive. The two MTVs depend upon each other. A music television station that was simply frivolous, playful, pleasure centered, and so forth would quickly be dismissed as corporate froth—not just by critics, but by music fans who expect more than "entertainment" from rock, pop, and rap culture. On the other hand, an environment that is too serious, worthy, and socially committed would be equally inappropriate for a rock culture that must also embody hedonism, self-expression, and so on

However, MTV (and services like it) are not determined solely by their relation to aesthetic forms and discourses. As outlined in chapter 2, music television services are also an advertising "environment." In the case of MTV, that environment will seem credible only if it seems to speak to (an increasingly fractured) youth culture—one that now includes people in their thirties and forties and that encompasses a generic "breakup" in terms of musical styles. (This fracturing explains MTV's announcement, in the spring of 1991, that it will divide up into three separate services in 1993. If this happens, it will inaugurate a *fourth* phase in MTV's history.) It is a paradox, then, that in order to function as a successful service for the delivery of viewers to advertisers and record companies, MTV must promote countercultural and antiestablishment points of view. Therefore, MTV aligns itself with liberal causes, mounts a critique of everyday life that is at times almost situationist,[17] sets itself apart from "mass culture" (especially network television),[18] and constantly emphasizes rock's roots in pantheism (see Pattison, 1987) through its strident pro-ecology spots, and in social concern (items and videos on the homeless, for instance).[19] This could be seen as the "incorporation" of counterhegemonic discourses in the name of corporate profit. (Although, in Williams's terms, "alternative," as opposed to dominant or oppositional, would be a better general summary of its politics; see Williams, 1973.) Yet this analysis reveals the inadequacy of such a reading, for one way of understanding MTV would be through an "innocent" framework that takes rock myths at face value and that goes beyond cynicism (either through ignorance or choice) in discarding the issue of MTV's broader economic concerns. As with the debate about rock philanthropy (Live Aid and so on), one interpretation simply insists that the message is more important than the motive. MTV is thus simultaneously involved in the incorporation *and* the promotion of dissent.

SEVEN

Aesthetics and Politics in Music Television
Postmodernism Reconsidered

Since there's been what people call a postmodern crisis — i.e.
language doesn't work like we thought it worked any more,
identity doesn't exist, reference doesn't work, truth doesn't
obtain, everything's adrift — then perhaps what music does against
that relief is quite significant.
                            — Green Gartside, Scritti Politti[1]

Music television is no more a coherent object than is "rock and roll" or
"pop music." It is impossible, therefore, to identify an all-encompassing
politics or aesthetics of music television. In the main body of this thesis I
have been concerned with stretching the limits of analysis in a particular
way, so that the critique of music videos takes into account a variety of
extratextual discourses and practices. In this chapter, however, I will concentrate instead on the specific elements introduced into popular culture
by music television itself, as a particular cultural form. Rather than attempting to enforce a unity here that does not exist, I will focus on particular issues in order to argue for a reengagement with the question of
ideology, through a reconsideration of postmodern analyses of music
television.

    There are a number of important absences in postmodern criticism
that leave spaces for scholars to bounce back and forth between cultural
pessimism and cultural optimism in a manner that is ultimately often un-
productive, since it implies that political criticism is a matter of *mood*.
First, the postmodern focus on surface, which I would argue has been
extremely productive and revealing, has sometimes leaked into the criticism itself, so that an observation about a cultural form has become in
some instances an epistemological (indeed, sometimes an ontological)
position.[2] This has frequently occurred at the expense of investigating the

possibilities for depth. I will pursue this issue in relation to intertextuality and pastiche, showing how the debate needs also to be related to a political economic and ideological analysis of music television.

Second, as I suggested in chapter 6, it is a problem for postmodern analysis that it is often largely ahistorical and therefore blind to the ways in which the televisual vehicle (in that instance, MTV) has changed. Similarly, at a greater level of abstraction, the development of music television needs to be read ideologically (as does the production of new kinds of television, such as *The Simpsons* and *Twin Peaks*), and I will argue that we need a political economy of the media in order to undertake that task, which includes a consideration of how economic and policy shifts may influence patterns of programming.

Third, there is the question raised by Edward Said (1985) concerning the often purely textual understanding of "politics" in cultural studies that sometimes occurs at the expense of what Said calls "Politics 2." Said has pointed out that postmodern theory has generally kept concrete political issues at arm's length, while embracing an aestheticized political discourse from the academy. (One symptom of this is the implied activism involved in giving journals titles such as *October, Strategies,* and *Textual Politics.*) Thus, "radicalism" in academic studies still tends to mean textual avant-gardism (breaking with naturalism/realism) or the corruption of hierarchies of taste. Exactly how these issues connect with social power often remains unexplained.

Ideology and Cultural Analysis

The political analysis of popular culture has in the last twenty years undergone a radical overhaul, in which elitist, economistic, reductionist, and pessimistic approaches have been replaced by emphases on relative autonomy, audience resistance, multiplicity of meaning, and a politics of pleasure. These arguments have sharpened our understanding of how ideological reproduction is dispersed throughout the social formation (it does not simply "trickle down" from a unified "ruling class"), and they have usefully pointed up the ways in which culture can be seen as a site of contest, rather than domination. In the relation to rock and pop culture, the critique of elitism has been especially important as a way of validating popular musical forms (see, for instance, Chambers, 1985). The effort to secure these new positions is open to the charge, however, that they have progressively marginalized a task that remains central to any historical materialist theory of culture. This is the project of ideological critique. It is the abandonment of this work (and, sometimes, its transformation into a project that explicates theory, rather than the world) that is identified by Lawrence Grossberg (1988) as the "scandal" of cultural studies.

By *ideology* I deploy here the fairly restrictive sense of the term (and I believe it is *useful* precisely because it *is* narrow) that suggests not just that ideas and culture are expressions of social interest, but that some forms of consciousness work to *sustain existing power relations.* I therefore agree with John B. Thompson's (1990) recent effort to rethink some of the unworkable or inadequate aspects of a materialist concept of ideology while preserving its essentially negative character:

> Ideology can be used to refer to the ways in which meaning serves, in particular circumstances, to establish and sustain relations of power which are systematically asymmetrical — what I shall call "relations of domination." Ideology, broadly speaking, is *meaning in the service of power.* (p. 7)

This definition does not imply that ideas and cultural practices always or only do this, but it does suggest that discovering where and how they interact with social power is a priority.[3]

It should be the case, however, that the ground-clearing operation of refining ideological analysis then opens up a way for better-informed political criticism that is more adequate to the real. Instead, the process of critiquing the old assumptions has itself become the intellectual *goal* of a new populism. What has happened in practice is that instead of researching key theoretical and political issues more thoroughly than before, media critics have continued to oscillate between cultural pessimism and cultural optimism. Postmodern analyses of music television and of popular music bear the marks of this unhelpful fracture in theory. For some postmodern critics, popular culture expresses ideological formations within late capitalism (Jameson, 1984a, 1984b). Reacting to this "pessimism," other postmodernists find resistant, counterhegemonic discourses to be of primary importance (for example, Kaplan, 1987).

One issue of central importance in the postmodernism debate concerns questions that are addressed through spatial metaphors — depth, distance, surface, and so on. What is at stake in these analogies is in essence political, since they raise the issue of whether or not postmodern cultural forms offer any position from which to understand (or, indeed, to sustain) social power. I will begin my analysis of ideology in music television by discussing the concept of "pastiche," since this concept is essential to the argument that the form lacks "depth," and is open to a reinterpretation that illustrates both the complexities of music television and some simplicities in postmodern analysis.

Blank Generations

Jean Baudrillard (1975, 1988b: 57-97) combines a deployment of semiotic theory and a critique of Marxist accounts of the commodity to arrive at a view of popular culture (see also Baudrillard, 1985, 1988b: 166-219) that has gained widespread currency in cultural criticism, especially through the concept of "pastiche." Just as semiotic theory eventually developed an analysis of "sliding signifiers" in which the signifier-signified relation was undermined when it was argued that signifiers in fact only ever refer to other signifiers, so Baudrillard views postmodern culture as one in which texts increasingly refer to each other, where "simulations" have replaced the real.[4]

Postmodern analyses often present this idea via a one-dimensional account of changing notions of history in pop music, tending to use all instances of quoting from pop's past as though they were simple examples of "pastiche" (see Goodwin, 1988). This argument is highly significant for a political analysis of music television, for two reasons. First, it is the basis for a model of readership in which viewers consume "on the surface," via a fragmented sense of self. Second, the argument overlooks some important economic determinations in the process of intertextuality. In fact, it can be shown that music television's intertextuality and its articulation of popular cultural history are often anything but blank.

Consider, for example, the variety of ways in which music video clips "quote" from other texts. This practice is pervasive in music television and is usually labeled "pastiche." This concept is characterized by Fredric Jameson (1984b) as "blank parody," by which he means that the referential element of parody is present, without the critical distance implied by that concept. E. Ann Kaplan and others have usefully cited this concept as an element in music video, in order to demonstrate the postmodern nature of the form. Kaplan instances the well-known Queen video RADIO GA GA as an example, where both the direct quotation of extracts from the Fritz Lang movie *Metropolis* and the referencing of discourses of nazism from films such as *The Triumph of the Will* are presented as part of the video, without providing for any apparent position from which to view them. The textual "quotes" are blank because we are asked neither to criticize nor to endorse them.[5]

It is possible to think of many other examples of this: the references to Truffaut's *Day for Night* in the Human League's DON'T YOU WANT ME, Dire Straits' invocation of MTV in MONEY FOR NOTHING, Ozzy Osbourne's rather tacky representation of *Dallas* in THE ULTIMATE SIN, Sigue Sigue Sputnik's references to *Blade Runner* and video games in LOVE MISSILE F-1 11, and the famous pastiche of a scene from the Howard Hawks movie *Gentlemen Prefer Blondes* in Madonna's MATERIAL GIRL.

However, the incorporation of other texts into music video does not always fit the category of pastiche, and might be seen as ranging across a continuum of positions, from social criticism to homage, as shown in Table 7.1, in relation to the appropriation of visual signifiers.[6]

Where postmodern theory uses the pervasive quoting from other texts in music video uniformly, as evidence for its postmodern status, this table shows that many examples of this phenomenon, perhaps even the majority of them, do not fit the category of pastiche. Central to that concept is the notion that music video textual incorporation tends to eschew any critical distance. No less than three of my alternative categories demonstrate that this is not so.

Social Criticism

It is clear that the inclusion of news footage in TWO TRIBES (in one of the song's numerous mixes, Godley and Creme use footage of Richard Nixon) does take up a position—in this case the position that all politicians (and, by implication, all politics) are phony/self-serving. In tapes such as SUN CITY, WAR, and LIVES IN THE BALANCE, the sociopolitical critique is more focused, establishing very clear antiracist and anti-Reagan positions and making them socially specific via the use of TV news clips. THIS IS RADIO CLASH is an interesting earlier example that might also be placed in the category of pastiche, depending on the politics we bring to it—including our reading of the meaning of the Clash. I have included it because it is contentious and serves to demonstrate that this categorization needs to be considered flexibly, since we know that any text may generate a range of readings. SISTERS ARE DOIN' IT FOR THEMSELVES and CULT OF PERSONALITY represent less trenchantly radical arguments, but

Table 7.1

Visual Incorporation in Music Video

Social Criticism	Self-Reflexive Parody	Parody
SUN CITY (AAA)	DON'T LOSE MY NUMBER (Phil Collins)	BAD NEWS BEAT (Neil Young)
WAR (Springsteen)	JUST A GIGOLO (David Lee Roth)	LIFE IN ONE DAY (Howard Jones)
LIVES IN THE BALANCE (Jackson Browne)	THIS NOTE'S FOR YOU (Neil Young)	RIGHT ON TRACK (Breakfast Club)
TWO TRIBES (FGTH)	EAT IT ("Weird Al" Yankovic)	
RADIO CLASH (the Clash)	POP SINGER (John Mellencamp)	
JAMMIN' ME (Tom Petty)	ON THE GREENER SIDE (Michelle Shocked)	
SISTERS ARE DOIN' IT FOR THEMSELVES (Eurythmics)		
CULT OF PERSONALITY (Living Colour)		
ONE (Metallica)		

Pastiche	Promotion	Homage
RADIO GA GA (Queen)	A VIEW TO KILL (Duran Duran)	DON'T GET ME WRONG (Pretenders)
THE ULTIMATE SIN (Ozzy Osbourne)	ABSOLUTE BEGINNERS (David Bowie)	CHAIN REACTION (Diana Ross)
MONEY FOR NOTHING (Dire Straits)	STAND BY ME (Ben E. King)	DR MABUSE (Propaganda)
MATERIAL GIRL (Madonna)	DANGER ZONE (Kenny Loggins)[a]	E = MC^2 (BAD)
THRILLER (Michael Jackson)	LAND OF CONFUSION (Genesis)[b]	TELL HER ABOUT IT (Billy Joel)
WHERE THE STREETS HAVE NO NAME (U2)	BATDANCE (Prince)	R.O.C.K. IN THE USA (John Cougar Mellencamp)
BIG TIME (Peter Gabriel)[c]	HEARTBEAT (Don Johnson)	ROCKIT (Def Leppard)
MEDIATE (INXS)		

[a]DANGER ZONE is especially interesting because it both promotes the film *Top Gun* and references (as pastiche?) the opening scene of Francis Ford Coppola's *Apocalypse Now*.

[b]LAND OF CONFUSION is not a move trailer, as the other examples here are, but it does indirectly promote the British TV series *Spitting Image*, through its use of puppets. It also contains pastiche, in its joking reference to the montage sequence in Stanley Kubrick's *2001: A Space Odyssey*, in which the chimp's bone becomes a spaceship (here it is transformed into a telephone receiver held by the Phil Collins puppet).

[c]BIG TIME uses a pastichelike reference to the television series *Pee-Wee's Playhouse* (through its distorted, playful mise-en-scène), but the complicating factor here is that this can be read as an auteurist discourse, since the clip's director, Stephen Johnson, has also directed that television program. Read in that light, the clip should more accurately be classified as (self-?) promotion or homage.

use images of politicians (Indira Ghandi, Joseph Stalin, Mahatma Ghandi) to draw attention to the social comment in the lyrics to each song. JAMMIN' ME is an explicit critique of television and media politics in the 1980s, while ONE uses excerpts from the film *Johnny Got His Gun* to make an antiwar statement.

Self-Reflexive Parody

A number of music video parodies take music video itself as the target. Partly I think this is because it is such an easy one, and also because it avoids any engagement with the institutions themselves: MONEY FOR NOTHING is the only example I know of, and it has to be classed as pastiche because of its studied ambiguity toward MTV—an economic determinant, if ever there was one.[7] Neil Young discovered this difficulty when his clip THIS NOTE'S FOR YOU was initially banished from the MTV airwaves because it referred to MTV advertisers (who are attacked in the song itself, which is against corporate sponsorship of rock). JUST A GIGOLO and POP SINGER both parody aspects of the music industry. EAT IT is a humorous clip based on Michael Jackson's BEAT IT. ON THE GREENER SIDE parodies some of Robert Palmer's clips, such as ADDICTED TO LOVE.

Parody

It is interesting that there are so few attempts at straight parody in music video. The only examples I can think of are Neil Young's BAD NEWS BEAT, in which he plays a TV news reporter on the spot at a traffic accident (although the extent to which the critique is directed toward TV is questionable), and Howard Jones's Godley and Creme-directed tape, LIFE IN ONE DAY, which includes parody of TV ads. RIGHT ON TRACK is framed with a similar device.

Pastiche

There is no need to say much about the category of pastiche, since most of the examples in Table 7.1 are discussed by Kaplan and others, and I am entirely in agreement with the attempt to establish this concept in relation to music video. Each of the examples cited utilizes other texts in a manner that might be read as "blank": *Metropolis* (RADIO GA GA), *Dallas* (THE ULTIMATE SIN), MTV (MONEY FOR NOTHING), *Gentleman Prefer Blondes*

(MATERIAL GIRL), horror movies (THRILLER), the rooftop scene from the Beatles film *Let It Be* (WHERE THE STREETS HAVE NO NAME), and *Pee-Wee's Playhouse* (BIG TIME). MEDIATE is based on Bob Dylan's famous "Subterranean Homesick Blues" sequence from D. A. Pennebaker's 1965 documentary film *Don't Look Back*.

Promotion

Music video analysis has generally overlooked the extent to which music video offers not parody minus critical distance, but something else altogether—promotion and homage. The various clips designed to promote movies cannot be seen as pastiche, because they usually reference texts with which most viewers are as yet unfamiliar—nonetheless, they are clearly seen to be quoting from other texts, in a multiplicity of ways that are extremely important for the analysis of music video, since this aspect of the form introduces new economic and narrative demands. The clip has to sell a film as well as a record, and must act as a taste of the cinematic narrative without giving too much away.

Homage

More interesting still are those tapes that abandon parody entirely in favor of a tribute to a particular director, TV show, or cultural form. The most obvious example is the Big Audio Dynamite clip E $=$ MC^2, which uses extracts from Nicolas Roeg movies (*Don't Look Now, The Man Who Fell to Earth, Insignificance*) in order to illustrate a song that is itself a tribute to that director, which is evident from the lyrics and song title alone. Propaganda's DR MABUSE is a similar example, where a German expressionist-style tape promotes a song whose title is taken from a Fritz Lang movie. And there are clips that pay tribute to TV, nearly all of them originating in the 1960s—the use of TV soul in CHAIN REACTION, Billy Joel's tribute to Ed Sullivan in TELL HER ABOUT IT, John Mellencamp's historicizing tribute to soul music in R.O.C.K. IN THE USA (framed with a mock TV interview), and the Pretenders' homage to *The Avengers*, with Chrissie Hynde cast in the role of Emma Peel, in DON'T GET ME WRONG.

There is, however, a problem in knowing how to distinguish between pastiche and homage. Is THRILLER a tribute to horror movies? Is MATERIAL GIRL likewise homage to Howard Hawks? I think the answer to both questions is no, just as some of my examples (for instance, $E = MC^2$) cannot be placed in the category of pastiche. Nonetheless, there is a methodological problem here in knowing quite where to place the emphasis. To some extent that will depend on reading competence in relation to popular culture generally and star-texts in particular. Def Leppard's ROCK-IT, for instance, celebrates the rock culture that the musicians grew up with by including *Top of the Pops* images of T. Rex, Elton John, and Sweet alongside shots of the 1977 Manchester United F.A. Cup victory. With this pop culture knowledge in mind, the visual images perfectly illustrate the song. Devoid of these references the visual rhetoric would appear merely random.

I am not, of course, seeking to establish a definitive categorization: all of the six categories described must inevitably allow for "slippage" among them, depending on viewer interpretation. These are precisely the subtleties that are missing from postmodern accounts of pastiche. My aim is to establish that there are categories that are not just devoid of any element of parody, but that do in fact endorse and celebrate the representations of representation that they offer. *Pastiche* is not the correct term for these phenomena.

Overriding the entire debate here is the vexed question of socially differentiated readings of cultural texts. And it is not only critics who disagree on the interpretation of such elements as parody and pastiche. Acts such as ABC and Frankie Goes to Hollywood played with irony and critical distance in order to create at least two kinds of readers — those who read the "commercialism" as an ironic comment on pop, and those who simply carried on consuming in blissful ignorance of any such irony. Duran Duran's involvement in video is important here, because their "playful" glamorous videos (RIO, HUNGRY LIKE THE WOLF) were read as crass exploitation by critics of the band, who nonetheless maintain that these clips were meant ironically:

> Whenever we do something tongue in cheek, people think we're being more serious than we are. Like when we went to Rio to make that video on a boat, which we thought was a big joke, wearing silk shirts on a yacht, everybody thought Duran Duran was trying to put over a jet-set image. (quoted in Cohen, 1987)

There are two points here. First, and more obvious, is that any categorization of music video texts around the concepts of parody and pastiche must allow for a range of interpretations, so that many clips will in fact be capable of generating readings that slide across the boundaries of irony, critical distance, homage, and so on. But, second, there is something peculiar about contemporary pop culture, in its eagerness to sell us a tease (this point was taken up briefly in chapter 2). Today's pop images attempt to construct a mass market by playing upon confusions about critical distance, so as to generate simultaneously two sets of images that can be read both innocently and self-consciously. The sexism of ZZ Top clips is one example, along with Duran Duran, the Pet Shop Boys, and developments such as Sigue Sigue Sputnik. While this is not new (for example, Richard Lester's Beatles movie *A Hard Day's Night*, or the Bob Rafelson/Jack Nicholson–directed Monkees movie *Head*), it is more pervasive than ever before. And it means that while the concept of pastiche is a very useful one, it needs to be placed more firmly within the contexts of music video production and consumption.

In terms of ideology, music television's sometimes blank intertextuality needs to be thought out in three ways. First, as I have just suggested, we need to consider the many ways in which textual incorporation leaves open the possibility of social criticism. In that respect, the emergence of music video is striking in two respects. The use of news and documentary footage can render the pop song more socially specific and at the same time represents the opening up of a new space in television, since music videos articulate political positions that might otherwise be absent (TWO TRIBES, ON THE GREENER SIDE, GIVE PEACE A CHANCE), except possibly in political satire (*Spitting Image, Saturday Night Live*).

Second, it is foolish to ignore the extent to which "pastiche" is merely a cover for cross-promotion. The quoting of other texts in order to advertise them is central to music video clips, and there is little that is "blank" about this; on the contrary, the practice seeks to construct a very clear reading position centered on the effort to create an obedient consumer who will take an interest in the text (usually a film) that is being advertised.

Third, there is the issue of what pastiche *means*, politically speaking, when it *is* present. For all its superficiality, the process may not be an innocent one, in ideological terms. I am struck here by the parallels between the description of pastiche offered in postmodernism and the critical account of modernism provided in Franco Moretti's (1987) analysis of the "spell of indecision," which revealingly links that aesthetic with Romanticism. Moretti describes this phenomenon using terms that sound like a description of music television pastiche:

> As for the stimulus, it has to be "evocative" more than
> "meaningful": it must possess as little determinacy as possible,
> and therefore be open to, or better still produce, such a plurality
> of associations that everybody may be able to "find something"
> in it. . . . Romantic irony is a frame of mind which sees in any
> event no more than an "occasion" for free intellectual and
> emotional play, for a mental and subjective deconstruction of the
> world as it is. Devoted to the category of "possibility,"
> Romantic irony is therefore incapable of a decision. (p. 19)

Moretti argues that this free play of meaning is linked to Romanticism
through its yearning to *daydream*, to create an alternative "inner" reality
that never challenges the social order. Pastiche, from this point of view,
while *technically* "blank," is nonetheless *socially* invested in a kind of pa-
ralysis of representation. Politically, in Moretti's view, it is associated not
with Marxism, but with consumerism: "Is it not the basic technique of
modern advertising, which took off shortly after the golden age of avant-
garde movements, and whose task is to endow commodities with a surprising and pleasant aesthetic aura?" (p. 18). This point dovetails with the
arguments of political economy, which will now be used to redress the
lack of historical context in postmodern accounts of music television.

Common Markets

Cultural studies has increasingly conceptualized ideological analysis in
such a way as to conflate political economy and cultural pessimism, so
that any attempt to understand contexts of production (and the wider issues concerning how political and economic forces shape these contexts)
is thought to be reductionist (not giving sufficient autonomy to the materiality of the text), disempowering of the audience, and elitist (implying a link between economic analysis and personal taste). Reversing this
logic, text and audience analysis has increasingly been associated with
finding sites of resistance in popular culture (thus, the loss of ideological
critique). Despite the fact that text and audience analyses *have* produced
many convincing studies of counterhegemonic discourses and interpretations in the mass media (for instance, Ang, 1985; Hobson, 1980), the
conflation of methodology and cultural attitude remains illegitimate.

What has been forgotten here is the notion that there might be levels of
mediation (see Sartre, 1963) between a mode of production and its culture. Because the new populism has shifted the emphasis of research onto

texts and audiences, the larger issues concerning how developments in the mode of production might be related to cultural production (which are surely central to any politics of culture) have been ignored. This is true even for Marxist critics. Stuart Hall (1980, 1986), for instance, pays lip service to the role of political economy here and there, but these questions never surface in his actual research. And the literature of postmodernism, while it sometimes celebrates popular forms, rarely demonstrates concrete, historical links between the aesthetic and its mode of production.

Postmodern writing on music television reproduces (often very crudely) precisely the kind of reductionism criticized by structuralist, semiotic, and post-Marxist thinkers. In other words, this is an unintentional exercise in vulgar Lukacsianism, in which readings are produced that show how individual music video clips "express" the dominant "postmodern" aesthetic/social structure. Fredric Jameson's (1983) account of historicism precisely describes the way in which postmodern theory has been used in relation to music television when he outlines this process:

> The construction of a historical totality necessarily involves the isolation and the privileging of one of the elements within the totality (a kind of thought habit, a predilection for specific forms, a certain type of belief, a "characteristic" political structure or form of domination) such that the element in question becomes a master code or "inner essence" capable of explicating the other elements or features of the "whole" in question." (pp. 27-28)

My point, congruent with Jameson's argument, is not that totalizing is illegitimate, but that it becomes irredeemably idealistic when criticism is used to "discover" textual elements that line up with the properties of a mode of production *when there is no account of actual, historical relations between the two levels.* To say this is simply to reiterate Theodor Adorno's criticism of Walter Benjamin, in his letter of November 10, 1938, when he takes Benjamin to task for idealizing base-superstructure relations, for instance, in relation to Baudelaire's wine poems. Claiming to be as "simple and Hegelian" as possible, Adorno (1977) carefully points out that "your dialectic lacks one thing: mediation." (p. 128)

I have already argued (in chapter 2) that music television needs to be understood in relation to its production context, which is of a very specific nature; video clips themselves are not primarily commodities, but must nonetheless embody use-values while also teasing the audience into seeking out further use-values in the product being advertised. This remains quite a local picture that is itself in need of contextualization. At issue here is the question of how the development of music television relates to the ideological aspects of changing patterns of production and consumption in broadcasting.

As noted in chapter 2, the development in the 1980s of a music television industry (both distribution networks such as MTV and the production companies who make the clips) was a result of considerable expansion of broadcast hours in television. This growth occurred in markets established beyond the remit of the traditional "over the air" networks and broadcasters, initially through cable television (in the United States) and home video (in the United Kingdom) and later extending into direct satellite broadcasting and new kinds of "independent" television services (Channel Four in the United Kingdom, local nonaffiliated stations and the Fox network in the United States). These institutional changes were part of a process that permeated political and social change during the 1980s: the rejection of state funding, regulation, or control in favor of "free market" mechanisms.[8] In such a climate, state funding for the expansion of the television industry was never likely. Indeed, in both the United Kingdom and the United States the state was pressuring publicly funded television to find alternative sources of revenue.[9] The only possible mechanisms for financing the new services were therefore advertising revenue and direct sales/rental fees. The "independent" nonaffiliates in the United States (and, to a limited extent, Channel Four) have used advertising revenue, even to the extent of screening a new kind of sponsored programming—the thirty-minute commercial (see Hayes & Rotfield, 1989). Direct sales and rentals operate for satellite broadcasting and home video. Cable television services usually survive on some combination of the two.

What is important here is the extent to which television in the 1980s broke with the traditions of "public service broadcasting," the ideals of which have been usefully summarized by Asa Briggs (1979) as follows: (a) no profit motive, (b) national service, (c) centralized control, and (d) "high standards." The marketplace organization of the new television services was designed as part of a package of "entertainment-led" cultural enterprises that were an explicit part of the project of Thatcherism (see Golding & Murdock, 1983) and that clearly broke most, if not all, of the public service ideals (see Ang, 1991; Scannell, 1990). In the United States, the Fox network (owned by Rupert Murdoch) represents the most striking overall break with that tradition yet attempted in network/broadcast television.

This political/economic context is extremely important for any understanding of music television that interprets ideological analysis as an exercise in locating the places where meaning serves power. For all the sophisticated work done in recent years on theories of subjectivity, very little has been said about the different ways in which contemporary culture attempts to restructure the subject-as-citizen (the public service model) along the lines of the subject-as-consumer (the "free market" model). This is especially important for advertising-funded services, where the viewer will constantly be addressed as a potential consumer, and where (especially in the United States, with its tradition of nonintervention in commercial activities) that address is likely to "leak" into the programming. "Commercials," writes Todd Gitlin (1987), "get us accustomed to thinking of ourselves and behaving as a market rather than a public" (p. 513; see also White, 1987). Many critics have observed that advertising sells more than individual commodities and services — it also promotes consumerism itself, and may constitute an ideology to the extent that it implies marketplace solutions to all social problems (Williams, 1980: 170-95). The development of "product placement" is also significant here, as is the growth of sponsorship in televised sports (see Whannel, 1986, 1988).

What is especially important about this is not that advertising may be ideological, but that the development of music television should be seen as an instance in the shift of power away from public service institutions. As Nicholas Garnham (1979b) wrote in the late 1970s:

> The current struggle throughout Western Europe, of which the post-Annan debate about a 4th UK television channel and local radio is only one instance, concerning the balance of force between commercial and non-commercial broadcasting, is an ideological struggle (ie, commercials, as an instance of signifying practice, carry a specific ideology); a political struggle over the forms and powers of the bourgeois state and its relationship to civil society, and an economic struggle by surplus capital seeking new areas for valorization. (p. 132)

In this context the development of new kinds of programming that are not only advertising funded but actually constitute advertising is of obvious significance. Music television services have a parallel in the way product placement expanded to the point where, in the U.S. market, children's programming was developed that was designed primarily to sell toys (see Engelhart, 1986). Like the thirty-minute commercial, the sponsorship of televised sports, and the new children's shows, music television delivers the message that messages must deliver. It is a form of television that inherently positions the viewer as consumer and that suggests the universality of the sales pitch (see Jhally, 1990: 93-102); this is true even where advertising revenue is not a factor (for instance, when public television screens video clips, or on the Video Jukebox Network, where viewers pay directly for their selections).

Garnham's position is based on a Marxist account of intellectual labor that argues that the disproportionate distribution of surplus value works ideologically (as well as economically) because it enables those in power (and the argument might be made about race or gender here, every bit as much as class) to employ intellectuals. The most blatant example of this is perhaps the funding of "think tanks" for policy development (which in their turn feed into a bias in media coverage, through their kudos as "expert" opinion), where the production of ideas in the service of the working class is hampered by a relative lack of funds. This is not to endorse the idea (and it is not advanced by Garnham, Murdock, or anyone else in the field of political economy) that this phenomenon magically "explains" ideology. However, it can be seen as a significant factor in the social production of ideas, since ideas involve intellectual work that needs to be paid for.

Applied to music television and the growth of post-public service broadcasting, this approach is suggestive because the kind of intellectuals who were employed to develop television programs in the 1980s were clearly very different from the people who were paid to do this in the more paternal pre-1970s era. It is not "reductionism" to suggest that this connects with the economic; it is an empirically observable and well-documented fact that the culture of a television institution and its resultant programming has something to do with the manner in which it is regulated and funded (see Burns, 1977; Altman, 1987; Garnham, 1978; Gitlin, 1983; Schlesinger, 1978). Read in the light of Garnham's application of *The German Ideology*, the sociological observations about broadcasting institutions can be understood in terms of a wide-ranging struggle over ideology that takes place inside the institutions of the state. In the case of music television services, the close fusion of programming and advertising, the mixing of promotional and critical/informational rhetorics, and the culture of cynicism that often comes out in the programming itself (see chapter 6) are clearly effects of its economic organization. Had the struggle identified by Garnham in the 1970s turned out differently, then we might expect that music television would be positioned differently in relation to ideology.[10]

Dave Laing's (1985a) comments on the lack of autonomy involved in music production are relevant here. Both the clips themselves and the television services that depend upon them remain highly dependent on music industry funding. Thus, in Garnham's terms, the "intellectuals" who are ultimately responsible for music television are not professional broadcasters, but sales and promotional staff in music industry corporations. It is important and necessary, therefore, to think about the professional ideologies that operate in the music business. The broader point I am making here, however, is that this represents a shift in institutional control that is intimately tied to wider political and economic changes. Politically speaking, music television must be seen as an ideological phenomenon through its capacity to extend the social relations of the marketplace and erode public service notions of culture. Of course, its meaning may not be reduced to this (other meanings are also present), but that is no reason to ignore or deny the importance of the economic–ideological nexus at this particular level of analysis.

More specifically, I wish to expand on the political economy of music television by using the work of Nick Browne (1987), who has studied the made-for-TV movie through the concept of a televisual "supertext." Browne proposes that a vital link between political economy and text analysis can be made if we consider all the material transmitted during a television broadcast as one text—that is to say, the advertisements, trailers, continuity, and station identification materials constitute, alongside the program itself, a televisual supertext. Browne then identifies coherence in the supertext at two levels of linkage between programming and commercials. First, in an allusion to Freud's comments on the *fort-da* game, he suggests that television's fragmentary and segmented form (which John Ellis, 1982b, has analyzed extensively) creates temporary disequilibriums that are resolved through the restoration of the "lost object"—the commodities advertised in commercial breaks: "Though interruptive, the ad, in its role as agent of symbolic restitution for a lack in the narrative proper, constructs a kind of narrative pleasure that assures formal resolution and confers on the represented object the status of good object" (p. 596). Second, Browne argues that the tacit contract between viewers and advertisers (that we will agree to be exposed to a sales pitch in exchange for the experience of "free" television) constitutes a naturalizing discourse that imports the alienated relations of production into our "leisure" time—a position that is very close to the arguments made by the Frankfurt School concerning the commodification of our so-called free time:[11]

> In "free" television, the general possibility of "entertainment" is exchanged for the willingness of the audience to be subjected to a view of something specific—the objects displayed in ads. . . . The literal circuit of exchange is closed when the viewer, through the relay of the represented object, purchases the actual object in whose price the invisible cost of the motivating ad is hidden. The actual commodity, then, is the ultimate referent of the television discourse. . . . Television presents and sustains consumption as an answer to the problems of everyday life. It articulates and, at the same time, dissolves the difference between the "supertext" and "supermarket." (Browne, 1987: 596)[12]

I do wish to lodge one reservation here, concerning the extent to which the "contract" between advertisers and audiences must be seen as a battleground: a struggle that is played out, for instance, through strategies such as exposing/ridiculing the commercials in conversation and through new technologies, such as the remote control unit—which allows us to consume advertising-funded television and radio programming while "zapping" away from, or muting out, the commercials—and VCRs—which allow for "zipping" through the commercial breaks with the fast-forward button (for a useful summary of relevant research on this topic, see Lull, 1982). However, applied to the development of music television, these arguments are extremely pertinent.

The notion of the commodity as a "lost object" that restores order to an imperfect world has dual applications in relation to music television, for while Browne's argument can be applied to, say, the advertisements on MTV (Stridex pimple cream as the magical solution to the romantic loss dwelt upon in countless clips), it is also highly suggestive of the relation between the clip and the commodity it promotes. As I showed in chapters 4 and 5, logos, album designs, and star imagery are central elements of the video clip, and may thus function as the clue to the object-to-be-restored within each segment.

Sometimes this device is actually narrativized. For instance, the Nelson clip AFTER THE RAIN opens with a male teenager crying in his room while in the next room his father argues with his mother. However, he then escapes into a fictional Nelson world, via a huge poster on his wall (a not-so-subtle example of product placement within what is already a commercial), where he finds (to borrow Richard Dyer's, 1977, terms) energy, abundance, and community in Nelson's performance of the song "After the Rain." As is often the case in music videos, this diegetic "fantasy" turns out to be "real": a feather obtained in the "fantasy" is present in his room when the teenager returns to the "real" world. (The same emblem is used, with a similar narrative device, in Pink Floyd's LEARNING TO FLY.) A similar trope is used in Poison's NOTHING BUT A GOOD TIME. Here, a male teenager is washing dishes in a restaurant while listening to rock music on the radio, when his boss enters to berate him for working too slowly. Disgruntled and upset, he escapes through a door and into an alternative reality, where Poison are performing their song. On his return to the kitchen, the dishes have magically been cleaned during his absence. ZZ Top's videos have often used this same technique, through the magical agent of the key (which contains the "ZZ" of the group's name) to their car, the Eliminator. In both GIMME ALL YOUR LOVIN' and LEGS this key/car provides a young male with access to sex, romance, and escape from his small-town life. Nick Browne's argument could hardly be made more explicitly relevant than it is in these clips.

Of course, this link takes on even greater significance when current songs (and perhaps their video imagery) are used in television commercials—for instance, in the Genesis Michelob spot that used "Tonight, Tonight, Tonight" or in Robert Plant's Coca-Cola ad, which used "Tall Cool One." During *MTV 10*, in November 1991, a commercial for Chic jeans raided the imagery for Chris Isaak's WICKED GAME clip, so that the product seemed to be the "solution" to the romantic angst of that song/clip.

Music video clips enhance television's ability to forge this ideological nexus between texts and commodities, since their narratives can stage dramas that offer the star/musical object as "solution" to a much greater degree than can a televised performance of a song. Furthermore, the development of dedicated music television services such as MTV opens up possibilities for programming that highlight consumption, through VJ/ host presentational material (an essential part of the "supertext" of music television), complementary star profiles and interviews (MTV's *Rock-line*), news and reviews of new tours, movies, videos and albums, and celebratory documentaries (such as MTV's *Rockumentary*).

Nick Browne argues that the political economy paradigm is especially important in the context of American television, whereas the British "cultural studies" school is more suitable for a broadcasting system in which commercial mechanisms are not predominant. However, as Garnham (1979a) has pointed out, it is a weakness in the arguments of Stuart Hall (1977) and others that their overarching theory of the media-ideology nexus tends to privilege state-funded and -regulated institutions during a period when private-enterprise commodity-based and advertising-funded media forms are in the ascendant. Thus, Browne's use of political economy is in fact highly relevant outside the context of U.S. broadcasting, including in Western Europe, where services such as MTV Europe and BSkyB have done precisely what the political economists predicted—they have extended market relations, the globalization of U.S. media forms, and the commodification of culture still further, in this case into "youth" culture and into public service broadcasting.

I have dwelt upon these highly generalized political economic arguments because it seems to me that they are currently undervalued in cultural studies analysis, for reasons that remain unconvincing—for instance, in the twin assumptions that political economic arguments are "pessimistic" and reductionist. (As I will show, political economic arguments do not necessarily lead to pessimistic diagnoses, but where they do, this cannot be a valid reason for disagreeing with them.) That is to say, the objection to such arguments is that they tell us too little about what particular television programs mean, what use-values are obtained in the consumption of popular culture, and so on. I agree that these counterarguments place some limits on what a political economy of the media can teach us. Nelson's AFTER THE RAIN is not only a little lesson in consumer behavior. However, to argue that diverse audience readings and real use-values must also be taken into account is not to argue that a politics of individual consumption, based around the promotion of market relations (in this case, a particular product), does not also operate. Indeed, to suggest that the former actually cancels out the latter is every bit as reductionist and simplistic as the most brazen economism.

We need to see popular culture as truly contradictory—not in some glib sense as meaning merely "complicated," but in the more precise sense that it works politically through disunity, at a number of levels, any or all of which might be in operation at different times, in different places, and in relation to different consumers. In the analysis of ideology, in consideration of how meaning serves power, it is transparently the case that during a period of ascendancy for free-enterprise ideologies, when the clusters of political attitudes embodied in Thatcherism and Reaganism sought to roll back state influence in favor of the marketplace, cultural critics need to pay attention to where and how that ideology might be reproduced, and perhaps promoted, in the mass media. This is all the more so because Browne's analysis suggests that the ideas advanced by the television supertext ultimately address the consumerist practices of everyday life.

The World Spins

A fully materialist account of ideological production in music television needs, however, to move from these general questions to particular issues, chiefly concerning production practices and professional ideologies.[13] Although I have shown, on the one hand, that music television is far from "depthless," and, on the other, that it not only *has* a history, but is a *part* of economically structured developments within the Anglo-American media system, the question of how to understand its representations is still somewhat open. If, as I have argued above, the ideological significance of the appeal to the viewer-as-consumer has been underestimated, that is not the whole story. The political implications of music television cannot be reduced to this one, very broad, point—and not only because other meanings may be in play, but because consumerism itself is a contradictory phenomenon (see the essay titled "The Culture Gap" in Hall, 1988a).

Thinking through the impact of music television in pop music culture, I want to take up Edward Said's (1985) demand that cultural analysis consider not just the more esoteric questions of narrative form, and so forth, but also some of the more immediate issues regarding political power. One way to do so would be to consider, for instance, ways in which music television has explicitly tackled political questions: for instance, in David Bowie's LET'S DANCE, Midnight Oil's BEDS ARE BURNING and BLUE SKY MINE, Michelle Shocked's ON THE GREENER SIDE, Metallica's ONE, or

Public Enemy's FIGHT THE POWER, or in music television programs such as some of the MTV programming considered in chapter 6. However, many of the questions of representation raised in such an analysis would merely tell us what we already know: that music television tends to reproduce many of the values of pop, rock, and rap music, and to the extent that the music, songs, and star-texts embody values that are Romantic, liberal, countercultural, alternative, and (very occasionally) oppositional, so does music television.

I want to finish this chapter on a more specific note, by pointing out some of the particular ways in which music television itself intervenes in the ideological climate of popular music. To return to postmodernism one last time, it has to be said that the approach offers us very little guidance in this respect, and this is partly because (as I suggested in chapter 1) its criticism is often merely a displaced, nonrational celebration of music itself. Despite their otherwise quite sophisticated arguments, the postmodernists tend to become strangely crude when the political dimension is confronted. For instance, despite a promise to break with the formalism of film theory, Kaplan concludes her discussion of representations of women by hailing the clips of Tina Turner on the grounds that they foreground the question of representation.

In more concrete terms, it is evident that production practices in music television are responsible for *particular* shifts in the representation of popular music, three of which must be seen as moving in a more conservative ideological direction. With regard to representations of sexuality, it has been argued by Sut Jhally, in his documentary tape *Dreamworlds*,[14] that MTV works systematically to deny women subjectivity and to construct them through the patriarchal discourse of "nymphomania" as ever-available objects in an endlessly repetitive male adolescent fantasy world.[15] Despite the presence of strong female images in music videos, it is hard to fault the essential truth in this position; indeed, it is so striking that even such postmodern critics as E. Ann Kaplan are forced to take account of it. This construction of woman-as-object was discussed in narrative terms in chapter 4. Central to my argument here, however, is the fact that this routine display of body parts via fragmentation and objectification is a technique more firmly rooted in advertising than in popular music. That is to say, while acknowledging that the techniques of fragmentation, objectification, and violation have been present in pop and rock music for many decades,[16] I believe it is necessary also to ask what specific changes music television has brought about in the representation of sexuality. Here I think it is evident that a political economic study of the topic should alert us to the increasing prevalence of these techniques, which arise out of the advertising function of the promotional clip.

Again, this is not to deny the gaps in this account, which occur every bit as much in relation to images of men as they do to transgressive representations in videos by Madonna or Pat Benatar. Robert Walser (1989) has written convincingly about male sexuality, pointing out that in heavy metal video clips the routinely sexist display of women's bodies is often accompanied by disruptive and transgressive images of masculinity, for instance, in the androgynous costuming and makeup of groups such as Kiss, Mötley Crüe, and Poison. Lisa Lewis (1987a, 1987b, 1990) has also made an important intervention in an effort to redress the dismissal of artists such as Madonna and Cyndi Lauper; her arguments do not, however, address the issue of how men and boys consume these and other images, whose "preferred meanings" explicitly draw on conventions of soft-core pornography and "cheesecake" popular imagery.[17]

Second, I want take up a point made by Curran and Sparks (1991) in their argument that a political economy of culture requires an analysis of a *repertory of texts*. This is especially relevant to music television, in that one debate about the form concerns how the high costs and centralized control (budgets are usually decided by record companies) involved in music video production may have adversely effected diversity. In terms of representations of ethnicity, it is a serious problem that clips for black artists tend to have significantly lower budgets than those for white artists (see Newman, 1991). This point links with the argument of chapter 3, because the process of stitching images into the music on the sound track requires long (and expensive) hours of editing time that are unavailable to lower-budget productions. To that extent, music television has become a powerful force for consolidation, rather than diversity, within the music industry.

Third, there is the issue of how pop stardom is represented. Music television offers a very particular, highly controlled version of events that contrasts with other possible ways of representing the star-text. On stage, in press interviews, and in documentaries (for instance, D. A. Pennebaker's *Depeche Mode 101*), stars often step out of the star-text and are revealed in a less flattering light (Dave Gahan of Depeche Mode using his power as a star to threaten an employee with dismissal for speaking in the wrong manner to a member of the band) and/or use the opportunity to critique the music industry itself—for example, Chris Heath's (1990) account of the Pet Shop Boys on tour, *Literally*. Music videos, on the other hand, in common with album covers and advertisements, engage in a particular kind of *affirmative vision* that usually denies space for a critical view of the industry. This is not at all surprising, but it is important, given that video clips are now one of the major channels through which mass-mediated meanings are circulated.

The issue of professional ideologies suggests two "breaks" on the conservative shifts outlined above. First, it is apparent from the analysis presented in chapters 5 and 6 that the Romantic aesthetic that continues to inform (and sometimes dominate) popular music creates spaces for oppositional texts and readings. In chapter 6 I showed how this created not just the *possibility*, but in fact the *necessity* for liberal/Romantic discourses on MTV. The development of MTV is very important in this regard. To the extent that MTV sets itself off from "normal" television and attempts to promote a rock "attitude," it has been far more resistant to censorship than has, say, the BBC (for examples of BBC censorship, see Street, 1985: 114-15). Where the BBC engaged in massive censorship during the Gulf War (banning dozens of records because they might allude to the conflict, for instance),[18] MTV screened GIVE PEACE A CHANCE. Because MTV is a dedicated service, committed to the promotion of an "alternative" culture (however cynically or self-servingly), it has an investment in risk taking that public service and commercial networks alike do not share. One result of this is that MTV has (in selected instances) opened up the political agenda on television, by using gatekeeping criteria that reflect the values of rock and roll rather than the values of a paternalist broadcasting institution. Second, professional ideologies in broadcast journalism—while they are by no means pervasive in music television—do surface (for instance, on *MTV News*) and thus open up a liberal space in which critical distance can sometimes occur between the music television text and the commodities it promotes.

This in its turn opens up the question of power relations in the music industry, where corporate/commercial concerns are dominant. The development of music video clips is interesting in this respect in that it represents a shift in the power to visualize music away from the musicians and their managers and toward record companies and media conglomerates. In other words, to refer back to the argument made in chapter 2, the promotional job of performing and visualizing music that once occurred in a concert or club performance left the creation of visual meaning to the musicians, their management, and (in the more elaborate shows) lighting and perhaps set designers. In the age of music television that task is increasingly taken over by the record company, through their control of the music video budget and through their economic relation with the video director. However, this is a dynamic process: one response (Madonna, Public Enemy, the Pet Shop Boys) has been to attempt to take control of this image-making machinery, so that music television then becomes an opportunity to articulate critical views through the mass media to an extent that was not previously possible (for example, Public Enemy's *Fight the Power—Live* long-form tape, Madonna's *Truth or Dare* movie, the Pet Shop Boys' DJ CULTURE video clip).

What this suggests is an increasing *convergence*, throughout the 1980s, of the field of popular music and popular television. Politically, this shift is far from one-dimensional. As I have already noted, the deregulation of television may also open up political spaces for oppositional messages that would not otherwise occur—for instance, due to the ideological policing that occurs at the BBC. Most interestingly, the late 1980s were a period of crisis for television in the United States, because of increasing competition among the networks, cable, and home video, and this led to some experiments with "risk taking" that defy an account of the political economy of the media that draws only pessimistic conclusions.[19] In an effort to coax viewers back to network television, U.S. broadcasters tried to innovate, and in doing so opened up prime time to a variety of aesthetic (*Twin Peaks, Cop Rock*) and political (*The Simpsons, In Living Color, The Morton Downey, Jr., Show*) experiments that broke with naturalism/realism and with the narrow terms of political "consensus." MTV must be seen in these terms as well as as a symptom of an expanding new American media world order.[20] Thus, as noted in chapter 6, MTV (and various individual video clips) searched for a new television audience, and in doing so sometimes offered a counterhegemonic critique of established power relations.

This economic drive combines with the more discursive forms of resistance inherent in the Romantic ideologies of rock music (or with the more explicitly oppositional social exposé that is common in rap and hip-hop)[21] to provide us with the beginnings of a materialist explanation of how mediations work in the production of music television to produce oppositional spaces as well as further opportunities for ideological enterprise. *The Simpsons* is a very pertinent example here: it generated music videos (DO THE BARTMAN, DEEP DEEP TROUBLE) that, like the cartoon television program, offer a child's-eye view that critiques the adult world in ways that are far from politically innocent.[22]

It is possible to see, through the three key absences that I have pointed to in postmodern analyses of the form, that there is an alternative (and, I would argue, more convincing) agenda that needs to be addressed. This agenda situates music television not as a completely new kind of television, but as a particular development that can be explained historically— partly in the terms set out in the political economy of culture. In its own referencing of music and popular cultural history, music television mixes "pastiche" with other kinds of address that (along with the anchoring mechanisms identified in previous chapters) demand a cultural studies analysis that engages the question of preferred meanings and that assumes that while different parts of the audience will be positioned *differently*, music television viewers are nonetheless still *positioned*. Finally, then, this allows us to consider political questions concerning the impact of music television upon the ideological formation of pop music culture. Contrary to the postmodern literature on this topic, music television does not, generally speaking, indulge in a rupture with the Symbolic; nor does it defy our understanding or attempt to elude logic and rationality through its refusal to make sense. Far from constituting a radical break with the social processes of meaning production, music television constantly reworks themes (work, school, authority, romance, poverty, and so on) that are deeply implicated in the question of how meaning serves (or resists) power.

Concluding Thoughts

This book addresses two constituencies, one an academic grouping, the other less campus-bound. Rather than summarize and rehearse the arguments of the book as a whole, I want to end by making some comments of a more general nature on the political and social significance of music television, taking into account some of the more public concerns of the second audience. (Of course, I am well aware that many of us feel at home in both camps. If only one could take that for granted at all times.)

Before reengaging those issues, however, I want to clarify what I am saying about postmodernism. The final chapter of this book builds on the preceding analyses to identify three gaps in the postmodern analysis of music television: in the account of "pastiche," in the absence of historical context for shifting ideological forms (especially in "patterns of programming"), and with regard to debates about actual, lived social relations of power. I have tried to advance and reframe that debate, first, by showing how the use of textual incorporation in music videos extends well beyond the fragments of pastiche. Ranging from radical social criticism through to promotional appeals of various kinds, these reappropriations are often far from blank, and certainly provide preferred reading positions that defy the assumptions about "depthlessness" that characterize most accounts of pastiche. Second, I have also demonstrated how the economic and regulatory basis of contemporary television can be used to explain some of the textual features of music television programming, most notably through changing patterns of programming and in the relations between pop commodities and the music television "supertext."

These arguments suggest at least a need for a reformulation of postmodern approaches to music television. However, some parts of the argument might be incorporated into a more informed postmodern investigation into music television. Pastiche, for instance, is sometimes utilized as a subset of an ironic discourse that is read as essentially postmodern; therefore my criticisms, alongside a demonstration of how textual reappropriation may be read more thoroughly, could be mobilized on behalf of a postmodern criticism that is interested in providing an account of the actually operative, historical mediations that structure the relations between a postmodern society and its culture. This is the second way in which my arguments could be used in relation to postmodernism: as an attempt to fill in some of the missing links in the argument— although parts of the argument, as I have shown, have to be rejected rather than revised. (Once again, I would stress that this critique is not aimed at postmodern theory in general, but takes issue with the specific attempt to apply these ideas to music television.)

In general, however, my conclusions about postmodern analysis are quite negative. My argument as a whole demonstrates that when music television is understood in relation to music and the music industry, the arguments of postmodernism falter. It shows how music television makes sense (not nonsense), both for consumers of pop and for the institutions that control its production. It would be foolish to deny that music videos and their distribution services break many of the rules of what MTV likes to call "*regular* TV." In its disruptive editing, its new postproduction computer effects, its modes of address, and so on, music television differs from prime time. My point (and this is the essential link between the two riffs I set into motion at the outset, pleasure and political economy, music and politics) is that most of these changes make perfect sense *in relation to contemporary popular music*.

But what kind of sense does music television make, politically speaking? It follows from what I have just stated that the politics of music television is essentially the politics of pop music itself. The kinds of intelligent discussion and analysis applied to the contradictions of pop politics that are attempted for instance by Simon Frith (1983), Greil Marcus (1976), Fred and Judy Vermorel (1985), Dave Laing (1985a), Lawrence Grossberg (1988), and Susan McClary (1991) are highly relevant to any understanding of how music television combines discourses of Romanticism, of modernist irony, of scopophilia and voyeurism, of compulsive consumerist obsession, of social action, and of temporary escapes from everyday life and its various oppressions.

As for the particular impact of music video itself, in the preceding chapter I tried to show how there are a number of *specific* areas where it can be shown that music television, and MTV in particular, has a negative impact, at least from the perspective of left/liberal and feminist politics. To be precise, these problems lie in the areas of music television's relation to consumerism, the climate of deregulation in contemporary broadcasting (I still believe, for instance, that the BBC is more intelligent, more fun, and more sexy than MTV), and the specific ways in which the female body is displayed. Historically, it has also been argued that MTV in particular has played a regressive role in suppressing black music—an argument that was briefly alluded to during *MTV 10* in November 1991, when Spike Lee appeared on screen to note that MTV "seriously avoided black music" in its early days. As noted in chapter 6, there have been important changes since then. However, Sut Jhally (1990) makes the important point that any advertising-funded services (such as MTV) necessarily underrepresents the tastes of less affluent consumers, who in most cases include the black community.

However, I do *not* endorse the view, and this book has not set out to demonstrate, that the "problem" with music television is that it commodifies pop music. I want to end, then, not with a "defense" of music television or MTV, but with an attack—an attack against one-dimensional notions of what this new form is supposed to have done to popular culture.

Sut Jhally (1990) has assisted me here, since he has outlined very clearly for us four areas of public concern regarding the impact of MTV (although my argument applies to music television in a more general sense). The first is the issue of whether or not music television has negatively influenced the signing of new acts. There are, I believe, at least three problems in posing the issue in these terms, and I hope that pop consumers who have bothered to read this far will ponder them. First, the extent to which most acts can be "successful" with music videos has less to do with how they *look* (ask Warrant, for instance), and far more to do with the available budget, the skills of the video director, and so on. The notion that only good-looking "videogenic" acts are signed these days is surely a myth. This is not to deny that looks *are* important, espe-

cially for women artists. However, this has always been so, since long
before MTV. And, furthermore, the conflation between "looks" and
"video"contains an important contradiction. Critics of MTV maintain
that videos *construct* false images of physical "perfection" (which is true)
and at the same time suggest that this mass-mediated construct restricts
musical diversity. However, since the video image *is* a fabrication (like
the publicity photograph, the album cover shot, advertising imagery),
the *actual* "looks" provided by artists are less important than we sometimes imagine. Second, to the extent that *some* acts aimed at *some* sections
of the pop market are signed for how they look, we should not make the
mistake of thinking this applies only to teeny pop audiences (don't Bruce
Springsteen's looks matter, too?). Nor should we imagine that this is a
post-MTV phenomenon. It is not, as I showed in chapter 2 of this book.
Third, if bands now submit demo videotapes to record companies instead of demo audiotapes, they do so because they have access to the
technology, and in hopes their videos will have the same impact that photographs once had. Anyone who thinks that videos have *introduced* a visual element into the signing of bands should see the letter that Bob Last
(of Fast Products) sent me in 1980, when I mailed him a tape of my band
without a photo. You never could get signed without being *seen*, and
video demos are simply the new shortcut, not an Orwellian plot hatched
by MTV Networks. By far the more important technological development is the high-fidelity and sonic complexity available through modern
recording techniques (CDs, twenty-four-track studios, DAT master
tapes)—this, more than video, has upped the stakes and inflated the costs
of selling a new act to a record company, because it has significantly
raised the ceiling of what a "professional" recording sounds like.

Even to the extent that video-friendly acts may have been signed since
the growth of music video, the results are not necessarily negative. Jhally
cites the example of Cyndi Lauper. If it is true that the artist who went on
to put "She Bop" (a song that pays homage to female masturbation) on
the charts got there because of video, then clearly we have something to
thank music television for. Indeed, if we consider that three of the areas
of pop most closely associated with videos are the New Pop (from ABC
to the Pet Shop Boys), the neofeminist pop divas (the culmination being
Madonna, of course), and rap (Public Enemy crossing over to a white
audience with a message of black power, partly via *Yo! MTV Raps*), then
it becomes clear that music television is not without blessings that are
both aesthetic and political.

Second, there is the issue of composition. The question of whether music television introduces visuals into pop production was briefly discussed in chapter 3. The only additional point I want to make here is to question whether we automatically assume that it is a bad thing for writers to envisage video images as they write songs. There are examples (the The's *Infected* long-form tape, for instance) of highly creative and politically interesting interplay of music and video production techniques.

Third, Jhally points to the other side of this coin, the question of the impact on the pop audience, and states rather boldly that "the visual interpretation of the song tends to fix the *meaning* that it comes to have for the audience" (p. 99). This is a common argument, but there is almost no evidence for it. In chapters 1 and 3 I tried to raise some of the counterarguments. Only new research can answer the question definitively, but I do want to argue very emphatically that it simply will not do to pose these questions as if prevideo music were image free.

Fourth, there is the question of the general impact of music television on popular culture as a whole, including the politics of its consumerism. I am very sympathetic to Jhally's suggestion that music video (and MTV in particular) works ideologically against nonmarket solutions to social problems, and that, therefore, like all advertising, it works *in part* (in this *particular area*) to sustain existing power relations.[1] Nick Browne's (1987) argument about the televisual "supertext" was deployed in chapter 7 to suggest a development of that argument.

However, even in this area there is some ambiguity. In chapters 2 and 7 I have tried to make very *specific* arguments about music television's relation to use-value and exchange-value, and to the practices of consumerism. I would also go even further than Jhally (or perhaps anyone else) in seeing MTV as a master manipulator. But that is different from making the often-heard complaint that music video has "sold out" the hitherto unblemished soul of rock and roll. Such arguments are nonsensical. Rock and pop were commodified practices of mass mediation long before the introduction of music television.

One area where music television is more clearly implicated in a reactionary vision of consumerism concerns the simplistic and banal way in which gender roles are used to sell products. I think that many of the comparisons between music television and pornography are misplaced, not least of all because the politics of the latter are a good deal more complex than many critics assume (see, for instance, Ross, 1989; Williams, 1989). However, it is clear that the shortcuts used by video directors to get the attention of the male audience have rendered vast tracts of music video uninteresting and/or offensive (far more offensive than pornography, in my view),[2] and that this is one very obvious problem that is specific to video itself, since the opportunities for a particular type of boring voyeurism are so much more in evidence here than in previous forms of pop promotion. It is also clear to me that this is one area where services such as MTV are engaging in bad faith when they claim to be powerless to control the content of video clips. MTV, *Top of the Pops, Friday Night Videos*, and so on have clear standards about, for instance, the promotion of violence, and these standards *are* enforceable; it then follows that the distribution networks could also exert influence on the promotion of images of women that reinforce existing gender power relations.

At issue here is not how explicit the clips are, nor even the pleasures of voyeurism, fetishism, and so on. And the nub of this debate is most certainly *not* the question of violence against women (which, as with pornography, is found more often in prime time and at the movie mall than in music video). What is at stake here is the routine denial of subjectivity to women in music videos and their repeated display as helpers, assistants, objects of lust, groupies, backup singers, and so on, without sufficient programming that redresses these representations.[3] (Men appear as objects, but *also* as actors.) In that respect, the common comparison between MTV and porn is in fact insulting to pornographers.

MTV itself has changed a good deal in its first decade, as I have shown. Far from being an ahistorical form with timeless features, MTV in fact resembles other areas of television and mass culture in its need to react to shifts in technologies, funding, policy-making, and so on. In chapter 6 I showed how particular changes at MTV Networks led the service to change programming and scheduling policies. I also offered an explanation for the contradictory politics of MTV, stressing the importance of "the other MTV" (in its socially conscious, sometimes liberal, appeals), which rock critics and postmodern theorists alike have tended to neglect. This argument should also act as a counterweight to the often heard but hardly ever argued belief in rock culture that television is inherently uninteresting, trivial, and dumb.

It is often suggested that MTV and/or music video is to blame for all manner of cultural phenomena, from *Miami Vice* to *Flashdance* to CNN to McDonald's commercials that feature rap music. Here again, we have to be careful. Apocryphal or not, the story is that *Miami Vice* was sold to NBC on the basis of its description as "MTV Cops." Unfortunately for

MTV's detractors, however, *Miami Vice* was not just innovative but also rather interesting, both politically and aesthetically, and hardly constitutes an effective argument for MTV's deleterious impact on the body pop-politic. In any case, questions of cause and effect are a good deal more complex than the average *Newsweek* cover story would have us believe. If MTV and *Dirty Dancing* and *Miami Vice* have certain features in common, it is probably because each speaks to shifts in Anglo-American popular culture (as Grossberg, 1987, implies), and not because MTV possesses some irresistible power to invade and transform other cultural institutions. One obvious way in which these examples function as a cultural symptom is that each expresses elements of rock music's new centrality in "mainstream" Western culture. This, obviously enough, is a mixed blessing.

I have argued in this book that music television must be understood in relation to the music industry and the music it produces. This is because of the importance of the contexts of both production and consumption. The circuit of exchange outlined in chapter 2 made this evident: without a successful encounter with the audience for music, there is no funding for promotional video clips. Therefore, we need to keep thinking about two central issues. On the one hand, the nature of the music television text (not just individual clips, but also long-form collections and dedicated music television services, such as MTV) arises out of the organization of the popular music industry and reproduces both its economic imperatives and its dominant critical discourses (e.g., Romanticism). On the other hand, the reception of music television is deeply rooted in the audience's involvement in pop music and its surrounding, ancillary practices (other media sites and media representations of pop).

It follows from this critique that analysis of music television must be grounded in an understanding of how pop music texts function: this is an *economic* as well as an aesthetic issue. In chapter 2, I stressed the essentially promotional function of pop performances. This point demonstrates the fundamental *continuity* of music television with practices inside the music industry. I showed how and why music videos emerged, not as an aberration, but as an outgrowth of this promotional function. The particular timing had as much to do with changing ideologies and technologies within the music industry as it did with the (equally necessary) search for new programming that occurred within the television industry.

What is going to be interesting, both politically and aesthetically, in the future development of pop music is how the current generation of musicians and consumers *react* to music video, whether or not videos can become economically independent of their promotional function, what kinds of competition emerge to challenge the cultural dominance of MTV, and how the new technologies of music production and consumption negotiate the sound-vision relation that has *always* been at the heart of popular music.

Music Television Time Line

The purpose of this time line is to help fill in some of the historical developments in music television and some of the possible forms that have been viewed as antecedents of the form. It is an aid to teaching/learning about music television. It is *not* a "history" of music television, nor is it even a full chronology. It does not attempt to trace the "influences" upon music video. What is actually *explained* in chronological accounts of the "evolution" of music television? Is history just "one goddam thing after another"?

Sources for the time line include Marcus (1980), Dellar (1981), Ehrenstein and Reed (1982), Shore (1985), Blacknell (1985), Berg (1987), Viera (1987), Denisoff (1988), and McNeil (1991).

1921   Oskar Von Fischinger begins making animated films synchronized to jazz and classical music, in Germany.

1927   *The Jazz Singer* (starring Al Jolson) is the world's first "talkie."

1934   Fischinger produces "Komposition in Blau."

1940   Fischinger works on Disney's *Fantasia*.

1941–47   Panoram Soundies produced by the Mills Novelty Co.

1952   *Bandstand* debuts on WFIL-TV in Philadelphia (August). The show features Soundies-like "concept" clips, made by George Snader.

1953   *The Wild One* (starring Marlon Brando).

Teleclub, first BBC "youth" program, debuts (October).

1955   Bill Haley & the Comets perform "Rock Around the Clock" in *The Blackboard Jungle*.

Rebel without a Cause (starring James Dean, directed by Nicholas Ray).

1956   Dick Clark begins hosting *Bandstand* (July).

Elvis Presley appears on U.S. TV for first time, on *Stage Show* (six appearances, beginning January).

Love Me Tender (Elvis Presley's cinematic debut).

Rock around the Clock (Bill Haley & the Comets).

The Girl Can't Help It (featuring Little Richard, directed by Frank Taslin).

1957   Elvis Presley appears on *The Ed Sullivan Show* (shot from waist up only).

Six-Five Special debuts on BBC TV (February).

Ricky Nelson sings for the first time on *The Adventures of Ozzie and Harriet* (April) (program debuted on ABC-TV in 1952.)

Jailhouse Rock (starring Elvis Presley).

American Bandstand makes national debut on ABC-TV.

1959   *Juke Box Jury* debuts on BBC TV.

NBC debuts *The Music Shop*, a prime time pop show.

1960   *G.I. Blues* (starring Elvis Presley).

Scopitone color video jukebox introduced in Europe.

1963   *Ready, Steady, Go!* debuts on ITV.

1964   *Top of the Pops* (BBC) begins transmission (January).

The Beatles appear on *The Ed Sullivan Show* (February).

Shindig debuts on ABC-TV (September).

Scopitone introduced into United States.

A Hard Day's Night (the Beatles, directed by Richard Lester).

1965   *Help!* (the Beatles, directed by Richard Lester).

Ready, Steady, Go! switches from lip-syncing to live studio performances.

The T.A.M.I. Show (directed by Steve Binder).

The Beatles' concert at Shea Stadium is televised.

Ferry cross the Mersey (Gerry and the Pacemakers, directed by Jeremy Summers).

Hullabaloo debuts on NBC (January).

1966   The Beatles make two clips: WE CAN WORK IT OUT and PAPER-BACK WRITER.

The Kinks make a clip: DEAD END STREET.

The Who make a clip: HAPPY JACK.

The Monkees (produced by Don Kirshner) debuts on NBC.

1967   PENNY LANE and STRAWBERRY FIELDS FOREVER clips produced for the Beatles.

Don't Look Back (directed by D. A. Pennebaker), a documentary account of Bob Dylan.

The Rolling Stones are forced to change the lyrics of "Let's Spend the Night Together" in an *Ed Sullivan Show* appearance.

The BBC produces the Beatles' "experimental" TV special *Magical Mystery Tour*.

The Beatles (and friends) perform "All You Need Is Love" live in a BBC TV transmission broadcast around the world to 200 million viewers (June).

1968   *Yellow Submarine* (Beatles cartoon movie).

The Archies cartoon show (produced by Don Kirshner) debuts.

Head (starring the Monkees, directed by Bob Raphelson and Jack Nicholson).

Colour Me Pop debuts on BBC-2. The first rock show in color on British TV, the first to emphasize "serious" rock music, it became *Disco 2* (1970) and then *The Old Grey Whistle Test* (1971).

Elvis Presley's *Elvis* TV special "comeback" (directed by Steve Binder).

1969   *Monterey Pop* (directed by D. A. Pennebaker).

One Plus One (Rolling Stones, directed by Jean-Luc Godard).

The Archies' "Sugar, Sugar" reaches No. 1, promoted by a cartoon clip (September).

1970   ABC's *Music Scene* attempts to bring "serious rock" to U.S. TV.

The Partridge Family debuts on ABC-TV.

The New Seekers make Coca-Cola TV ad, featuring the song "I'd Like to Teach the World to Sing," which becomes a worldwide hit single.

Captain Beefheart makes a one-minute TV commercial (never shown) to promote his LP *Lick My Decals Off, Baby*.

Woodstock (Oscar-winning documentary).

Gimme Shelter (Rolling Stones, directed by David and Albert Maysles).

Elvis — That's the Way It Is (documentary, directed by Denis Sanders).

Let It Be (final Beatles movie).

Performance (starring Mick Jagger, directed by Nicholas Roeg).

1971   *200 Motels* (Frank Zappa movie).

Jimi Plays Berkeley (Jimi Hendrix in concert).

Pink Floyd at Pompeii (concert film).

Soul Train goes nationwide in the United States in syndication; began in Chicago as a local program in 1970.

1972   *Concert for Bangladesh* (movie of 1971 aid concert).

David Bowie's *The Rise and Fall of Ziggy Stardust and the Spiders from Mars* introduces new elements of characterization and theatrical staging into rock music.

The Harder They Come (starring Jimmy Cliff).

Lady Sings the Blues (Diana Ross as Billie Holiday).

1973   Three rock shows debut: *In Concert* (ABC), *Midnight Special* (NBC), and *Rock Concert* (Don Kirshner, syndicated).

Mean Streets (starring Robert De Niro, directed by Martin Scorsese).

American Graffiti (directed by George Lucas).

c. 1973 Russell Mulcahy begins making video clips for Australian bands.

1974   Pink Floyd undertake highly theatrical, multimedia world tour to promote *Dark Side of the Moon*.

1975   Jon Roseman/Bruce Gowers produce BOHEMIAN RHAPSODY clip for Queen.

Bruce Gowers makes clip for Rod Stewart, HOT LEGS.

Rock Follies (British TV series about fictional female rock group, written by Howard Breton).

Tommy (directed by Ken Russell, from the Who's rock opera).

The Residents produce LAND OF 1,000 DANCES clip.

The Tubes make debut LP; their live show parodies TV.

Nightclubbing video program opens on Manhattan cable TV.

1976   Mike Nesmith (ex-Monkees) produces RIO.

Devo produce JOCKO HOMO and SECRET AGENT MAN clips.

Genesis make ROBBERY, ASSAULT AND BATTERY clip (directed by Bruce Gowers).

The Jacksons debuts on CBS.

The Man Who Fell to Earth (starring David Bowie, directed by Nicolas Roeg).

The Song Remains the Same (Led Zeppelin), featuring fictional "fantasy" sequences.

The Sex Pistols cause uproar when they use obscene language on Bill Grundy's Granada TV show.

1977   *Saturday Night Fever* (starring John Travolta).

Abba — The Movie.

1978   *The Last Waltz* (directed by Martin Scorsese) is shot in San Francisco.

The Wiz (starring Michael Jackson).

Grease (starring John Travolta and Olivia Newton-John).

Rock and Roll High School (directed by Allan Arkush).

Jubilee (directed by Derek Jarman).

Devo's *The Men Who Make the Music* anthology is first U.S. long-form video.

Kevin Godley and Lol Creme make AN ENGLISHMAN IN NEW YORK clip.

Steve Barron directs the Jam's STRANGE TOWN clip.

Notable clip: David Bowie, HEROES.

1979   *America's Top Ten* begins to play video clips.

David Bowie makes clips D.J., BOYS KEEP SWINGING, and LOOK BACK IN ANGER.

Quadrophenia (movie of rock opera by the Who).

Notable clips: Buggles, VIDEO KILLED THE RADIO STAR (Russell Mulcahy); Boomtown Rats, I DON'T LIKE MONDAYS (David Mallet).

1980   *The Great Rock and Roll Swindle* (directed by Julien Temple).

Solid Gold debuts, in syndication (September).

Blondie's *Eat to the Beat* collection is first long-form video to sell in significant numbers.

Notable clips: Devo's WHIP IT; Visage, WE FADE TO GRAY (Godley/Creme); Duran Duran's GIRLS ON FILM (Godley/Creme); David Bowie, ASHES TO ASHES (David Mallet).

1981   The Gang of Four are told they cannot say "rubbers" on TV, and walk off the set of the BBC's *Top of the Pops*.

The Decline of Western Civilization (directed by Penelope Spheeris).

The USA Network debuts *Night Flight* (March).

Home Box Office (HBO) cable network begins simulcasts of rock concerts.

MTV begins transmission (August 1). Owned by Warner-Amex. First clip: VIDEO KILLED THE RADIO STAR (Buggles).

Mike Nesmith's Pacific Arts company begins packaging clips into a half-hour show titled *Popclips*, in collaboration with Warner Cable. *Popclips* airs on Nickelodeon.

Nesmith also releases a full-length video album, *Elephant Parts*.

Jovan sponsors Rolling Stones U.S. tour (first corporate sponsorship of a major rock tour).

BBC's *Top of the Pops* bans the Police clip INVISIBLE SUN.

Notable clip: Duran Duran's HUNGRY LIKE THE WOLF (Russell Mulcahy).

1982   *Fame* (based on 1980 film directed by Alan Parker) debuts on NBC.

Mantrap (ABC, directed by Julien Temple) is first U.K. long-form music video.

Pink Floyd make a movie of *The Wall* (directed by Alan Parker, starring Bob Geldof).

Notable clips: Captain Beefheart's self-directed ICE CREAM FOR CROW; The Tubes' TALK TO YA LATER (which cashes in their TV-derived imagery).

1983   Sony introduces Video 45s (January).

Devo tour with live video synchronization (January).

Michael Jackson's THRILLER is produced. The long-form tape *The Making of Michael Jackson's "Thriller"* becomes the biggest-selling music video to date.

MTV repeatedly accused of racism for failing to screen clips by black artists.

The Country Music TV Network begins transmission (March).

Flashdance (directed by Adrian Lynne).

First American Video Awards (June).

WTBS launches *Night Tracks* (June).

NBC's *Friday Night Videos* debuts (June).

Pete Shelley releases a single ("Telephone Operator") with encoded visual animation and lyrics for home computer screens.

1984   National Coalition on Television Violence publishes critical report on MTV (January).

Nickelodeon's *Nick Rocks* debuts.

Purple Rain (Prince).

This Is Spinal Tap (directed by Rob Reiner).

MTV signs exclusivity deals with six major record labels.

Joe Jackson writes *Billboard* column condemning music videos (June).

Europe's Music Box all-music satellite/cable service begins transmission (July).

Miami Vice (working title: "MTV Cops") debuts on NBC.

Michael Jackson's first Pepsi-Cola TV ad.

Ted Turner launches the Cable Music Channel.

Band Aid's "Do They Know It's Christmas?" (December).

1985   VH-1 (MTV Networks) begins transmission (January 1). First clip: THE STAR SPANGLED BANNER (Marvin Gaye).

USA for Africa releases "We Are the World" (April).

Live Aid concert transmitted around the world from London and Philadelphia (July).

MTV Networks sold to Viacom International (August).

New York's Museum of Modern Art begins collecting music video clips (first exhibition in September).

1986   MTV begins repeats of *The Monkees* (February).

Sid and Nancy (directed by Alex Cox).

Robert Pittman leaves MTV (August).

Absolute Beginners (starring David Bowie, directed by Julien Temple).

1987   MTV Europe (owned by MTV Networks, British Telecom, and Maxwell Communications) begins transmission from London (August). First clip: MONEY FOR NOTHING (Dire Straits).

Abortive attempt to launch *The New Monkees* sitcom.

Dirty Dancing movie.

Sony introduces the CD-V (CDs with video images).

1988   MTV tours shopping malls with "The Museum of Unnatural History."

BAD (Michael Jackson, directed by Martin Scorsese) is promoted via a CBS prime-time special, *Michael Jackson — The Legend Continues*.

Worldwide transmission of a London concert to honor Nelson Mandela's seventieth birthday is marred in the United States by accusations that the Fox network censored the broadcast (June).

Dirty Dancing TV series.

MTV denies that Neil Young's THIS NOTE'S FOR YOU (directed by Julien Temple) has been banned, but it is rarely screened.

1989   *Depeche Mode 101* (documentary directed by D. A. Pennebaker).

Pepsi-Cola pulls its Madonna TV commercials after controversy arises concerning her LIKE A PRAYER clip.

Batman (the movie, the album, the cereal).

Do the Right Thing (directed by Spike Lee, with music by Public Enemy).

Public Enemy's *Fight the Power* long-form tape.

Andrew Dice Clay is banned for life from MTV, following his offensive performance on MTV's Video Music Awards program (September).

1990   *Elvis* (TV series) debuts on ABC (February). Widely publicized as the most expensive series ever made, it is canceled before the season's end.

MTV Networks launches HA!, an all-comedy channel (April).

The Power Station (twenty-four-hour music videos) is launched as a satellite and cable TV service in Europe (run by British Satellite Broadcasting).

Rolling Stones *Steel Wheels* concert from Atlantic City is broadcast on the Fox network with 3-D sequences.

Amid growing controversy about the lip-syncing of "live" vocals in performance, legislators in New Jersey (and, later, California) call for laws to inform the public where vocal lip-syncing is used in concert.

Roger Waters and friends stage *The Wall* at the Berlin Wall (July).

David Bowie's summer concert tour features extensive use of live video synchronization.

New TV season features more pop/TV fusions than ever: *Fresh Prince of Bel-Air, Cop Rock, Hull High* (September).

Madonna's JUSTIFY MY LOVE clip is banned by the BBC and by MTV, and is released as a video single (December).

1991   Pet Shop Boys tour with highly choreographed show.

Madonna's documentary film *Truth or Dare* (titled *In Bed with Madonna* outside the United States) is released (May).

Michael Jackson's new video BLACK OR WHITE debuts in prime time, on the Fox network (November).

MTV celebrates tenth anniversary with *MTV 10* screened in prime time on the ABC television network (November).

Notes

Introduction

1. The notion of "distraction" is widely known through the cultural criticism of Walter Benjamin and has recently been taken up in the debate about postmodernity. My deployment of the term *distraction factory* is, however, taken from an essay by Siegfried Kracauer titled "The Mass Ornament," published in the *Frankfurter Zeitung* in 1927. This essay, an analysis of the "Tiller Girls," is reprinted in Bronner and Kellner (1989).

2. I am grateful to Richard Johnson for casting the problem in these terms and thus clarifying what had been upsetting (and obsessing) me for some time.

1. Silence! Academics at Work

1. Quoted in *Musician* (February 1987: 56).

2. The problems with the empiricist tradition of audience studies have been usefully summarized by Morley (1980a: 1-11). The most notorious and debilitating aspect of such studies is of course the failure to analyze *meaning* systematically. In the study of music television this limitation is neatly exemplified in Vincent, Davis, and Boruszkowski's (1987) attempt to establish a "sexism index," whereby four "levels" of sexism are established ("Condescending," "Keep Her Place," "Contradictory," and "Fully Equal") and tabulated to arrive at one conclusion that is banal ("Females are portrayed as submissive, passive, yet sensual, and physically attractive") and another that seems to take no account of the androgynous disruption of masculinity (see Walser, 1989) that occurs in many heavy metal clips ("the clothing . . . tends to reinforce traditional gender roles"). "It is revealing to find," conclude the authors, "that rock videos perpetuate social norms so effectively."

An audience study that is, however, more in the tradition of Morley's bid to take account of socially differentiated readings is offered in Brown and Schulze's (1990) study of reaction to Madonna's music videos PAPA DON'T PREACH and OPEN YOUR HEART.

3. A few analysts have tried to locate music television in the context of pop's codes, conventions, and aesthetics (Berland, 1986; Burns & Thompson, 1987; Frith, 1988a, 1988b; Hodge, 1984; McClary, 1988a; Marcus, 1987; J. Walker, 1987). None of these beginnings tackles the music-vision relation in a systematic way, however.

4. It is noticeable that Tania Modleski's (1988) critique of some of these readings—for instance, of *Rear Window*—pays closer attention to the dialogue and, therefore, the plot. The issue of film music is addressed in special issues of *Yale French Studies* (No. 60, 1980) and *Screen* ("On the Soundtrack," Vol. 25, No. 3, May-June).

5. The resistance to analysis so often encountered in the study of music has been discussed psychoanalytically (Flinn, 1986), sociologically (Wolff, 1987), and in musicological terms (McClary & Walser, 1990). Rodowick (1991b) argues that the contemporary culture of the plastic arts needs to be approached not via linguistic models, but through the notion of the "figural," thus opening up a new and very suggestive line of inquiry that avoids some of the traps of postmodernism.

6. In Neil Postman's *Amusing Ourselves to Death: Public Discourse in the Age of Show Business* (1985), it is specifically television that is held responsible for the decline of reason. Postman argues that "the epistemology created by television not only is inferior to a print-based epistemology but is dangerous and absurd" (p. 27). His argument echoes a more general complaint that is summarized thus by Stanley Aronowitz (1987): "Profound illiteracy has afflicted large segments of the American population. . . . the (deeper) problem is a gradual but relentless growth of anti-intellectualism in American life, born in part of the traditional antipathy of American ideology to ideas themselves . . . and in part from the rise of what I will call a *visual culture*, which has increasingly replaced other types of communication, particularly the written and verbal forms" (p. 466). This debate is encountered again in postmodern cultural analysis, and has been usefully explored by Martin Jay (1988) and Stuart Hall (1988b).

7. Kaplan sees MTV's schizophrenia as a function of its disruption of realist narrative codes. Postman (1985) uses the ideas of Marshall McLuhan to argue: "Embedded in the surrealistic frame of a television news show is a theory of anticommunication, featuring a type of discourse that abandons logic, reason, sequence and rules of contradiction. In aesthetics, I believe the name given to this theory is Dadaism; in philosophy, nihilism; in psychiatry, schizophrenia" (p. 105). Ferguson (1991) elaborates the parallels between McLuhan's ideas and postmodern theory.

8. Joe Jackson made a trilogy of promotional videos midway through his career to promote his 1982 album *Night and Day* (STEPPIN' OUT, REAL MEN, and BREAKING US IN TWO, each directed by Steve Barron). In June 1984 he authored a column in *Billboard* condemning the clips as a "shallow, tasteless, formulized way of selling music which, often, can't stand on its own" (quoted in Denisoff, 1988: 263). By 1989 Jackson had abandoned this stance (long after every other major pop act had reneged on the promise to avoid videos), participating in some MTV programming to promote a North American tour and making a video clip for the single "Nineteen Forever."

The Smiths, on the other hand, were both quicker and more circumspect in their negotiation of the video age: in 1987 they hired independent filmmaker Derek Jarman to produce a "film" for the single "Panic." "I don't even use the word 'video,' " said the band's lead singer Morrissey in an interview. "Sometimes it will slip out, but I prefer to say 'film' or 'promotional device.' Anything we've done has been under *extreme* pressure" (quoted in *Creem*, July 1987: 7).

9. Rock musicians often criticize the business of video promotion in their media interviews (which, ironically, are usually nothing more than a promotional chore). The members of Bon Jovi, for instance, have repeatedly criticized their early video clips and boasted

that they had refused to "act" in any further videos, having taken charge of such productions (which thereafter emphasized performance footage and "on the road" clips).

10. On the iconography of pop music, see Laing's (1985a: 82-98) discussion of the visual representation of punk rock.

11. Since this is such a key myth in rock history (it was recently invoked, for instance, in Prefab Sprout's song "Jordan: The Comeback," on their 1990 album of that name), it is perhaps worth noting that Elaine Dundy (1986) points out that the January 6, 1957, telecast was "the *only one* in which the cameras cut him off at the waist" (p. 290; emphasis added). Presley had appeared on *The Ed Sullivan Show* the previous year.

12. Sampling music computers problematize the relation between sound and vision because they can store and then generate sounds whose *embodiment* is visually absent. The sampler may be used to generate sounds that seem incompatible with the established "look" of an instrument—for instance, a keyboard may store backing vocals, a guitar may trigger the sampled sounds of a cello, and so forth. Since this technology can now be used in live performance, it has become increasingly difficult to align what is seen and what is heard. See Goodwin (1991c).

13. Pat Aufderheide (1986) takes a similar position when she reports that Richard Lester's *A Hard Day's Night* "turned the Beatles into a visual experience" (p. 60). However, numerous Beatles biographies (e.g., Norman, 1981) have shown that the construction of a visual image for the group first began during their early days in Germany and Liverpool.

14. "I Didn't Mean to Turn You On" was originally a hit for Cherelle, and in the accompanying video clip she sings the song to a cartoon ape (thus recalling filmic memories of King Kong and the myth of beauty and the beast). The clip is briefly discussed in the context of black representation in music video by Peterson-Lewis and Chennault (1986: 54). Robert Palmer's subsequent cover of the song, plus its clip, is a further instance of the shifting of meaning through video imagery. It would be interesting to know whether or not Cherelle's version of the song now conjures up visual images of Palmer's video clip.

15. On Band Aid/Live Aid, see Rijven, Marcus, and Straw (1985). In a less cyncial encounter with this pheonomenon, Charles Hamm (1989) points out that the Band Aid/USA for Africa songs may take on meanings in an African context that defy Western-oriented readings.

16. See Flinn (1986) and Silverman (1988) for a critical review of the suppression of music and the voice in psychoanalytic theory.

17. See, for instance, Paglia (1990) for an example of Madonna's canonization as "the future of feminism." Goodwin (1991a) presents a different reading, focusing on the JUSTIFY MY LOVE clip. See also Bordo (1990). For another view, see Lisa Lewis (1987a, 1987b, 1990).

2. From Anarchy to Chromakey: Developments in Music Television

1. Quoted in *Rolling Stone* (October 5, 1989: 52).

2. The "aura" of pop music is partially located at the moment of "raw" creation, and it is this moment that many record producers strive to capture on tape. It is for this reason that critics, musicians, and producers often celebrate the composition of songs and the production of records in relatively short periods of time. Quick, inspired writing and performing tend to be privileged over long, drawn-out attempts to make "flawless" music.

A case study in the marketing of this ideology could be mounted in relation to countless recordings: one recent case in point was the promotion of the Rolling Stones LP *Steel Wheels* (CBS Records, 1989), which was widely publicized for (a) the speed with which Mick Jagger and Keith Richards wrote the songs and (b) the relative speed (three months) with which it was recorded. These auratic moments are mirrored in the ideology of recording technologies, in which there is debate about the relative merits of analog (tape) and digital (DAT, CD) methods of recording and reproduction, centering on their fidelity to the original moment of performance and the relative "warmth" of the two processes (see Goodwin, 1988).

3. The fact that performance is essentially about promotion is starkly revealed in the economics of live performance, which for many new acts involves the phenomenon of "pay to play." Numerous music clubs require acts to buy a certain number of tickets (which are then given away free to friends, fans, and family) and offer no fee to the performers—a practice that has raised protest and campaigns against "pay to play" clubs (for instance, in Los Angeles in 1989). Support acts are often obliged to buy their way onto major tours in order to gain exposure. I have myself attended meetings with rock management at which the costs of buying onto a national British tour were discussed in terms of what the support act (of which I was a member) would pay for the privilege of touring with British group Aztec Camera. These payments are often disguised as "fees" for the main act's supply of a sound and/or lighting system.

4. The 1986 BBC program *Video Juke Box* cited the 1934 film *Komposition in Blau* by Von Oskar Fischinger as a music video antecedent. This work is also referenced by Shore (1985) and Berg (1987).

5. The Soundies were brief black-and-white films that illustrated popular jazz tunes and ballads. They were shown on Panoram machines, and manufactured by the Mills Novelty Co. (in the United States) from 1941 to 1947. More than two thousand Soundies were made, some culled from Hollywood musicals. In the early days of U.S. television, Soundies were sometimes screened between programs. The clips were usually made in one day, with the music recorded first, followed by the filming of the musicians lip-syncing and miming instrumental parts. Sometimes narrative elements were introduced into the clips, and some of these examples look remarkably like today's pop videos, albeit without the *pace* that advanced editing techniques permit. The Soundie "Texas Strip" (made in 1942) appears to be the source of the imagery for Devo's WHIP IT! (I am grateful to Noah Landis for pointing this out to me.)

The Scopitone clips made in France in the 1960s were shot in color and featured pop artists such as Johnny Halliday, Petula Clark, Dionne Warwick, and Neil Sedaka. For more details, see Shore (1985) and Berg (1987).

It is clear that both the Soundies machine and the Scopitone jukebox died out because as a commodity form (in which the consumer pays directly for the commodity) they could not compete with television. In that respect, little has changed; music videos today remain a form whose economic base is usually reliant on additional forms of revenue, above and beyond the use-value/exchange-value transaction.

6. There are, for instance, segments that resemble the pop video (because that form is sometimes based upon song-and-dance conventions from the Hollywood "musical" and from the musical as "biography") in movies such as *The Blackboard Jungle, Rock Around the Clock, Blue Hawaii, A Hard Day's Night, Help!, Yellow Submarine, Performance,* and *Let It Be.*

7. On the New Pop, see Simon Reynolds (1985) for an analysis and Neil Tennant (1985) for a collection of *Smash Hits* journalism (which usefully illustrates many of the themes identified by Reynolds).

8. In the case of Frankie Goes to Hollywood, it was producer Trevor Horn (whose earlier work included production for ABC's classic New Pop album, *The Lexicon of Love,* Phonogram, 1982) who was responsible for their automated, machinelike gloss. The link with "progressive rock" is made concrete here, since Horn had previously been a member of prog rock group Yes, for a brief period, and went on to produce their commercial come-

back album *90125*. Trevor Horn is a key figure in these debates and it is thus not accidental that he was one half of the New Pop act Buggles, whose video clip VIDEO KILLED THE RADIO STAR was the first to air on MTV in the United States, on August 1, 1981.

9. Controversies about who played what on the Frankie Goes to Hollywood records eventually led to acrimony and an unsuccessful lawsuit brought against lead singer Holly Johnson by ZTT Records.

10. A similar fracas has occurred in relation to the dance group C + C Music Factory, whose recordings use the voice of Martha Wash extensively, while the group is co-fronted in performance by Zelma Davis. In an MTV News item (broadcast in May 1991), Davis was interviewed backstage insisting that she *does* sing live, even going so far as to give MTV a live demonstration of her vocal talents.

11. The New Pop prefigured rap in its reliance on computers and machines, and in its use of video to sell an image of performance through the construction of a "community" of musicians whose contribution to the recording process is negligible or nonexistent. Compare, for instance, the extramusical role of Andrew Ridgley in Wham! with the iconographic functions of Professor Griff and the Security of the First World crew in the performance imagery of rap group Public Enemy. Rap, like the New Pop, was also initiated as a low-tech musical form independently of the later use of sophisticated and expensive recording technologies (see Costello & Wallace, 1991; Toop, 1984). The role of the technology itself is debated in Goodwin (1991c).

12. Simon Frith's developing critique of rock's myths of authenticity is articulated generally in *Sound Effects* (1983); in relation to technology, see Frith's "Art versus Technology" (1986); as regards style, see *Art into Pop* (Frith & Horne, 1987); and concerning particular artists, most notably Bruce Springsteen, see "The Real Thing" (in Frith, 1988a: 94-104).

13. Fitzgerald (1982) quotes an average cost of £10,000 per clip, in the early 1980s. Qualen (1985) gives a figure of £15,000, in the mid-1980s. Quarry (1987) reports that the average cost of most video clips made in the United Kingdom in the mid- to late 1980s was £15,000-£25,000. Major artists may, however, spend larger amounts: Sting's RUSSIANS (directed by Jean-Baptiste Mondino) cost £140,000, according to Quarry.

14. The Warner/Atari story has often been cited as a cautionary tale by writers discussing music video. In 1983, Atari reported losses of more than $536 million following a huge investment in a video game fad, which proved to be more ephemeral than they had hoped. MTV's corporate masters at the time (Warner Communications) were involved in this venture (see Denisoff, 1988: 124).

15. Press reports in the spring of 1991 suggested that record companies were beginning to scale down production costs. According to Music Video Producers Association spokesperson Len Epland: "Certain videos that may have been budgeted at $75,000 one or two years ago are often edging to $60,000. Now we're hearing of $30,000-$35,000 videos when those didn't exist two years ago—you didn't do anything for under $40,000" (quoted in Newman, 1991b; see also stories in *Billboard*, November 6, 1990, and April 6, 1991).

16. In April 1991 the Recording Industry Association of America reported a jump in music video sales, from $115.4 million in 1989 to $172.3 million for 1990. This compares with cassette sales of $3,472.4 million. Rachel Powell (1991) reports that "music videos still account for only a tiny part of the business, just 1 percent of all music units shipped."

17. Sales of JUSTIFY MY LOVE were variously reported as 400,000 (Newman, 1991a) and 500,000 (Powell, 1991).

18. As MTV executive Robert Pittman put it: "Our core audience is the television babies who grew up on TV and rock & roll" (quoted in Levy, 1983).

19. Shore (1985) surveys the work of some key music video clip directors, suggesting that the range of costs in the mid-1980s in the United States was $20,000-$60,000, with a

few of the more famous directors (Bob Giraldi, David Mallet, Russell Mulcahy) working with budgets as high as $100,000. See Newman (1991a) for more details on up-to-date U.S. costs.

20. BAD's television presentation was a classic example of vertical integration. Michael Jackson's record company is Epic, which was a part of Columbia Records, ultimately owned by CBS. (CBS was later bought by Sony, and the Columbia label was abolished.) Since the CBS television network is a part of the same media entity, this television program was virtually a thirty-minute commercial that cross-promoted another CBS product—Jackson's latest LP, Bad (Epic, 1987).

21. In 1984 MTV signed "exclusivity" deals with six major record companies: CBS, RCA, MCA, Geffen, Elektra/Asylum, and Polygram. Under these agreements, MTV pays a flat fee for rights to choose a given number of clips from each company's output, which it may then screen exclusively for a thirty-day period. As Viera (1987) points out, this period effectively ties up the clip for the most active period of the sales life of the single it promotes.

22. I am very grateful to Roger Wallis and his students at San Jose State University for suggesting the notion of the music video "circuit."

23. "Manufacturers say that music video of any length still remains the domain of the loyal fan and has yet to be proven as a way to enlarge an act's fan base" (Newman, 1991a: MV-8).

24. Mark Booth, managing director of MTV Europe, made this remark in an interview I conducted with him in London on August 12, 1987. Booth left MTV Europe in 1989, to work for Rupert Murdoch's Sky TV operation.

3. A Musicology of the Image

1. Quoted in SPIN (1989).

2. While the concept of synaesthesia refers broadly to the displacement of sensory experiences, I will use the term in the specific sense that is usually employed in relation to music—where we "see" sounds.

3. To offer two rather contrasting pieces of autobiographical "evidence": I tend to "see" the Yes album Fragile (Atlantic, 1972) as a clean, crystal, light blue experience—a synaesthetic phenomenon that is suggested by the clear, discrete lines set up in the music itself, by the clarity of the recording, and in the album cover. The Sex Pistols debut album Never Mind the Bollocks Here's the Sex Pistols (Virgin Records, 1977) sounds as wonderfully brash and gaudy as its cover art, which mixes colors with an appropriate lack of "good taste" that is, for me, an essential part of the experience of listening to the music.

4. For instance, artist Jenny Holzer, whose work appears in this book, has made an "art-break" station identification segment promoting MTV.

5. This study was undertaken in the Broadcast Communication Arts Department at San Francisco State University, in February 1988. My thanks to the students on BCA 221 ("The Electronic Culture") for their participation. Clearly this informal feedback is subject to an important determinant—the students had been asked to concentrate on what they "saw." I tried to minimize this factor in a number of ways; I chose a class that had not previously discussed music television, picking a group who were not mainly communications majors, since this was a general education class drawn from throughout the university system. Of course, the concept of synaesthesia was not discussed before the study, which was conducted very rapidly in order to discourage self-conscious analysis of the process. The students had between twenty and fifty seconds to respond to each extract, as it played, and then the exercise was over.

6. The study was done prior to the use of "Moments in Love" in an AIDS-awareness television commercial made by the U.S. Centers for Disease Control in 1990.

7. Of course, it may be that students were downplaying mass-mediated influences because they felt they should demonstrate their resistance to the media.

8. See an interesting article by rock critic Jon Pareles (1989), "Her Style Is Imitable, but It's Her Own."

9. The artificiality of the recording process is usually masked by the presence of electronic "reverberation" introduced at the mix-down stage of production. This makes the sounds appear "wet," framed by an ambience that suggests the realism of a prior moment of performance. When this convention is rejected (for instance, on the Prince track "Kiss"), the recording sounds very stark, "dry," and unreal, precisely because the synaesthetic function of reverb has been exposed through its absence.

10. The question of placing of sounds also has implications in live performance iconography. On Bruce Springsteen's Tunnel of Love world tour of 1988 a great deal of significance was attributed to the placement of musicians on the stage. The shifting of saxophone player Clarence Clemons from center stage to a stage-right position and the placing of backing vocalist Patty Scialfa in his place were taken as signs of the musicians' respective importance in Springsteen's new music—and played a part in signifying a partial shift in the sexual politics of the *Tunnel of Love* (CBS, 1987) album. I cite this, of course, because it so explicitly demonstrates that the physical placing of musicians on stage contributes in important ways to the meaning of the music.

11. As my informal survey suggests, songs and acts are also associated with places and signs anchored in both personal memory and a collective pool of rock myths. One hitherto unexplored avenue is the undeveloped relation between a global pop culture and tourism. An important synaesthetic moment that is taken up in music video concerns the regional and/or national location of pop stars.

Just as important, although neglected thus far in the study of music television, are the meanings that come with specific regional identities, and which are represented in clips that link rock acts with places such as New York (Blondie's UNION CITY BLUES, Madonna's INTO THE GROOVE, Public Enemy's FIGHT THE POWER), New Jersey (Bruce Springsteen's ATLANTIC CITY, Bon Jovi's IN AND OUT OF LOVE), London (the Jam's IN THE CITY), Los Angeles (Guns N' Roses' WELCOME TO THE JUNGLE, N.W.A's STRAIGHT OUTTA COMPTON), and Australia (Men at Work's DOWN UNDER, Midnight Oil's BEDS ARE BURNING). Indeed, one video clip centers its visual rhetoric on this process of regional recognition, when the Fat Boys/Beach Boys cover of WIPE OUT uses comic inversion, by presenting images of the Fat Boys in California and the Beach Boys in New York City (in other words, in locations that jar with their conventionally estabished regional identities).

12. Chuck D sees rap as a mass-mediated *visual* medium, because it allows rap fans to "see" each other's communities. Commenting on the raps of Oakland's Too Short, he observes: "I know what kind of car he drives, I know the police give him a hard time, I know that there's *trees* in the area, you know what I'm saying? It's like a CNN that black kids never had" (quoted in *Newsweek*, March 19, 1990: 61).

13. "It is sometimes extremely important to expose some familiar and seemingly already well-studied phenomenon to fresh illumination by reformulating it as a problem, i.e., to illuminate new aspects of it with the aid of a set of questions that have special bearing upon it. It is particularly important to do so in those fields where research has become bogged down in masses of meticulous and detailed—but utterly pointless—descriptions and classifications" (Volosinov, 1986: 112).

14. *Ready, Steady, Go!* videotapes are now publicly available for rental and demonstrate many such instances. For example, in a performance by the Who, rapid zooming in and out

is used to illustrate the anarchic musical breakup that occurs midway through "Anyway, Anyhow, Anywhere."

15. The emphases are different, however, for other musical genres—soul music and reggae clearly depart from this placing of the beat. The point, however, is that images may be used to reinforce rhythmic accents, wherever they occur.

16. See Toop (1984) for an explanation of the "scratching" technique and its origins.

17. There may be tensions between the staging of the music itself and the mechanics of stardom. According to Peter Wynne Wilson, Pink Floyd's lighting operator in their early days, the importance of lighting was certainly understood by the man who went on to become the central focus of the group: "They put a lot of pressure on me. . . . Roger [Waters] would often complain that he was not illuminated as a star. I specifically didn't illuminate any of them as 'rock stars' because I did the lighting to blend with the music rather than accentuate somebody as a personality" (quoted in Schaffner, 1991: 35).

Video technologies at live performances now exaggerate these conventions when live video relays onto large TV screens are used (usually at outdoor venues) to concentrate attention on vocalists and soloists. Cheering at live concerts is now often triggered not by aural events, but by the appearance of particular images on the venue's video screens (such as a close-up of an instrumentalist whose fingers are moving at speed across a fret board or keyboard).

18. For a review of the issues concerning lyrics in pop songs, see Frith's "Why Do Songs Have Words?" (1988a: 105-28).

19. See Said (1979) on Orientalism, which has clear implications for the representation of Asian culture in popular music, especially in the fetishizing of images of Japan that was eventually deployed by the band who took on that name and utilized familiar Western images of "Japan" in promotional materials such as album covers.

4. The Structure of Music Video: Rethinking Narrative Analysis

1. Quoted in *New Musical Express*, (March 16, 1991: 3).

2. Shaun Moores (1990) provides an accessible and cogent summary of these issues.

3. There are of course instances in which other media narratives are framed so as to conflate the real and implied narrator. One instance arises from popular criticism of Francis Ford Coppola's *Godfather* trilogy, which is frequently written about in terms of the parallels between the fictional Corleone family and Coppola's own familial and personal circumstances. The documentary *Hearts of Darkness* (uncritically) crystallizes this same link, in relation to Coppola's *Apocalypse Now*.

4. The star-as-narrator position does not necessarily derive from authorship, at least as it relates to the song. There are many examples of pop singers who do not always write their own songs (Elton John, Madonna), and of acts in which the singer is not the lyricist/ songwriter (Depeche Mode, for instance).

5. N.W.A. (*Straight Outta Compton*, Ruthless Records, 1989), Ice Cube (*AmeriKKKa's Most Wanted*, Priority, 1990), Ice-T (*Freedom of Speech . . . Just Watch What You Say*, Sire, 1989; *OG: Original Gangster*, Sire, 1991), and the Geto Boys (*Geto Boys*, Geffen, 1990) are the most well-known examples of "gangster rap." N.W.A.'s video STRAIGHT OUTTA COMPTON was banned by MTV because it was thought to promote gang violence. For an account of how this has spilled over into the policing of live rap concerts, see Smith (1991).

6. I pursued this question in some detail in my master's thesis, with regard to television drama-documentary (see Goodwin, 1981).

7. An especially striking example of this occurred on *American Bandstand* when Sam Cooke sang "You Send Me" directly to the camera.

8. On repetition in popular music, see the special issue of *ONETWOTHREEFOUR: A Rock 'n' Roll Quarterly* (No. 4, Winter 1987).

9. This beat ultimately derives from West African and Afro-Cuban musics.

10. Soho's "Hippychick" is also a literal example of part interchangeability, since its "Bo Diddley" beat is a sampled guitar loop by Johnny Marr, from the Smiths' "How Soon Is Now."

11. See Levin (1990) for an account of Adorno's music criticism that downplays his "pessimism" and argues for a more sympathetic reading of his attitiude toward mass culture. The essay introduces three pieces by Adorno (1990) that deal with mass-produced music. See also Hullot-Kentor (1991) and Berman and D'Amico (1991).

12. Qualen (1985) charts the emergence of the twelve-inch single as a commodity form.

13. The latest figures available in the United States, reported by the Recording Industry Association of America, indicate a decline in sales of 18.9 percent in the seven-inch single market from 1989 to 1990 (see Powell, 1991).

14. Given the decline in sales of singles (which is especially significant in the U.K. market), the video that once promoted a single increasingly *replaces* it, promoting the album directly and working as perhaps a "simulation" of the seven-inch record.

15. It is a possibly apocryphal but nonetheless essentially truthful tale among songwriters that publishing agents will actually time a song in order to ensure that the chorus is reached within a given number of seconds (usually about twenty).

16. The problem with so much contemporary cultural analysis is, however, that scholars have forgotten that popular culture *is* also a tease. The problem can be illustrated as follows. One critic of an earlier draft of this book observed that perhaps the "populists" I criticize are reacting to the arguments of scholars such as Wolfgang Haug. To which the answer is perhaps so, but his arguments are nonetheless a valid critique of that populism. We can thus go around in circles forever, playing the name-calling game of optimist versus pessimist. But surely the point is that both sets of arguments are true (making optimist/pessimist a fruitless distinction), since the tease of popular culture delivers real pleasures, while that pleasure remains always ideological to the extent that it buttresses capitalist social relations.

17. One interesting attempt to defy this is the music of the Jesus and Mary Chain, whose debut album *Psychocandy* (Blanco Y Negro, 1985) reversed the established relation of foreground and background in pop, by burying the vocals in a wall of distorted guitars and drums saturated in reverberation. Just as interesting, however, from the Adornian perspective advocated here, is that the Jesus and Mary Chain eventually had to abandon this approach, providing more conventionally mixed recordings on the subsequent albums *Darklands* (WEA, 1987) and *Automatic* (WEA, 1990).

18. In the terms set out by some narratologists, music cannot be discussed in terms of narrative theory at all. For instance, Robert Scholes (1981) insists that "a narrated event is the symbolization of a real event: a temporal icon. A narration is the symbolic presentation of a sequence of events connected by subject matter and related by time" (p. 205). In these terms, it is hard to see how music could constitute a narrative at all, but this is especially so for the nonlinear, highly repetitive forms of rock and pop. However, since I maintain that music clearly *does* engage in conflict and resolution, I will argue for some stretching of the terms here. One can argue both that music *does* represent something (including interior realities) and that there are causal connections between the different parts of the song structure, in that the verse seems to lead into the chorus. Nonetheless, this remains rather thin conceptual ice, since the rhythmic nature of pop renders its structure more like a brief repeated loop than a linear chain.

19. I am reminded here of the "Nice Video, Shame About the Song" sketch performed by the BBC's *Not the Nine O'Clock News* team, which admirably satirized the problem of the overly cryptic video clip.

20. This example was suggested in an unpublished paper written by Holly Kindel, Department of Film, San Francisco State University.

21. Other examples include USA for Africa, WE ARE THE WORLD; Ferry Aid, LET IT BE; and the Take-It-Back Foundation, YAKETY-YAK TAKE IT BACK.

22. There are four versions of "Relax." ITV's show *The Tube* first made a film of Frankie Goes to Holywood performing the song, which was seen by producer Trevor Horn and led to the band being signed to ZTT Records. Then a video was made for the song that contained erotic scenarios considered unfit for broadcast by the BBC's *Top of the Pops*. A less explicit version was then made for broadcast TV. Finally, the band appeared miming the song in Brian De Palma's movie *Body Double*. See Jackson (1985) and Gross (1984b).

23. The armadillo may have other significance. Pattison (1987: 114) reminds us of the line from *This Is Spinal Tap* ("the armadillos in our trousers—it's quite frightening") that suggests a comic phallic allusion!

24. For parallel forms of product placement in children's television programming, see Engelhardt (1986).

25. Propp (1968) identifies thirty-one functions in a syntagmatic analysis of narratives, one of which is the receipt of a magical agent by the hero. This is precisely the function of the ZZ Top key: for instance, in GIMME ALL YOUR LOVIN' this key becomes the agent whereby the hero (a young male garage attendant) is able to escape the clutches of the villains (a motorbike gang) with his princess (a young girl who works in a shoe store) in ZZ Top's "Eliminator" car.

5. Metanarratives of Stardom and Identity

1. Quoted in an interview by Tom Hibbert in Q (February 1989: 34).

2. A more critical feminist response is provided by Susan Bordo (1990).

3. This reading has often been underscored by Madonna herself, for instance, in her famous ABC *Nightline* television interview (December 3, 1990), when she happily boasted about her material success—a topic that rock stars are usually quite coy about—and then turned on host Forrest Sawyer to ask rhetorically, "Isn't that what feminism is about?"

4. Philip Hayward's (1991) account of CHERISH is, in my view, a credible context for understanding JUSTIFY MY LOVE: "The Cherish single/video and its two predecessors, Like a Prayer and Express Yourself were produced in 1989. At this time, Madonna was trying to revive her career as a pop star after the lull produced by the critical and commercial failure of her role in the film *Shanghai Surprise*, her much publicized marital break-up with Sean Penn and her failure to produce new musical product during this period. In this context, the controversial nature of her first two big budget music video productions of 1989, Like a Prayer (which drew on both religious and Ku Klux Klan imagery) and Express Yourself (which combined soft-pornographic images with elaborate sets based on Fritz Lang's 1926 film *Metropolis*) can be seen as (literally) spectacular attempts to re-promote Madonna as star" (pp. 101-2). This comment turned out to be an extremely prescient articulation before the fact of the motivation behind the next clip, which was JUSTIFY MY LOVE.

5. I am aware that there are other precedents, such as the Who's rock opera *Tommy*, the Genesis recording *The Lamb Lies Down on Broadway*, and the performances of Pink Floyd, most obviously *The Wall*. However, none of the classic rock or progressive rock examples really displaced the singer/musician. On the contrary, these recordings and performances celebrated virtuosity; when I saw Genesis perform *The Lamb Lies Down on Broadway* in

1974, a power failure led drummer Phil Collins to fill in time with a drum solo! While these performances focused on the songs and their lyrical themes, the musicians continued to function as storytellers. Indeed, the fact that the musicians are inherently more fascinating, for their fans, than any of the characters they create explains why rock operas and narrative-based performances are nearly always overshadowed by the storyteller.

6. David Alden reports on the impact of MTV thus: "I'm always very influenced by MTV anyway. Sometimes when I'm working on an opera by Mozart or Verdi or someone I play the record of the opera and I turn on MTV with the sound off, so I'm listening to classical images but seeing these pop images" (quoted in program notes for Pet Shop Boys' Performance tour, spring 1991).

7. See Chris Heath (1990) for a biographical account of the Pet Shop Boys that illustrates their own self-consciousness about the group's relation to a rock aesthetic. Heath is especially perceptive in showing the contradictions of espousing an antirock attitude in a touring situation that inevitably involves many of the rituals and practices of the rock industry.

8. In the 1990s, however, there is considerable concern, especially within the British music industry, regarding the growth of a dance music culture (hip-hop, hi-NRG, techno, acid house) that generates sales of singles (through dance clubs and "raves") without establishing star identities. See Thornton (1990) for an analysis.

9. The Residents are an act who formed in San Francisco in 1974. They have released a series of albums and have infrequently played live, but they have never revealed their identities. In performance and in publicity shots they are disguised in costumes such as "skulls; neo-KKK hoods and robes made from newspapers; huge bloodshot-eyeball masks" (Pareles & Romanowski, 1983: 466).

10. Janet Jackson's deal with Virgin Records was reported in *Rolling Stone* as being worth more than $50 million, for as few as two albums (with Virgin able to take up an option on further releases). Michael Jackson's deal with Sony is more complex and involves the creation of his own record company and Sony's advancing him about $12 million just for the promotional videos for his album *Dangerous*. Epic Records (now owned by Sony) has the rights to Jackson's next six albums, with a reported advance of $5 million on each, plus a $4 million bonus on delivery of his next release. See Goldberg (1991).

11. This is used by Lawrence Grossberg (1988) as evidence for his contention that we need a category of "authentic inauthenticity."

12. As Lester Bangs has put it: "One thing I have learned both through observation and personal experience is that the myth of rock 'n' roll bands as four or five happy-go-lucky guys just bouncing through the world is just that: a lie" (Nelson & Bangs, 1981: 84).

13. The promotion of Led Zeppelin long after the band's demise also illustrates the usefulness of videos as a means of marketing artists and bands who are no longer recording. For example, Atlantic Records marketed Led Zeppelin's four-CD boxed set (*Led Zeppelin*, Atlantic, 1990) ten years after the band split up (following the death of drummer John Bonham) by including one or two rare, previously unreleased tracks (a common practice designed to make boxed sets essential to "completists"). New video clips were then made for some of these songs—including OVER THE HILLS AND FAR AWAY and TRAVELLIN' RIVERSIDE BLUES, a reworking of a Robert Johnson song—using old footage of the band.

14. The star-text is thus both unique in its finer details and often made up of common elements, very much in the manner identified by Adorno (1941).

15. On the Monkees, see Lefcowitz (1985). This account contains some interesting detail on the production of the movie *Head* (see pp. 55-62).

16. This aspect of Cher's appeal to young men was played up via her public persona when she became romantically involved with a younger man—Richie Sambora, lead gui-

tarist in Bon Jovi. Their relationship was given extensive coverage in tabloid publications such as the *National Enquirer*, in the gossip sections of music magazines, and on MTV.

17. Richard Marx had previously worked as a jingle writer and within a year of his success had struck a deal with Kodak for use of his songs in television advertisements, raising the interesting possibility that pop stardom may now be merely a transitional stage between one kind of promotional endeavor and another.

18. Advertisers play on these ideologies, too. Michelob beer has been promoted in the United States by a string of television commercials featuring pop musicians on "the street," from Genesis standing in the shadows by a wire fence singing "Tonight, Tonight, Tonight" to Eric Clapton walking in off the street to perform "After Midnight" in a small club.

19. John Ellis's argument that live performance completes the star-text contradicts my position, outlined in chapter 2, that live performance itself remains incomplete, since it is designed to stimulate desire for *another* product—the single/album. Of course, it may be that sound recordings are often used to replay a live experience. However, albums generally sound a good deal better (in terms of fidelity, mixing, and so on) than live performance, and also offer a moment of aural intimacy that is usually unavailable at a pop concert. Pop remains, then, multidiscursive: Ellis's position needs to be read, and perhaps criticized, in this light.

20. This interview appeared originally in *Smash Hits*, May 24, 1984. The interviewer was Neil Tennant, whose work with the Pet Shop Boys was discussed earlier in this chapter, and his reply, which closed the article, was prescient: "And that is a difficult question to answer."

21. David Fricke's (1986) *Rolling Stone* interview is subtitled "The Main Man in Wham! Alters His Image" and is peppered with an auto-critique of Wham! that helps estabish George Michael's revised star-text. For instance: "I totally threw away my personal credibility for a year and a half in order to make sure my music got into so many people's homes. . . . It was a calculated risk, and I knew I would have to fight my way back from it" (p. 88).

22. Lindsay Anderson is presumably trying to make a political point when he takes the song "Freedom" (which is about sexual freedom within a relationship, and how the narrator prefers monogamy) and illustrates it with shots of Chinese people dancing, marching, and so forth. The sequence in *Wham! in China: Foreign Skies* and the FREEDOM promotional clip are thus good, if rather unsubtle, examples of a disjunctive relation between song and video.

23. I am grateful to Greg Sandow for pointing this out to me.

6. A Televisual Context: MTV

1. Quoted in an interview by David Wild in *Rolling Stone* (March 7, 1991: 36).

2. Phil Hardy (1983: 19-20)/John Qualen (1985: 14-16), who are actually the same person, argues that music video was consciously used by the British record industry as a cost-effective way into the U.S. market.

3. Denisoff (1988) quotes Les Garland, then vice-president of programming, talking in August 1982, thus: "About 30 to 40 percent of the music we play is not on the typical AOR radio station" (pp. 84-85). Note, therefore, how much of the playlist was AOR! In early 1983, Garland told a reporter: "We can show REO Speedwagon and Duran Duran. We can show Kenny Loggins and Haircut One Hundred. We've been able to invent our own format, because we're the only ones doing it" (quoted in Jackson, 1983).

4. Denisoff (1988) and others have reported that CBS was able to persuade MTV to screen Michael Jackson's BEAT IT only by threatening to withdraw all CBS clips from the station. The problem of black airplay persisted beyond this early period. At a Gill Chair

Seminar at San Jose State University (held November 6, 1986), Polygram Records president Dick Asher reported that his company experienced great difficulty in gaining MTV airplay for the 1986 WORD UP clip, by black dance act Cameo. By the late 1980s MTV's promotion of rap music (on *Yo! MTV Raps*) significantly changed attitudes toward its negotiation of race, leading many musicians and executives to credit the channel with playing a major role in the national success of that genre of black music. In that respect it is certainly true that MTV has been more adventurous in its programming than radio, including stations with formats focusing on "black" and "urban contemporary" music. MTV was also very visible in its promotion of the radical black hard rock group Living Colour, especially during 1989.

5. The history of white appropriations of black music is intrinsic to the development of rock, as Gillett (1983) and Harker (1980) have shown. More particular accounts of racism are delineated, for example, in Chuck Berry's (1987) autobiography, in Gerri Hirshey's (1984) account of soul, and in Dave Hill's (1989) analysis of Prince.

6. It is also important to note the contribution of American New Wave and punk acts, whose clips also tended to fall in the nonnarrative category (Devo's WHIP IT, SATISFACTION, and SECRET AGENT MAN, the Cars' YOU MIGHT THINK, Talking Heads' PSYCHO-KILLER and ONCE IN A LIFE-TIME) or to utilize a New Pop-like self-consciousness (see Blondie's long-form tape, *Eat to the Beat*, Chrysalis, 1983).

7. The liberal/feminist arguments against MTV were frequently articulated in the newsletter *Rock and Roll Confidential* (see, for example, Marsh, 1985: 204-8).

8. MTV ratings are often miscited as the figure that derives from the number of basic cable-subscribing households on systems that offer the service. By December 1990, MTV was the seventh-largest cable service in the United States, with a potential audience of 52.9 million (*Channels*, December 3, 1990: 48). However, this figure has only a distant correlation with the number of viewers. MTV's actual audience has usually been less than 1 percent of this figure. For instance, in August 1990, MTV averaged a 0.6 percent share in prime time and a 0.7 percent share during the hours of 7 A.M. to 1 A.M. (see *Channels*, August 13, 1990). A "share," in the U.S. cable market, represents the percentage of potential viewers who watched.

9. Public Enemy, De La Soul, Ice-T, and Hammer subsequently emerged as black rap acts with mass appeal who sell in large quantities to white audiences.

10. In the spring of 1991 MTV began broadcasting a coproduced show titled *Liquid Television* (an episodic cartoon series), made in association with the BBC, for *DEF II*.

11. For instance, introducing a clip from the group Bad English (formed by two veteran members of Journey and the Babies), Seal refers dryly to their ambitions to emulate Blind Faith—the 1970s "supergroup" featuring Ginger Baker, Eric Clapton, Steve Winwood, and Rick Gretch, whose music notoriously failed to add up to the sum of its parts.

12. The VJs' linking segments are recorded in blocks ahead of time and then edited in, live, with the videos, commercials, station IDs, and so on.

13. Young's song attacks corporate sponsorship and names names (including some MTV advertisers, such as Coca-Cola and Budweiser), which resulted in a controversy concerning MTV's failure to screen the video, directed by Julien Temple (see Reed, 1988). Typically, MTV then nominated the clip for its 1989 *Video Music Awards* show, where it won the award for Best Video of the year. Neil Young appeared live on camera (from backstage at a gig) to thank MTV for the award. MTV's chief executive, Tom Freston, subsequently acknowledged that the decision to ban the clip was an error (see *SPIN*, 1992).

14. John Street (1985) contextualizes some debates about politics and popular music.

15. The political force of this intervention was diluted somewhat by the subsequent revelation that many of the featured stars did not themselves vote, because of their recording and touring commitments!

16. Personal communication with Judianne Atencio of MTV Networks, January 24, 1991.

17. In addition to the "Words" art-break cited below, MTV runs many station identification sequences that critique everyday life and attempt to expose the society of the spectacle. (This was once incorporated into an "I Hate My Miserable Life" contest.) Many such art-breaks satirize television, advertising, and mass culture. In one sequence the words EAT, WORK, and SLEEP are repeated with increasing speed (and appropriate imagery) until the whole segment blurs into indistinguishable montage and stops only with the arrival (of course) of the legend "MTV."

18. The apotheosis of this address is MTV's "Words" art-break, which is mainly silent and consists entirely of the following white-on-black captions. WORDS / THESE ARE WORDS / BLIND PEOPLE CAN'T [blank space] THEM / FOREIGNERS DON'T UNDERSTAND THEM / BUT YOU CAN / NOWADAYS PEOPLE WHO MAKE TV / COMMERCIALS / USE WORDS JUST LIKE THESE / TO COMMUNICATE / A / MESSAGE / SO THOSE PEOPLE WHO DO NOT / LISTEN / UNDERSTAND / THIS PRACTICE IS SUPPOSED TO BE / SIMPLE / AND / EFFECTIVE / THESE WORDS CAN'T REALLY SAY ANYTHING / THEY COULD BUT THEY'RE NOT / THEY WANT TO BUT THEY CAN'T / SO, THEY WILL HANG OUT FOR FIFTEEN SECONDS / UNTIL IT'S TIME / FOR / ANOTHER / COMMERCIAL / THESE ARE WORDS / THAT COULD BE SAYING SOMETHING / FUNNY OR COOL OR INTERESTING / BUT THEY'RE NOT / THEY'RE JUST SITTING THERE / LIKE YOU / mtv.

19. Homelessness figures prominently in videos such as DAY IN, DAY OUT (David Bowie), BORN IN THE USA (Bruce Springsteen), MAN IN THE MIRROR (Michael Jackson), ANOTHER DAY IN PARADISE (Phil Collins), and SOMETHING TO BELIEVE IN (Poison).

7. Aesthetics and Politics in Music Television: Postmodernism Reconsidered

1. Quoted in an interview by Roberts (1991).

2. This is not the place to debate those issues, which have been addressed critically by Peter Dews (1987) and Janet Wolff (1990).

3. Neither am I suggesting that this is the only (or, indeed, the correct) interpretation of Karl Marx or his legacy.

4. Following Stuart Hall (1980: 36-37), this conceptual shift seems to parallel the slippage from "Semiotics I" to "Semiotics II." More radically, it can be argued that the roots of this tendency to collapse the real and its referent (of which postmodernism is but one of many recent examples in cultural theory) lie in Saussure's theory of signification, with its stress upon the arbitrary dualism of signifier and signified. Raymond Williams (1977b), implicitly, and Anthony Giddens (1979), more explicitly, both follow this line of thinking. It is explained by Robert Scholes (1981) thus: "Saussure demonstrated that the link between 'sound-image' and concept in language, that is, between the signifier and the signified, was arbitrary in most cases, which is unexceptional; but he went on to assume that he had demonstrated the arbitrariness of all concepts themselves, which he had not" (p. 200). Scholes argues for the tripartite system of Charles Saunders Peirce (which includes an "interpretant"), echoing Giddens's point that the problem with Saussure's famous example of the Geneva-to-Paris Express train as an example of a sign is that the arbitrary nature of its sig-

nifier does not apply to some "readers" (e.g., train spotters, engineers). It is worth noting here also that in the work of Nattiez (1990), where semiotics is applied systematically to music, it is Peirce's system, and not Saussure's, that is developed.

This way into the debate about signification is important for anyone wishing to criticize postmodernism's interest in "simulations." It would provide a different starting point for the critique of postmodernism-as-theory than is afforded, for example, by the critique of Lacanian psychoanalysis offered by Nicholas Garnham (1979b), whose critical assessment of *Screen* raises many of the same issues.

5. Franco Moretti's (1987) argument about the "spell of indecision" implied by modernism's "free play" of signifiers, developed later in this chapter, is obviously relevant to the concept of pastiche.

6. Pastiche also relates to the sound track, in that music and lyrics may also be reappropriated from other texts. See McRobbie (1986a), Born (1987), Stratton (1989), Lipsitz (1986–87), Straw (1988), and Goodwin (1988) for some ways in which this happened in pop music in the 1970s and 1980s.

Costello and Wallace (1991) put it like this: "Long before digital multitracked sampling erased boundaries between genres, we were all multitracking in our heads, sampling together everything we ever saw in TV or heard on the stereo, including stuff made by people who, before making it, loved the TV and music we ourselves loved, and couldn't help but sample it, just as Aerosmith so loved the Stones they couldn't help but copy them. . . . there is first 1 band called The Rolling Stones, then 2 Rolling Stones copycat bands, begetting 4 who copy the copiers, begetting 8, 16, 32, 64. This math unfolds nightly on MTV: keeping score is the last fascination remaining there" (p. 89). Their footnote 36 is priceless: "Somewhere in the Midwest, kids sit watching music videos & playing a drinking game called 'MTV,' which is swiftly supplanting Russian roulette and chicken fights as *the* teenage danger game. The game's rules: (1) IF the lame white boy (badly) rips off Muddy Waters's famous solo from "Mannish Boy," YOU chug half a Bud; UNLESS the lame white boy is too dumb to know who Muddy Waters is (or was), in which case YOU chug the whole Bud; (2) IF on the other hand, the lame white boy (badly) rips off Mick Jagger ripping off Muddy Waters, YOU chug the whole Bud; UNLESS the lame white boy *is* Mick Jagger (badly) ripping off Mick Jagger, in which case it's a Bud commercial, in which case YOUR punishment: watch."

7. That is to say, parts of MONEY FOR NOTHING appear to criticize MTV (the fictional sexist "video clips," for instance), but the satire remains directed mainly at the song's narrator. Of course, the song also begins with a line (sung by Sting) that was originally an MTV slogan: "I want my MTV."

8. I have included Channel Four as an example here because although it represented a commitment to state regulation and intervention (see Harvey, 1989), it may also be deployed as an example of less benign forces — through, for instance, its well-documented casualization of labor in the television industry (see Sparks, 1989).

9. These pressures have included the appointment of conservative ideologues to run regulatory bodies, such as Ronald Reagan's appointment of Mark Fowler as chairman of the Federal Communications Commission in the United States. See Katz (1989), Scannell (1990), Porter (1989)m and Gomery (1986, 1989).

10. Alternative possibilities were explored, for instance, in 1983, by the Sheffield TV Group (1983: 54–101), of which I was a member.

11. The notion of the valorization process at work in "leisure time" is taken up by Adorno and Horkheimer (1977) and developed by Jhally (1990). Recent programming on American television (such as the highly rated ABC show *America's Funniest Home Videos*) indicates a new stage in this process — the development of the mass mediation of the com-

modification of "free time," which can now be captured on videotape and sold to the networks in exchange for fame and cash prizes.

12. Nick Browne's analogy, in which the audience is the *object* of a gaze cast by advertisements (following the Marxist analysis of the commodity), usefully *reverses* the terms of Laura Mulvey's argument regarding the male gaze, and suggests that even the revision of this approach in terms of a "glance" at the television screen (Ellis, 1982a) inadequately considers the extent to which advertising-funded television is designed to capture the viewer (see Altman, 1987). These ideas are developed conceptually by Haug (1986, 1987).

13. I am grateful here to Garry Whannel, who suggests this breakdown of levels in his "Notes on Determinations" (1980).

14. *Dreamworlds* was subsequently the object of legal threats from MTV, citing infringement of their copyrights—the tape uses the MTV logo, for instance. This action is not resolved at the time of writing, and includes a demand that Jhally no longer distribute the (nonprofit) tape. My copy was obtained from Sut Jhally, University of Massachusetts, Department of Communication, Machmer Hall, Amherst, MA 01003, USA.

15. Jon Pareles (1991: 31) has criticized *Dreamworlds* (correctly, in my opinion) for taking images out of narrative context. However, Pareles goes too far in his defense of MTV and quite illegitimately suggests that feminist arguments are no different from Moral Majoritarian demands for censorship. Jhally's tape argues that women are denied subjectivity, and Pareles responds that the same is true for men, since music video lacks characterization. Of course, the weakness in this argument is that it systematically overlooks the problem of the male gaze. Men are infrequently imaged purely as erotic objects (whereas women are routinely represented in this way) and when this does occur (Michelle Shocked's ON THE GREENER SIDE) the effect is strikingly different from what is usually expected of MTV videos.

16. An infamous example was the initial promotion of Blondie in the United Kingdom, which featured a photograph of Deborah Harry and the caption "Rip Her to Shreds."

17. For a feminist discussion of pornography in cinema that takes account of theories of narrative and subjectivity, see Linda Williams (1989).

18. The BBC banned dozens of records that might be interpreted as referring to the war, including seemingly innocuous songs such as Phil Collins's "In the Air Tonight." This is certainly a firm lesson in the narrative openness of the pop song.

19. The declining audience for the networks not only stimulated a drive to move "down-market" (where the Fox strategy was taking them), but also provoked a search for upscale viewers: hence, *Twin Peaks*, which was coproduced by Mark Frost, who also produced *Hill Street Blues*—a program that famously changed the way American television thought about audiences, since its up-market viewership was highly attractive to advertisers. On audience trends in the United States, which are deeply relevant to developments in Europe, see Ang (1991: 68-77, 85-97).

20. It is important to consider the extent to which the globalization of MTV may *not* constitute "one-way flow." When I observed production at MTV Europe in August 1987, it was clear that many people working there hoped that a more diverse and critical European version of MTV would have an impact upon the U.S. network itself, partly through the sharing of programs, news items, art-breaks, and so on.

21. This discourse, albeit diluted in some respects (but only in some) has now found a place in mainstream U.S. television. Examples are the NBC prime-time situation comedy *Fresh Prince of Bel Air*, starring Fresh Prince (who, with DJ Jazzy Jeff, made the 1988 rap hit/video PARENTS JUST DON'T UNDERSTAND), and Fox's *In Living Color*—a daring, prime-time sketch comedy show that has featured appearances by Flavor Flav, Queen Latifah, and 3rd Bass.

22. Bart Simpson's "Underachiever and Proud of It" slogan was banned as a T-shirt logo by some U.S. department stores, and students in some U.S. schools were prohibited from wearing this item.

Concluding Thoughts

1. However, see Schudson (1984) for a sophisticated and nuanced discussion of the *limits* of advertising power.

2. Linda Williams (1989) and others have convincingly shown that what is "offensive" about pornography is often not its "bad" politics, but its transgressive force in challenging bourgeois discourses about sexuality and the body. Unsurprisingly, hard-core porn and music TV techniques have now been fused, as, for instance, in the work of porn director Andrew Blake. (I am grateful to Laura Miller for alerting me to this development.)

3. Sut Jhally makes this point in his *Dreamworlds* video critique of MTV. See note 14 for chapter 7.

Bibliography

Abrams, M. (1953) *The Mirror and the Lamp: Romantic Theory and the Critical Tradition.* London: Oxford University Press.

Adorno, T. (1941) "On popular music" [with the assistance of George Simpson]. *Studies in Philosophy and Social Science*, No. 9. (Reprinted in S. Frith & A. Goodwin [eds.], *On Record: Rock, Pop and the Written Word* New York: Pantheon, 1990.)

Adorno, T. (1977) "Letters to Benjamin," in E. Bloch et al., *Aesthetics and Politics.* London: New Left.

Adorno, T. (1978) "On the fetish-character in music and the regression of listening," in A. Arato & E. Gebhardt (eds.), *The Essential Frankfurt School Reader.* Oxford: Basil Blackwell.

Adorno, T. (1990) "The curves of the needle"; "The form of the phonograph record"; and "Opera and the long-playing record." *October*, No. 55 (Winter).

Adorno, T., & Horkheimer, M. (1977) "The culture industry: Enlightenment as mass deception," in J. Curran, M. Gurevitch, & J. Woolacott (eds.), *Mass Communication and Society* (abridged ed.). London: Edward Arnold.

Allan, B. (1990) "Musical cinema, music video, music television." *Film Quarterly*, Vol. 43, No. 3.

Allen, R. (1983) "On reading soaps: A semiotic primer," in A. Kaplan (ed.), *Regarding Television: Critical Approaches — An Anthology.* Los Angeles: American Film Institute.

Altman, R. (1980) "Introduction," in "Cinema/Sound" (special issue). *Yale French Studies*, No. 60.

Altman, R. (1987) "Television Sound," in H. Newcomb (ed.), *Television: The Critical View* (4th ed.). London: Oxford University Press.

Ang, I. (1985) *Watching Dallas.* London: Methuen.

Ang, I. (1991) *Desperately Seeking the Audience.* London: Routledge.

Aronowitz, S. (1987) "Mass culture and the eclipse of reason: The implications for pedagogy," in D. Lazere (ed.), *American Media and Mass Culture: Left Perspectives.* Berkeley: University of California Press.

Attalah, P. (1986) *Music Television* (Working Paper in Communications). Montreal: McGill University.

Attali, J. (1985) *Noise: The Political Economy of Music.* Minneapolis: University of Minnesota Press.

Aufderheide, P. (1986) "Music videos: The look of the sound," in T. Gitlin (ed.), *Watching Television.* New York: Pantheon.

Barthes, R. (1977a) "The death of the author," in R. Barthes, *Image-Music-Text* (S. Heath, ed.). London: Fontana.

Barthes, R. (1977b) "The rhetoric of the image," in R. Barthes, *Image-Music-Text* (S. Heath, ed.). London: Fontana.

Barthes, R. (1982) "The photographic message," in R. Barthes, *Roland Barthes: A Reader* (S. Sontag, ed.). New York: Hill & Wang. (Original work published 1961.)

Baudrillard, J. (1975) *The Mirror of Production.* St. Louis: Telos.

Baudrillard, J. (1985) "The ecstasy of communication," in H. Foster (ed.), *Postmodern Culture.* London: Pluto.

Baudrillard, J. (1988a) *America.* London: Verso.

Baudrillard, J. (1988b) *Selected Writings* (M. Poster, ed.). Cambridge: Polity.

Baudrillard, J. (1990) *Cool Memories.* London: Verso.

Beatbox. (1984–85) London: Argus Specialist Publications.

Berg, C. (1987) "Visualizing music: The archaeology of music video." *ONETWO-THREEFOUR: A Rock 'n' Roll Quarterly,* No. 5 (Spring).

Berland, J. (1986) "Sound, image and social space: Rock video and media reconstruction." *Journal of Communication Inquiry,* Vol. 10, No. 1.

Berman, R., & D'Amico, R. (1991) "Introduction: Popular music from Adorno to Zappa." *Telos,* No. 87 (Spring).

Berry, C. (1987) *Chuck Berry: The Autobiography.* New York: Harmony.

Blacknell, S. (1985) *The Story of Top of the Pops.* London: Patrick Stephens.

Bloom, A. (1987) *The Closing of the American Mind: How Higher Education Has Failed Democracy and Impoverished the Souls of Today's Students.* New York: Simon & Schuster.

Bordo, S. (1990) " 'Material Girl': The effacements of postmodern culture." *Michigan Quarterly Review,* No. 29 (Fall).

Born, G. (1987) "On modern music: Shock, pop and synthesis." *New Formations,* No. 2 (Summer).

Briggs, A. (1979) *The History of Broadcasting in the United Kingdom: Volume 4, Sound and Vision.* London: Oxford University Press.

Bronner, S., & Kellner, D. (1989) *Critical Theory and Society: A Reader.* New York: Routledge.

Brown, A. (ed.) (n.d.) *The History of Rock* (Rock and Art, No. 65). London: Orbis.

Brown, J., & Campbell, K. (1986) "Race and gender in music videos: The same beat but a different drummer." *Journal of Communication,* Vol. 36, No. 1.

Brown, J., & Schulze, L. (1990) "The effects of race, gender and fandom on audiences' interpretations of Madonna's music videos." *Journal of Communication,* Vol. 40, No. 2.

Brown, M. & Fiske, J. (1987) "Romancing the rock: Romance and representation in popular music videos." *ONETWOTHREEFOUR: A Rock 'n' Roll Quarterly,* No. 5 (Spring).

Browne, N. (1987) "The Political Economy of the Television (Super)Text," in H. Newcomb (ed.), *Television: The Critical View* (4th ed.). Oxford: Oxford University Press.

Brunsdon, C., & Morley, D. (1978) *Everyday Television: "Nationwide."* London: British Film Institute.

Burns, G. (1983) "Music video: An analysis at three levels." Paper presented at the meeting of the International Association for the Study of Popular Music, Montreal.

Burns, G., & Thompson, R. (1987) "Music, television, and video: Historical and aesthetic considerations." *Popular Music and Society*, Vol. 11, No. 3.

Burns, T. (1977) *The BBC: Public Institution and Private World.* London: Macmillan.

Burt, R. (1983) *The Tube.* Bristol: Purnell.

Buxton, D. (1990) "Rock music, the star system and the rise of consumerism," in S. Frith & A. Goodwin (eds.), *On Record: Rock, Pop and the Written Word.* New York: Pantheon.

Caughie, J. (1980) "Progressive television and documentary drama." *Screen*, Vol. 21, No. 3.

Caughie, J. (1981) *Theories of Authorship.* London: British Film Institute.

Chambers, I. (1985) *Urban Rhythms: Pop Music and Popular Culture.* London: Macmillan.

Chang, B. (1986) "A hypothesis on the screen: MTV and/as (postmodern) signs." *Journal of Communication Inquiry*, Vol. 10, No. 1.

Chatman, S. (1981) "What novels can do that films can't (and vice versa)," in W. Mitchell (ed.), *On Narrative.* Chicago: University of Chicago Press.

Chen, K. (1986) "MTV: The (dis) appearance of postmodern semiosis, or the cultural politics of resistance." *Journal of Communication Inquiry*, Vol. 10, No. 1

Cohen, S. (1987) "All dressed up and everywhere to go." *SPIN*, Vol. 2, No. 11.

Collins, J. (1989) *Uncommon Cultures: Popular Culture and Post-Modernism.* New York: Routledge.

Connor, S. (1989) *Postmodernist Culture: An Introduction to Theories of the Contemporary.* Oxford: Basil Blackwell.

Cook, P. (1979-80) "Star signs." *Screen*, Vol. 20, Nos. 3-4.

Corbett, J. (1990) "Free, single and disengaged: Listening pleasure and the popular music object." *October*, No. 54 (Fall).

Corliss, R. (1983) "The medium is the maximum." *Film Comment*, Vol. 19, No. 4.

Costello, M., & Wallace, D. (1991) *Signifying Rappers: Rap and Race in the Urban Present.* New York: Ecco.

Cubbitt, S. (1984) "*Top of the Pops*: The politics of the living room," in L. Masterman (ed.), *Television Mythologies: Stars, Shows and Signs.* London: Comedia.

Curran, J., & Sparks, C. (1991) "Press and Popular Culture." *Media, Culture & Society*, Vol. 13, No. 2.

Dannen, F. (1987) "MTV's great leap backwards." *Channels* (July/August).

Davis, S. (1985) *The Hammer of the Gods.* New York: Ballantine.

Dawson, K. (1989) "Making music." *Cable Television Business*, May 15.

Dellar, F. (1981) *The NME Guide to Rock Cinema.* London: Hamlyn.

Denisoff, S. (1988) *Inside MTV.* New Brunswick, N.J.: Transaction.

Dews, P. (1987) *Logics of Disintegration: Post-structuralist Thought and the Claims of Critical Theory.* London: Verso.

Dundy, E. (1986) *Elvis and Gladys: The Genesis of the King.* London: Futura.

Dunn, R. (1986) "Television and the commodity form." *Theory, Culture & Society*, Vol. 3, No. 1.

Dupler, S. (1986) "MTV's Garland speaks out on clips, ratings." *Billboard*, May 24.

Durant, A. (1984) *Conditions of Music.* London: Macmillan.

Dyer, R. (1973) *Light Entertainment.* London: British Film Institute.

Dyer, R. (1977) "Entertainment and Utopia." *Movie*, No. 24.

Dyer, R. (1979) *Stars.* London: British Film Institute.

Dyer, R. (1986) *Heavenly Bodies: Film Stars and Society*. London: British Film Institute.

Eagleton, T. (1983) *Literary Theory: An Introduction*. Oxford: Basil Blackwell.

Eco, U. (1972) "Towards a semiotic inquiry into the television message." *Working Papers in Cultural Studies*, No. 3 (Autumn).

Ehrenstein, D., & Reed, B. (1982) *Rock on Film*. New York: Delilah.

Elg, P., & Roe, K. (1986) "The music of the spheres: Satellites and music video content." *Nordicom*, No. 2.

Ellis, J. (1982a) "Star/industry/image," in C. Gledhill (ed.), *Star Signs*. London: BFI Education.

Ellis, J. (1982b) *Visible Fictions: Cinema, Television, Video*. London: Routledge & Kegan Paul.

Ellsworth, E., Larson, M., & Selvin, A. (1986) "MTV presents: Problematic pleasures." *Journal of Communication Inquiry*, Vol. 10, No. 1.

Engelhardt, T. (1986) "Children's television: The shortcake strategy," in T. Gitlin (ed.), *Watching Television*. New York: Pantheon.

Evans, M. (1979) *Soundtrack: The Music of the Movies*. New York: De Capo.

Fabbri, F. (1982) "A theory of musical genres: Two applications." *Popular Music Perspectives*, No. 1.

Ferguson, M. (1991) "Marshall McLuhan revisited: 1960s zeitgeist victim or pioneer postmodernist?" *Media, Culture & Society*, Vol. 13, No. 1.

Fiske, J. (1984) "Videoclippings." *Australian Journal of Cultural Studies*, Vol. 2, No. 1.

Fiske, J. (1986) "MTV: Post structural post modern." *Journal of Communication Inquiry*, Vol. 10, No. 1.

Fiske, J. (1987) "British cultural studies and television," in R. Allen (ed.), *Channels of Discourse: Television and Contemporary Criticism*. Chapel Hill: University of North Carolina Press.

Fiske, J., & Hartley, J. (1978) *Reading Television*. London: Methuen.

Fitzgerald, D. (1982) "Pop video." *Stills* (Winter).

Flinn, C. (1986) "The 'problem' of femininity in theories of film music." *Screen*, Vol. 27, No. 6.

Foucault, M. (1977) "What is an author?" in M. Foucault, *Language, Counter-Memory, Practice*. Oxford: Basil Blackwell.

Fricke, D. (1986) "The second coming of George Michael: The main man in Wham! alters his image." *Rolling Stone*, November 20.

Frith, S. (1983) *Sound Effects: Youth, Leisure and the Politics of Rock 'n' Roll*. New York: Pantheon.

Frith, S. (1984) "Can You Dance to It? Rock on TV." *Collusion*, No. 4.

Frith, S. (1985) "Confessions of a rock critic." *New Statesman*, August 23.

Frith, S. (1986) "Art versus technology: The strange case of pop." *Media, Culture & Society*, Vol. 8, No. 3.

Frith, S. (1987a) "Copyright and the music business." *Popular Music*, Vol. 7, No. 1.

Frith, S. (1987b) "Towards an aesthetic of popular music," in R. Leppert & S. McClary (eds.), *Music and Society: The Politics of Composition, Performance and Reception*. Cambridge: Cambridge University Press.

Frith, S. (1988a) *Music for Pleasure*. London: Methuen.

Frith, S. (1988b) "Video pop," in S. Frith (ed.), *Facing the Music*. New York: Pantheon.

Frith, S. (1990) "What is good music?" *Canadian University Music Review*, Vol. 10, No. 2.

Frith, S., & Horne, H. (1987) *Art into Pop*. London: Methuen.

Fry, V., & Fry, D. (1986) "MTV: The 24 hour commercial." *Journal of Communication Inquiry*, Vol. 10, No. 1.

Garfield, S. (1986) *Money for Nothing: Greed and Exploitation in the Music Industry.* London: Faber & Faber.

Garnham, N. (1972) "Television documentary and Ideology." *Screen,* Vol. 13, No. 2.

Garnham, N. (1978) *Structures of Television* (2nd ed.). London: British Film Institute.

Garnham, N. (1979a) "For a political economy of communications." *Media, Culture & Society,* Vol. 1, No. 2.

Garnham, N. (1979b) "Subjectivity, ideology, class and historical materialism." *Screen,* Vol. 20, No. 1.

Garnham, N. (1983) *Concepts of Culture, Public Policy and the Cultural Industries* (Discussion Paper). London: GLC.

Gehr, R. (1983) "The MTV aesthetic." *Film Comment,* Vol. 19, No. 4.

Gendron, B. (1986) "Theodor Adorno meets the Cadillacs," in T. Modleski (ed.), *Studies in Entertainment: Critical Approaches to Mass Culture.* Bloomington: Indiana University Press.

Giddens, A. (1985) *Central Problems in Sociological Theory.* London: Macmillan.

Giles, J. (1991) "The Milli Vanilli wars." *Rolling Stone,* January 10.

Gillett, C. (1983) *The Sound of the City: The Rise of Rock and Roll* (2nd ed.). New York: Pantheon.

Gitlin, T. (1983) *Inside Prime Time.* New York: Pantheon.

Gitlin, T. (1986) "We build excitement: Car commercials and *Miami Vice,*" in T. Gitlin (ed.), *Watching Television.* New York: Pantheon.

Gitlin, T. (1987) "Prime time ideology: The hegemonic process in television entertainment," in H. Newcomb (ed.), *Television: The Critical View* (4th ed.). Oxford: Oxford University Press.

Gitlin, T. (1989) "Postmodernism: Roots and politics." *Dissent* (Winter).

Glassner, B. (1991) "The medium must not deconstruct: A postmodern ethnography of *USA Today Television Show.*" *Media, Culture & Society,* Vol. 13, No. 1.

Gledhill, C. (1978) "Recent developments in feminist film theory." *Quarterly Review of Film Studies,* Vol. 3, No. 4.

Goldberg, M. (1991) "The Jacksons score big." *Rolling Stone,* May 2.

Goldie, G. (1977), *Facing the Nation: Television and Politics, 1936-75.* London: Bodley Head.

Golding, P., & Murdock, G. (1983) "Privatising pleasure." *Marxism Today* (October).

Goodwin, A. (1981) *British Television Drama-Documentary, 1946-1980.* Unpublished master's thesis, University of Birmingham, Centre for Contemporary Cultural Studies.

Goodwin, A. (1988) "Sample and hold: Pop music in the digital age of reproduction." *Critical Quarterly,* Vol. 30, No. 3.

Goodwin, A. (1991a) "Material woman." *East Bay Express,* January 4.

Goodwin, A. (1991b) "Popular music and postmodern theory." *Cultural Studies,* Vol. 5, No. 2.

Goodwin, A. (1991c) "Rationalization and democratization in the new technologies of pop production," in J. Lull (ed.), *Popular Music and Communication* (2nd ed.). Newbury Park, Calif.: Sage.

Gomery, D. (1986) "Vertical integration, horizontal regulation: The growth of Rupert Murdoch's US media empire." *Screen,* Vol. 27, Nos. 3-4.

Gomery, D. (1989) "The Reagan record." *Screen,* Vol. 30, Nos. 1-2.

Gorbman, C. (1980) "Narrative film music," in "Cinema/Sound" (special issue). *Yale French Studies,* No. 60.

Gross, J. (1984a) "What you can't see on MTV." *Rock Video* (August).

Gross, J. (1984b) "What you can't see on MTV." *Rock Video* (December).

Grossberg, L. (1986) "Is there rock after punk?" *Critical Studies in Mass Communication*, Vol. 2, No. 3. (Reprinted in S. Frith & A. Goodwin [eds.], *On Record: Rock, Pop and the Written Word*. New York: Pantheon, 1990.)

Grossberg, L. (1987) "The in-difference of television." *Screen*, Vol. 28, No. 2.

Grossberg, L. (with T. Fry, A. Curthoys, & P. Patton) (1988) *It's a Sin: Postmodernism, Politics and Culture*. Sydney: Power.

Guitar Player. (1989) "Steve Stevens' six-string platinum." December.

Hall, S. (1977) "Culture, the media and the 'ideological effect,' " in J. Curran, M. Gurevitch, & J. Woolacott (eds.), *Mass Communication and Society*. London: Edward Arnold.

Hall, S. (1978) "Debate: Psychology, ideology and the human subject." *Ideology and Consciousness*, No. 3 (Spring).

Hall, S. (1980) "Cultural studies and the Centre: Some problematics and problems," in S. Hall, D. Hobson, A. Lowe, & P. Willis (eds.), *Culture, Media, Language*. London: Hutchinson.

Hall, S. (1986) "Preface" in W. Haug, *Critique of Commodity Aesthetics: Appearance, Sexuality and Advertising in Capitalist Society*. Cambridge: Polity.

Hall, S. (1988a) *The Hard Road to Renewal: Thatcherism and the Crisis of the Left*. New York: Verso.

Hall, S. (1988b) [Interview]. *Block*, No. 14 (Winter).

Hall, S. (1989) "Ideology and communication theory," in B. Levin, L. Grossberg, & E. Wartella (eds.), *Re-thinking Communication: Paradigm Exemplars* (Vol. 2). London: Sage.

Hamm, C. (1989) "Afterword," in S. Frith (ed.), *World Music, Politics and Social Change*. Manchester: Manchester University Press.

Handelman, D. (1990) "Is it live, or . . . ," *Rolling Stone*, September 6.

Handelman, D. (1991) "Sold on Ice." *Rolling Stone*, January 10.

Hanna, J. (1988) *Dance, Sex and Gender: Signs of Identity, Dominance, Defiance and Desire*. Chicago: University of Chicago Press.

Hardy, P. (1983) *The Record Industry* (Economic Policy Group Strategy Document No. 16). London: GLC.

Harker, D. (1980) *One for the Money: Politics and Popular Song*. London: Hutchinson.

Hart, H. (1986) "MTV: Towards visual domination—a polemic." *Journal of Communication Inquiry*, Vol. 10, No. 1.

Harvey, S. (1978) *May '68 and Film Culture*. London: British Film Institute.

Harvey, S. (1989) "Deregulation, innovation and Channel Four." *Screen*, Vol. 30, Nos. 1-2.

Haug, W. (1986) *Critique of Commodity Aesthetics: Appearance, Sexuality and Advertising in Capitalist Society*. Cambridge: Polity.

Haug, W. (1987) *Commodity Aesthetics, Ideology and Culture*. New York: International General.

Hayes, R., & Rotfield, H. (1989) "Infomercials and cable network programming." *Advancing the Consumer Interest*, Vol. 1, No. 2.

Hayward, P. (1991) "The unlikely return of the Merman in Madonna's *Cherish*." *Cultural Studies*, Vol. 5, No. 1.

Heath, C. (1990) *Pet Shop Boys, Literally*. London: Viking.

Heath, S. (1977-78) "Notes on suture." *Screen*, Vol. 18, No. 4.

Hebdige, D. (1979) *Subculture: The Meaning of Style*. London: Methuen.

Hebdige, D. (1988) *Hiding in the Light: On Images and Things*. London: Comedia/Routledge.

Hennion, A. (1990) "The production of success: An anti-musicology of the pop song," in S. Frith & A. Goodwin (eds.), *On Record: Rock, Pop and the Written Word*. New York: Pantheon.

Hernadi, P. (1981) "On the how, what and why of narrative," in W. Mitchell (ed.), *On Narrative*. Chicago: University of Chicago Press.

Hibbert, T. (1985) "Square-eyed and legless." *Beatbox*, March.

Hilburn, R. (1986) "MTV's creator tackles new goals." *Los Angeles Times*, September 5.

Hill, D. (1986) "First, make your video." *The Observer*, March 9.

Hill, D. (1989) *Prince: A Pop Life*. New York: Harmony.

Hirshey, G. (1984) *Nowhere to Run: The Story of Soul Music*. London: Pan/Macmillan.

Hobson, D. (1980) *Crossroads: Drama of a Soap Opera*. London: Methuen.

Hodge, R. (1984) "Videoclips as a revolutionary form." *Australian Journal of Cultural Studies*, Vol. 2, No. 1.

Holdstein, D. (1984) "Music video: Messages and structures." *Jump Cut*, No. 29.

Hughes, P. (1990) "Today's television, tomorrow's world," in A. Goodwin & G. Whannel (eds.), *Understanding Television*. London: Routledge.

Hullot-Kentor, R. (1991) "The impossibility of music: Adorno, popular and other music." *Telos*, No. 87 (Spring).

Hustwitt, M. (1985) *Sure Feels Like Heaven to Me: Considerations on Promotional Videos*. Working Paper No. 6, International Association for the Study of Popular Music.

Hutcheon, L. (1987) "Beginning to theorize postmodernism." *Textual Practice*, Vol. 1, No. 1.

Huyssen, A. (1986) *After the Great Divide: Modernism, Mass Culture and Postmodernism*. London: Macmillan.

Jackson, B. (1983) "America gets its MTV!" (interview with Les Garland, MTV). *BAM (Bay Area Music Magazine)*, February 11.

Jackson, D. (1985) *Frankie Say: The Rise of Frankie Goes to Hollywood*. New York: Simon & Schuster.

Jameson, F. (1983) *The Political Unconscious: Narrative as a Socially Symbolic Act*. London: Methuen.

Jameson, F. (1984a) "The politics of theory: Ideological positions in the postmodernism debate." *New German Critique*, No. 33 (Fall).

Jameson, F. (1984b) "Postmodernism and the cultural logic of late capitalism." *New Left Review*, No. 146.

Jay, M. (1988) "Scopic regimes of modernity," in Hal Foster (ed.), *Vision and Visuality*. Seattle: Bay.

Jencks, C. (1986) *What Is Post-Modernism?* New York: St. Martin's Press.

Jhally, S. (1990) *The Codes of Advertising: Fetishism and the Political Economy of Meaning in the Consumer Society*. New York: Routledge.

Jivani, A. (1987) "I want my MTV" (interview with Mark Booth, MTV Europe). *Time Out*, August 5-12.

Jones, S. (1988) "Cohesive but not coherent: Music videos, narrative and culture." *Popular Music and Society*, Vol. 12, No. 4.

Journal of Communication. (1986) [Special issue on music television]. Vol. 36, No. 1.

Journal of Communication Inquiry. (1986) [Special issue on music television]. Vol. 10, No. 1.

Kaplan, E. A. (1985) "A postmodern play of the signifier: Advertising, pastiche and schizophrenia in MTV," in Drummond & Paterson (eds.), *Television in Transition*, London: British Film Institute.

Kaplan, E. A. (1986) "History, the historical spectator and gender address in music television." *Journal of Communication Inquiry*, Vol. 10, No. 1.

Kaplan, E. A. (1987) *Rocking around the Clock: Music Television, Postmodernism and Consumer Culture*. London: Methuen.

Kaplan, E. A. (ed.) (1988) *Postmodernism and Its Discontents: Theories, Practices*. London: Verso.

Katz, H. (1989) "The future of public broadcasting in the US." *Media, Culture & Society*, Vol. 11, No. 2.

Keil, C. (1966) "Motion and feeling through music." *Journal of Aesthetics and Art Criticism*, No. 26.

Kinder, M. (1984) "Music video and the spectator: Television, ideology and dream." *Film Quarterly*, Vol. 38, No. 1.

Kinder, M. (1987) "Music video and the spectator: Television, ideology and dream," in H. Newcomb (ed.), *Television: The Critical View* (4th ed.). Oxford: Oxford University Press.

Kowalski, R. (1986) "Woman is the message." *ONETWOTHREEFOUR: A Rock 'n' Roll Quarterly*, No. 3 (Autumn).

Kozloff, S. (1987) "Narrative theory and television," in R. Allen (ed.), *Channels of Discourse: Television and Contemporary Criticism*. Chapel Hill: University of North Carolina Press.

Kumar, K. (1977) "Holding the middle ground: The BBC, the public and the professional broadcaster," in J. Curran, M. Gurevitch, & J. Woolacott (eds.), *Mass Communication and Society*. London: Edward Arnold.

Laing, D. (1985a) "Music video: Industrial product, cultural form." *Screen*, Vol. 26, No. 1.

Laing, D. (1985b) *One Chord Wonders: Power and Meaning in Punk Rock*. London: Open University Press.

Langer, J. (1981) "Television's 'personality system.' " *Media, Culture & Society*, Vol. 3, No. 4.

Laurence, P. (1974) "Synaesthesia . . . seen any good records lately?" *Recording Engineer/Producer*, Vol. 5, No. 2.

Lefcowitz, E. (1985) *The Monkees Tale*. Berkeley: Last Gasp.

Lehnerer, M. (1987) "Music video: A uses approach." *ONETWOTHREEFOUR: A Rock 'n' Roll Quarterly*, No. 5 (Spring).

Leppert, R. (1988) *Music and Image: Domesticity, Ideology and Socio-Cultural Formation in Eighteenth-Century England*. Cambridge: Cambridge University Press.

Levin, T. (1990) "For the record: Adorno on music in the age of its technological reproducibility." *October*, No. 55 (Winter).

Levy, S. (1983) "Ad nauseum: How MTV sells out rock and roll." *Rolling Stone*, December 8.

Lewis, L. (1987a) "Consumer girl culture: How music video appeals to women," *ONETWOTHREEFOUR: A Rock 'n' Roll Quarterly*, No. 7 (Spring).

Lewis, L. (1987b) "Female address in music video." *Journal of Communication Inquiry*, Vol. 10, No. 2.

Lewis, L. (1990) *Gender Politics and MTV: Voicing the Difference*. Philadelphia: Temple University Press.

Lipman, A. (1985) "The world of Salvador Disney." *City Limits*, May 24–30.

Lipsitz, G. (1986-87) "Cruising around the historical block: Postmodernism and popular music in East Los Angeles." *Cultural Critique*, No. 12 (Spring).

Lipsitz, G. (1987) "A world of confusion: Music video as modern myth." *ONETWOTHREEFOUR: A Rock 'n' Roll Quarterly*, No. 7 (Spring).

Loewenthal, S. (1983) "The popular song analyzed," in G. Martin (ed.), *Making Music: The Guide to Writing, Performing and Recording*. London: Pan.

Lorch, S. (1988) "Metaphor, metaphysics and MTV." *Journal of Popular Culture*, Vol. 22, No. 3.

Los Angeles Times. (1988) "MTV goes global." December 18.

Lovell, T. (1980) *Pictures of Reality.* London: British Film Institute.

Lull, J. (1982) "The social uses of television," in G. Gumpert & R. Cathcart (eds.), *Intermedia: Interpersonal Communication in a Media World* (2nd ed.). New York: Oxford University Press.

Lynch, J. (1984) "Music videos: From performance to Dada-Surrealism." *Journal of Popular Culture,* Vol. 18, No. 1.

MacCabe, C. (1974) "Realism and the cinema: Notes on some Brechtian theses." *Screen,* Vol. 15, No. 2.

MacCabe, C. (1976) "Principles of realism and pleasure." *Screen,* Vol. 17, No. 3.

McClary, S. (1988a) "Living to tell: Madonna's resurrection of the fleshly." Paper presented at the Feminism and Mass Culture conference, SUNY-Buffalo.

McClary, S. (1988b) "Towards a feminist criticism of music: The Whitesnake paradigm and the classics." Paper presented at the Alternative Musicologies conference, Ottawa.

McClary, S. (1989) "Terminal prestige: The case of avant-garde music composition." *Cultural Critique,* No. 12 (Spring).

McClary, S. (1991) *Feminine Endings: Music, Gender and Sexuality.* Minnesota: University of Minnesota Press.

McClary, S., & Walser, R. (1990) "Start making sense: Musicology wrestles with rock," in S. Frith & A. Goodwin (eds.), *On Record: Rock, Pop and the Written Word.* New York: Pantheon.

McGrath, J. (1977) "TV Drama: The case against naturalism." *Sight and Sound* (Spring).

McNeil, A. (1991) *Total Television* (3rd ed.). New York: Penguin.

McRobbie, A. (1984) "Dance and social fantasy," in A. McRobbie & M. Nava (eds.), *Gender and Generation.* London: Macmillan.

McRobbie, A. (1986a) "Postmodernism and popular culture," in L. Appignanesi (ed.), *Postmodernism: ICA Documents 4.* London: Institute for Contemporary Arts.

McRobbie, A. (1986b) "Slave to the image." *New Socialist* (January).

Marcus, G. (1976) *Mystery Train: Images of America in Rock 'n' Roll Music.* New York: E. P. Dutton.

Marcus, G. (1980) "Rock films," in J. Miller (ed.), *The Rolling Stone Illustrated History of Rock & Roll.* New York: Rolling Stone Press.

Marcus, G. (1985) "One star per customer." *Artforum* (November).

Marcus, G. (1987) "MTV—DOA—RIP." *Artforum* (January).

Marsh, D. (ed.) (1985) *The First Rock and Roll Confidential Report.* New York: Pantheon.

Martin, W. (1986) *Recent Theories of Narrative.* Ithaca, N.Y.: Cornell University Press.

Mercer, K. (1986) "Monster metaphors: Notes on Michael Jackson's *Thriller.*" *Screen,* Vol. 27, No. 1.

Metz, C. (1975) "The imaginary signifier." *Screen,* Vol. 16, No. 2.

Meyer, J. (1989) [Interview with Julien Temple]. *Minnesota Daily,* April 21.

Middleton, R. (1985) "Articulating musical meaning/reconstructing musical history/locating the 'popular.' " *Popular Music,* No. 5.

Mifflin, M. (1991) "The auteur theory of music video means no more pretty cliches." *New York Times,* January 20.

Mitchell, W. (ed.) (1981) *On Narrative.* Chicago: University of Chicago Press.

Mix. (1987) "The big time sledgehammer road to the playhouse of life." Vol. 11, No. 6.

Modleski, T. (1988) *The Women Who Knew Too Much: Hitchcock and Feminist Theory.* New York: Routledge.

Moores, S. (1990) "Texts, readers and context of reading: Developments in the study of media audiences." *Media, Culture & Society,* Vol. 12, No. 1.

Moretti, F. (1987) "The spell of indecision." *New Left Review*, No. 164 (July-August).

Morley, D. (1980a) *The "Nationwide" Audience*. London: British Film Institute.

Morley, D. (1980b) "Texts, readers, subjects," in S. Hall, D. Hobson, A. Lowe, & P. Willis (eds.), *Culture, Media, Language*. London: Hutchinson.

Morley, D., & Silverstone, R. (1990) "Domestic communication: Technologies and meanings." *Media, Culture & Society*, Vol. 12, No. 1.

Morley, P. (1983) "Video and pop." *Marxism Today* (May).

Morris, M. (1988a) "Asleep at the wheel." *New Statesman*, June 26.

Morris, M. (1988b) "Banality in cultural studies." *Block*, No. 14 (Autumn).

Morse, M. (1986) "Postsynchronising rock music and television." *Journal of Communication Inquiry*, Vol. 10, No. 1.

Mower, S. (1986) "That old blue magic." *Guardian*, April 10.

Mulvey, L. (1975) "Visual pleasure and narrative cinema." *Screen*, Vol. 16, No. 3.

Mulvey, L. (1989) "Afterthoughts on 'Visual pleasure and narrative cinema' inspired by King Vidor's *Duel in the Sun*," in L. Mulvey, *Visual and Other Pleasures*. Bloomington: Indiana University Press.

Murdock, G. (1989) "Cultural studies: Missing links." *Critical Studies in Mass Communication*, Vol 6, No. 4.

Myers, K. (1982) "Towards a feminist erotica." *Camerawork*, No. 24 (March).

Nattiez, J.-J. (1990) *Music and Discourse: Toward a Semiology of Music*. Princeton, N.J.: Princeton University Press.

Nelson, P., & Bangs, L. (1981) *Rod Stewart*. New York: Delilah.

Newman, M. (1991a) "Impact: What was once a luxury is now a necessity." *Billboard*, May 11.

Newman, M. (1991b) "Vidclip makers see red in label deals." *Billboard*, April 20.

Norman, P. (1981) *Shout! The True Story of the Beatles*. London: Corgi/Hamish Hamilton.

Oglesbee, F. (1987) "Eurythmics: An alternative to sexism in music videos." *Popular Music and Society*, Vol. 11, No. 2.

Oliver, B. (1983) "Can a promotion rethink save the music business?" *Campaign*, April 22.

Option. (1989) "Summit talk." No. 27 (July-August).

Paglia, C. (1990) "Madonna—finally, a real feminist." *New York Times*, December 14.

Pareles, J. (1989) "Her style is imitable, but it's her own." *New York Times*, November 12.

Pareles, J. (1990) "How rap moves to television's beat." *New York Times*, January 14.

Pareles, J. (1991) "Sex, lies and the trouble with videotapes." *New York Times*, June 2.

Pareles, J., & Romanowski, P. (1983) *The Rolling Stone Encyclopedia of Rock and Roll*. New York: Rolling Stone Press/Summit.

Parsons, T. (with George Michael) (1991) *George Michael: Bare*. London: Penguin.

Pattison, R. (1987) *The Triumph of Vulgarity: Rock Music in the Mirror of Romanticism*. Oxford: Oxford University Press.

Pfeil, F. (1985) "Making flippy-floppy: Postmodernism and the baby-boom PMC," in M. Davis (ed.), *The Year Left*. London: Verso.

Pfeil, F. (1986) "Postmodernism and our discontent." *Socialist Review*, Nos. 87-88.

Pfeil, F. (1988) "Postmodernism as a 'structure of feeling,' " in C. Nelson & L. Grossberg (eds.), *Marxism and the Interpretation of Culture*. London: Macmillan.

Peterson-Lewis, S., & Chennault, S. (1986) "Black artists' music videos: Three success strategies." *Journal of Communication*, Vol. 36, No. 1.

Pittman, R. (1990) "We're talking the wrong language to 'TV Babies.' " *New York Times*, January 24.

Polan, D. (1986) "SZ/MTV." *Journal of Communication Inquiry*, Vol. 10, No. 1.

Porter, V. (1989) "The re-regulation of television: Pluralism, constitutionality and the free market in the USA, West Germany, France and the UK." *Media, Culture & Society*, Vol. 11, No. 1.

Postman, N. (1985) *Amusing Ourselves to Death: Public Discourse in the Age of Show Business*. London: Penguin.

Powell, R. (1991) "Making the jump from MTV to the retail shelves." *New York Times*, April 21.

Price, K. (1988) "Does music have meaning?" *British Journal of Aesthetics*, Vol. 28, No. 3.

Propp, V. (1968) *Morphology of the Folktale* (2nd ed.). Austin: University of Texas Press.

Qualen, J. (1985) *The Music Industry: The End of Vinyl?* London: Comedia.

Quarry, P. (1987) "Pop promos: Why the music industry's problem child has to grow up fast." *Direction* (May).

Reed, C. (1988) "Pop too near beer." *Guardian*, August 29.

Reimer, B. (1989) "Postmodern structures of feeling: Values and lifestyles in the postmodern age," in J. Gibbins (ed.), *Contemporary Political Culture: Politics in a Postmodern Age*. London: Sage.

Reynolds, S. (1985) "The New Pop and its aftermath." *Monitor*, No. 4.

Reynolds, S. (1990) *Blissed Out: The Raptures of Rock*. London: Serpent's Tail.

Rijven, S., Marcus, G., & Straw, W. (1985) *Rock for Ethiopia*. Working Paper No. 7, International Association for the Study of Popular Music.

Rimmer, D. (1985) *Like Punk Never Happened: Culture Club and the New Pop*. London: Faber & Faber.

Roberts, C. (1991) "Scritti Politti: Intellectual hooliganism." *Melody Maker*, March 2.

Robins, J. (1989) "Into the groove." *Channels* (May).

Robins, J. (1990) "MTV News hits skid row." *Channels*, April 23.

Rock Video. (1985-86) New York: Lamplight.

Rodowick, D. N. (1988) *The Crisis of Political Modernism: Criticism and Ideology in Contemporary Film Theory*. Urbana: University of Illinois Press.

Rodowick, D. N. (1991a) *The Difficulty of Difference: Psychoanalysis, Sexual Difference and Film Theory*. New York: Routledge.

Rodowick, D. N. (1991b) "Reading the figural." *Camera Obscura*, No. 24.

Ross, A. (1989) *No Respect: Intellectuals and Popular Culture*. New York: Routledge.

Rolling Stone. (1988) "Random notes." March 24.

Said, E. (1979) *Orientalism*. New York: Pantheon.

Said, E. (1985) "Opponents, audiences, constituencies and community," in H. Foster (ed.), *Postmodern Culture*. London: Pluto.

Sandall, (1988) "Watch this space." *Q* (October).

Sartre, J.-P. (1965) *Search for a Method*. London: Methuen.

Savan, L. (1987) "Rock rolls over." *Village Voice*, August 11.

Savan, L. (1989) "Desperately seeking soda." *Village Voice*, March 5.

Scannell, P. (1990) "Public service broadcasting: The history of a concept," in A. Goodwin & G. Whannel (eds.), *Understanding Television*. London: Routledge.

Schaffner, N. (1991) "The crack-up: How Pink Floyd lost its leader." *Musician*, No. 149 (March).

Schlesinger, P. (1978) *Putting 'Reality' Together: BBC News*. London: Macmillan.

Scholes, R. (1981) "Language, narrative and anti-narrative," in W. Mitchell (ed.), *On Narrative*. Chicago: University of Chicago Press.

Schwichtenberg, C. (1991) "Madonna's postmodern feminism: Strategies of simulation and the sexual politics of style." Unpublished paper.

Screen. (1984) "On The Soundtrack." Vol. 25, No. 3.

Sheffield TV Group. (1983) *Cable and Community Programming*. Sheffield/London: Sheffield City Council/GLC.

Sherman, B., & Dominick, J. (1986) "Violence and sex in music videos: TV and rock 'n' roll." *Journal of Communication*, Vol. 36, No. 1.

Shore, M. (1985) *The Rolling Stone Book of Rock Video*. London: Sidgwick & Jackson.

Shore, M. (1987) *Music Video: A Consumers' Guide*. New York: Ballantine.

Shore, M. (with Dick Clark). (1985) *The History of American Bandstand*. New York: Ballantine.

Silverman, K. (1988) *The Acoustic Mirror: The Female Voice in Psychoanalysis and Cinema*. Bloomington: Indiana University Press.

Simmonds, D. (1985) "Madonna." *Marxism Today* (October).

Smith, D. (1991) "Banned in the USA." *The Source* (January).

Smythe, D. (1977) "Communications: Blindspot of Western Marxism." *Canadian Journal of Political and Social Theory*, Vol. 1, No. 3.

Snow, M. (1988) *The Fame Game*. London: Penguin.

Sparks, C. (1989) "The impact of technological and political change on the labour force in British television." *Screen*, Vol. 30, Nos. 1-2.

SPIN. (1989) "Dropping Science" (roundtable discussion). Vol. 5, No. 5, August.

SPIN. (1992) "Mr. MTV." January.

Stratton, J. (1983) "Capitalism and Romantic ideology in the record business." *Popular Music*, No. 3.

Stratton, J. (1989) "Beyond art: Postmodernism and the case of popular music." *Theory, Culture & Society*, Vol. 6, No. 1.

Straw, W. (1988) "Music video in its contexts: Popular music and postmodernism in the 1980s." *Popular Music*, Vol. 7, No. 3.

Street, J. (1985) *Rebel Rock: The Politics of Popular Music*. Oxford: Basil Blackwell.

Sun, S., & Lull, J. (1986) "The adolescent audience for music video and why they watch." *Journal of Communication*, Vol. 36, No. 1.

Tagg, J. (1989) "Introduction: Postmodernism and the born-again avant-garde," in J. Tagg (ed.), *The Cultural Politics of "Postmodernism."* Binghamton: State University of New York, Deptartment of Art History.

Tagg, P. (1983) *'Nature' as a Musical Mood Category*. Gotenburg: International Association for the Study of Popular Music.

Talking Heads & Olinsky, F. (1987) *What the Songs Look Like*. New York: Harper & Row.

Tasker, P. (1982) "Over the points and off the rails: Pop music and British TV." *Prime Time*, Vol. 1, No. 4.

Tennant, N. (ed.) (1984) *Smash Hits Yearbook 1984*. London: EMAP.

Tennant, N. (ed.) (1985) *The Best of Smash Hits*. London: EMAP.

Tetzlaff, D. (1986) "MTV and the politics of postmodern pop." *Journal of Communication Inquiry*, Vol. 10, No. 1.

Théberge, P. (1989) "The 'sound' of music: Technological rationalization and the production of popular music." *New Formations*, No. 8 (Summer).

Thompson, H. (1987) "A spin on the vid-kids" (interview with Mark Booth, MTV Europe). *Guardian*, June 22.

Thompson, J. (1990) *Ideology and Modern Culture: Critical Social Theory in the Era of Mass Communication*. Stanford, Calif.: Stanford University Press.

Thomson, P. (1982) "Promotion candidates." *New Musical Express*, April 10.

Thornton, S. (1990) "Strategies for reconstructing the popular past." *Popular Music*, Vol. 9, No. 1.

Toop, D. (1984) *The Rap Attack: African Jive to New York Hip-Hop*. London: Pluto.

Turner, G. (1983) "Video clips and popular music." *Australian Journal of Cultural Studies*, No. 1 (May).

Variety. (1989) "Corporate sponsorship is now vital for touring rock acts." July 26–August 1.

Vermorel, F., & Vermorel, J. (1985) *Starlust: The Secret Fantasies of Fans*. London: Comet/W. H. Allen.

Viera, M. (1987) "The institutionalization of music video." *ONETWOTHREEFOUR: A Rock 'n' Roll Quarterly*, No. 5 (Spring).

Vincent, R., Davis, D., & Boruszkowski, L. (1987) "Sexism on MTV: Portrayal of women in rock videos." *Journalism Quarterly*, Vol. 64, No. 4.

Volosinov, V. (1986) *Marxism and the Philosophy of Language*. Cambridge, Mass.: Harvard University Press. (Original work published 1929.)

Walker, J. (1987), *Crossovers: Art into Pop/Pop into Art*. London: Comedia/Methuen.

Walker, J. R. (1987) "The context of MTV: Adolescent entertainment media use and music television." *Popular Music and Society*, Vol. 11, No. 3.

Walser, R. (1989) "Forging masculinity: Heavy metal sounds and images of gender." Unpublished paper.

Walters, B. (1987) "MTV lives!" *Village Voice*, June 2.

Weber, M. (1958) *The Rational and Social Foundations of Music*. Carbondale: Southern Illinois University Press.

Weinstein, D. (1989) "The Amnesty International concert tour: Transnationalism as cultural commodity." *Public Culture* (Bulletin for the Project of Transnational Cultural Studies), Vol. 1, No. 2.

Whannel, G. (1980) "Notes on determinations." Discussion Paper, CCCS Media Group.

Whannel, G. (1986) "The unholy alliance: Notes on television and the remaking of British sport, 1965-85." *Leisure Studies*, No. 5.

Whannel, G. (1988) "Seoul searching." *New Statesman*, September 9.

Whelan, B. (1988-89) " 'Furthur': Reflections on counterculture and the postmodern." *Cultural Critique*, No. 11 (Winter).

White, M. (1987) "Ideological analysis and television," in R. Allen (ed.), *Channels of Discourse: Television and Contemporary Criticism*. Chapel Hill: University of North Carolina Press.

Williams, L. (1989) *Hard Core: Power, Pleasure, and the "Frenzy of the Visible."* Berkeley: University of California Press.

Williams, R. (1973) "Base and superstructure in Marxist cultural theory." *New Left Review*, No. 82 (November-December).

Williams, R. (1974) *Television: Technology and Cultural Form*. London: Fontana.

Williams, R. (1977a) "A lecture on realism." *Screen*, Vol. 18, No. 1.

Williams, R. (1977b) *Marxism and Literature*. Oxford: Oxford University Press.

Williams, R. (1980) *Problems in Materialism and Culture*. London: Verso.

Williamson, J. (1985) "The making of a material girl." *New Socialist* (October).

Willis, P. (1976) *Profane Culture*. London: Routledge & Kegan Paul.

Willis, P. (1990) *Common Culture: Symbolic Work at Play in the Everyday Cultures of the Young*. Boulder, Colo.: Westview.

Wolfe, A. (1983) "Rock on cable: On MTV: Music Television, the first music video channel." *Popular Music and Society*, Vol. 9, No. 1.

Wolff, J. (1987) "The ideology of autonomous art," in R. Leppert & S. McClary (eds.), *Music and Society: The Politics of Composition, Performance and Reception*. Cambridge: Cambridge University Press.

Wolff, J. (1990) *Feminine Sentences: Essays on Women and Culture*. Cambridge: Polity.

Wollen, P. (1986) "Ways of thinking about music video (and postmodernism)." *Critical Quarterly*, Vol. 28, Nos. 1-2.

Yale French Studies. (1980) "Cinema/Sound" (special issue). No. 60.

Young, C. (1986) "Soda pop." *Musician* (December).

Zimmer, D. (1988) "Madison Avenue buys a big piece of the rock." *BAM* (*Bay Area Music Magazine*), February 12.

Index

Compiled by Robin Jackson

Andrew Goodwin is associate professor of communication arts at the University of San Francisco. His criticism appears regularly in the *East Bay Express*, the *San Francisco Bay Guardian*, and the *Chicago Reader*. He is coeditor, with Garry Whannel, of *Understanding Television*. He is a corresponding editor of the international communications journal, *Media, Culture & Society*.